We R the

Champions

No!

I AM A Not

CHAMPION

PACEMAKER

Basic English

by Bonnie Walker

PEARSON
AGS Globe

Shoreview, MN

About the Author

Bonnie L. Walker taught for 16 years in secondary schools and college. She holds a Ph.D. in curriculum theory and instructional design from the University of Maryland, an M.Ed. in secondary education, and a B.A. in English. She studied psycholinguistics at the University of Illinois Graduate School and was a curriculum developer at the Model Secondary School for the Deaf at Galludet University. She is the author of Pacemaker® *Basic English Composition,* Pacemaker® *Basic English Grammar, Life Skills English,* and numerous curriculum materials in written expression, grammar, and usage. Since 1986, Dr. Walker has been president of a research and development company specializing in the development of training and educational materials for special populations.

Reading Consultant

Timothy Shanahan, Ph.D., Professor of Urban Education, Director of the Center for Literacy, University of Illinois at Chicago; Author, AMP Reading System

Reviewers

The publisher wishes to thank the following educators for their helpful comments during the review process for Pacemaker® *Basic English*. Their assistance has been invaluable. **Lori Andrews,** Resource Teacher, Cullman High School, Cullman, AL; **Sylvia Berger,** Special Education Resource Teacher, Markham District High School, Markham, ON, Canada; **Raequel Gadsden,** ESE Teacher, Chamberlain High School, Tampa, FL; **William P. LeNoble,** English Instructor, Soledad High School, Soledad, CA; **Wendy Mason,** Special Education Teacher, Magnolia High School, Anaheim, CA; **John Petitt,** Special Education Resource Teacher, Culver Elementary School, Niles, IL; **Monica M. Thorpe,** Language Arts Teacher, El Paso, TX

Acknowledgments appear on page 494, which constitutes an extension of this copyright page.

ISBN-13: 978-0-7854-6312-2
ISBN-10:   0-7854-6312-7

1 2 3 4 5 6 7 8 9 10   11 10 09 08 07

1-800-992-0244
www.agsglobe.com

Table of Contents

How to Use This Book: A Study Guide

Welcome to *Basic English*. Why study the English language? Think about how many times each day you read, write, or speak English. To become a better reader, writer, and speaker, you need to understand sentences and how they are built. As you read this book, you will learn the correct way to put a sentence together. You will practice writing sentences. Then you will learn how to use sentences to build paragraphs. You will practice the steps in the writing process. Your study of English will help you express your ideas clearly—whether you are writing an e-mail, an assignment, or a phone message.

As you read this book, notice how each lesson is organized. Information is presented and then followed by Examples and Practices. Read the information. Study the Examples. Then do the Practice activities. If you have trouble with a lesson, try reading it again. If you still do not understand something, ask your teacher for help.

It is important that you understand how to use this book before you start to read it. It is also important to know how to be successful in this class. This study guide can help you to achieve these things.

How to Study

These tips can help you study more effectively:
- Plan a regular time to study.
- Choose a desk or table in a quiet place where you will not be distracted. Find a spot that has good lighting.
- Gather all of the books, pencils, paper, and other materials you will need to complete your assignments.
- Decide on a goal. For example: "I will finish reading and taking notes on Lesson 1-1, by 8:00."
- Take a five- to ten-minute break every hour to stay alert.

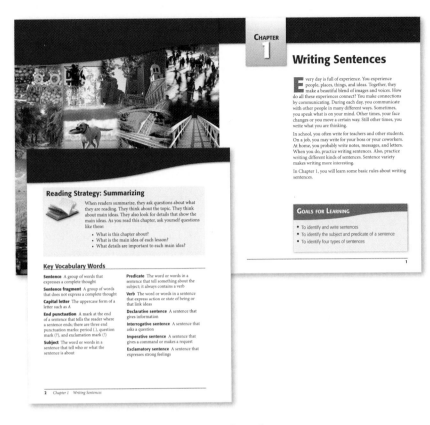

Before Beginning Each Chapter

■ Read the chapter title and study the photo.

■ Read the opening paragraphs. How is the photo related to the chapter?

■ Read the Goals for Learning. These are the main objectives of the chapter. Each goal represents one lesson.

■ Read the Reading Strategy feature. There are seven different strategies described in this book. They are also summarized in Appendix F. As you read the chapter, try to use the strategy. It will help you become a better reader.

■ Study the Key Vocabulary Words. Say each one aloud. Read its definition. These words will also be defined and explained in the chapter.

Note These Features

▶ **EXAMPLE 1**

Example
Example sentences that show a lesson idea

Practice A

Practice
An activity designed to practice a lesson skill

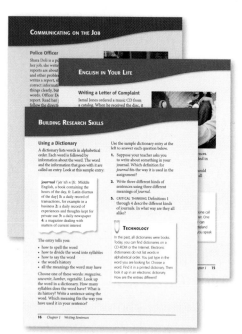

Communicating on the Job
Information about a job that requires writing skills

English in Your Life
A practical application of writing skills

Building Research Skills
Information about a research tool or a research skill

Vocabulary Builder
Vocabulary practice

Spelling Builder
Spelling practice

Putting It All Together
A writing activity that uses skills taught in the chapter

Group Activity
A writing activity designed for a small group

Reading Strategy

A prompt to help you use the chapter's reading strategy (See Appendix F for a description of these strategies.)

Six Traits of Writing:

Ideas message, details, and purpose

Six Traits of Writing

A prompt to remind you about a trait of good writing (See Appendix A for a description of the six traits.)

 **Writing Tip**

Writing Tip

A writing tip related to the lesson

 **Grammar Tip**

Grammar Tip

A grammar tip related to the lesson

 Test Tip

Test Tip

A tip to help you do your best on tests

NOTE

Note

Additional information related to the lesson

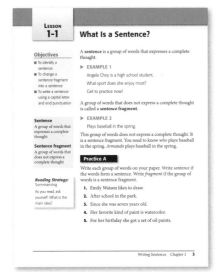

Before Beginning Each Lesson

Read the lesson title and restate it in the form of a question. For example, write: What is a sentence?

Look over the entire lesson, noting the following:

- Objectives
- bold words
- text organization
- notes and features in the margins
- Examples
- Practices
- Lesson Review

As You Read the Lesson

- Read the lesson title.
- Read the subheadings and paragraphs that follow.
- Study the Examples.
- Do the Practices.
- Complete the Lesson Review.
- Make sure you understand the concepts in the lesson. If you do not, reread the lesson. If you are still unsure, ask for help.

Using the Bold Words

Bold type
Words seen for the first time will appear in bold type.

Glossary
Words listed in this column are also found in the glossary.

Knowing the meaning of the red vocabulary words in the left column will help you understand what you read. These words are in **bold type** the first time they appear in the text. They are defined in the lesson text.

A **sentence** is a group of words that expresses a complete thought.

All of the boxed vocabulary words are also defined in the **glossary.**

Sentence (sen´ təns) A group of words that expresses a complete thought

Word Study Tips

- Start a vocabulary file with index cards to use for review.
- Write one term on the front of each card. Write the definition, chapter number, and lesson number on the back.
- You can use these cards as flash cards by yourself or with a study partner to test your knowledge.

Taking Notes

It is helpful to take notes during class and as you read this book.

- Use headings to label the main sections of your notes. This organizes your notes.
- Summarize important information, such as main ideas and supporting details.
- Do not try to write every word your teacher says or every detail in a chapter.
- Do not be concerned about writing in complete sentences. Use short phrases.
- Use your own words to describe, explain, or define things.
- Sometimes the best way to summarize information is with a chart or an example. Use simple word webs, charts, and diagrams in your notes. Write your own example sentences.
- Try taking notes using a three-column format. Draw two lines to divide your notebook page into three columns. Make the middle column the widest. Use the first column to write headings or vocabulary words. Use the middle column to write definitions and examples. Use the last column to draw diagrams, write shortcuts for remembering something, write questions about something you do not understand, record homework assignments, or for other purposes. An example of three-column note-taking is shown at the left.
- After taking notes, review them to fill in possible gaps.
- Study your notes to prepare for a test. Use a highlighter to mark what you need to know.

Purposes of sentences		
Declarative	Amber and I are in the same English class.	⊙
Interrogative	Do we have to cover our new textbook?	?
Imperative	Please make a cover for this book tonight.	⊙
Exclamatory	The school year is off to a great start!	!

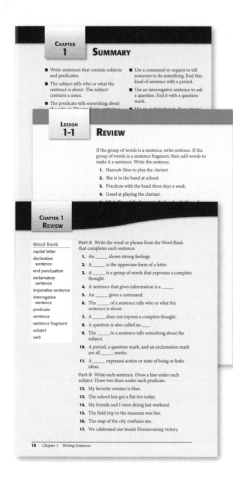

Using the Chapter Summaries

■ Read each Chapter Summary to be sure you understand the chapter's main ideas.

Using the Reviews

■ Complete each Lesson Review. It covers the most important ideas and skills from the lesson.

■ Complete the Chapter Review. Part A covers the chapter vocabulary words. The rest of the review covers the main ideas and skills taught in the chapter.

■ Read the Test Tip. Try to remember this tip when you take a test.

Using the Appendixes

This book contains six appendixes. Become familiar with them before starting your study of English.

■ Appendix A is a Writing Process Handbook. It describes six traits of good writing. Then it explains the five steps in the writing process: prewriting, drafting, revising, editing and proofreading, and publishing and presenting.

■ Appendix B is a Capitalization and Punctuation Handbook. If you have a question about how to use capital letters or punctuation marks, look for the answer here.

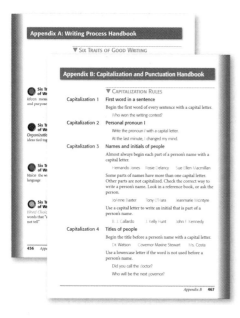

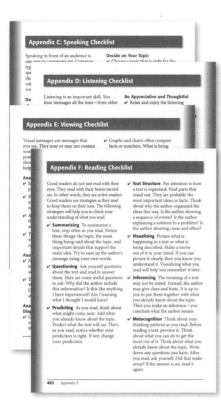

- Appendix C is a Speaking Checklist. Use this list to help you become a better speaker.
- Appendix D is a Listening Checklist. Use this list to help you become a more careful listener.
- Appendix E is a Viewing Checklist. Use this list to help you evaluate a visual message.
- Appendix F is a Reading Checklist. It summarizes the seven reading strategies that are described on the chapter opener pages. Review this list as you read. Use these strategies to become a better reader.

Preparing for Tests

- Read the Goals for Learning at the beginning of the chapter. A test may ask questions related to these goals.
- Review the Examples in each lesson. Ask yourself: What main idea does each one show?
- Complete the Practices in each lesson. Review your work.
- Study the Key Vocabulary Words at the beginning of the chapter. If you made flash cards, use them to study.
- Complete the Lesson Reviews and the Chapter Review.
- Read the Chapter Summary.
- Use a chart, list, or word web to summarize main ideas.
- Review your notes. Highlight key ideas and examples.
- Review Appendix A, the Writing Process Handbook.
- Make a sample test. You may want to do this with another student and share your test questions.

Writing Sentences

E very day is full of experience. You experience people, places, things, and ideas. Together, they make a beautiful blend of images and voices. How do all these experiences connect? You make connections by communicating. During each day, you communicate with other people in many different ways. Sometimes, you speak what is on your mind. Other times, your face changes or you move a certain way. Still other times, you write what you are thinking.

In school, you often write for teachers and other students. On a job, you may write for your boss or your coworkers. At home, you probably write notes, messages, and letters. When you do, practice writing sentences. Also, practice writing different kinds of sentences. Sentence variety makes writing more interesting.

In Chapter 1, you will learn some basic rules about writing sentences.

GOALS FOR LEARNING

- To identify and write sentences
- To identify the subject and predicate of a sentence
- To identify four types of sentences

Reading Strategy: Summarizing

When readers summarize, they ask questions about what they are reading. They think about the topic. They think about main ideas. They also look for details that show the main ideas. As you read this chapter, ask yourself questions like these:

- What is this chapter about?
- What is the main idea of each lesson?
- What details are important to each main idea?

Key Vocabulary Words

Sentence A group of words that expresses a complete thought

Sentence fragment A group of words that does not express a complete thought

Capital letter The uppercase form of a letter such as A

End punctuation A mark at the end of a sentence that tells the reader where a sentence ends; there are three end punctuation marks: period (.), question mark (?), and exclamation mark (!)

Subject The word or words in a sentence that tell who or what the sentence is about

Predicate The word or words in a sentence that tell something about the subject; it always contains a verb

Verb The word or words in a sentence that express action or state of being or that link ideas

Declarative sentence A sentence that gives information

Interrogative sentence A sentence that asks a question

Imperative sentence A sentence that gives a command or makes a request

Exclamatory sentence A sentence that expresses strong feelings

What Is a Sentence?

A **sentence** is a group of words that expresses a complete thought.

▶ **EXAMPLE 1**

Angela Choy is a high school student.

What sport does she enjoy most?

Get to practice now!

A group of words that does not express a complete thought is called a **sentence fragment**.

▶ **EXAMPLE 2**

Plays baseball in the spring.

This group of words does not express a complete thought. It is a sentence fragment. You need to know *who* plays baseball in the spring. *Armando* plays baseball in the spring.

Practice A

Write each group of words on your paper. Write *sentence* if the words form a sentence. Write *fragment* if the group of words is a sentence fragment.

1. Emily Watson likes to draw.
2. After school in the park.
3. Since she was seven years old.
4. Her favorite kind of paint is watercolor.
5. For her birthday she got a set of oil paints.

 Writing Tip

People often use sentence fragments in informal writing. You should use complete sentences in school assignments and formal writing.

Practice B

Look at each group of words from Practice A that you labeled *fragment*. Add words to each fragment to make it a sentence. Write the sentences on your paper. Begin each one with a capital letter. Use correct end punctuation.

Beginning and Ending a Sentence

When you write a sentence, there are two important rules to follow.

Rule 1 Every sentence starts with a **capital letter**. The capital letter tells the reader that you are beginning a new idea.

▶ **EXAMPLE 3**

Some people like to read about the past.

They like history books.

You might like to read a book about a president.

Rule 2 Every sentence ends with an **end punctuation** mark. It can be a period, a question mark, or an exclamation mark. It tells the reader where the sentence ends.

▶ **EXAMPLE 4**

George Washington was the first president of the United States.

Do you know who the second president was?

Yes, I do!

Practice C

Rewrite each sentence. Use capital letters and end punctuation.

1. for years, Cory had wanted a car
2. how could he earn the money to buy it
3. he got a job at the supermarket
4. it took a long time to save enough money
5. at last, he had enough

Practice D

Find five sentences in the paragraph below. Write them on your paper. Start the first word in each sentence with a capital letter. End each sentence with an end punctuation mark.

the library has many history books some people like to read about the past other people like to read about the future those books are in the science fiction section new books are added to this section every day

Gina likes to read books about life during the Civil War.

REVIEW

If the group of words is a sentence, write *sentence*. If the group of words is a sentence fragment, then add words to make it a sentence. Write the sentence.

1. Hannah likes to play the clarinet.

2. She is in the band at school.

3. Practices with the band three days a week.

4. Good at playing the clarinet.

5. Michelle and Carlos are in the band with Hannah.

Rewrite each sentence. Use capital letters and correct end punctuation.

6. did you bring your lunch

7. let me see it, please

8. that was the scariest movie I ever saw

9. the band is getting ready for a show

10. do you think they will be ready in time

VOCABULARY BUILDER

Understanding Antonyms

An **antonym** is a word that means the opposite of another word: cold–hot   small–large   none–all
For each item, read the first word. Then choose the word that is an antonym of the first word. Write the letter of your answer.

1. same   A alike   B nearly   C different
2. question   A example   B answer   C problem
3. angry   A important B young   C calm
4. arrive   A stay   B leave   C start

Subjects and Predicates

The Subject

Every sentence has a **subject.** The subject is the part of a sentence that tells who or what the sentence is about.

▶ **EXAMPLE 1**

Emily enjoys oatmeal for breakfast.

(Who enjoys oatmeal for breakfast? Emily does.)

Practice A

Write each sentence on your paper. Underline the subject in each one.

1. The school is on the corner.
2. Armando attends the school.
3. The bus goes to the school.
4. It arrives at 8:45 AM.
5. School starts at 9:00 AM.

The subject can be one word or many words. Every subject contains a word that names a person, place, or thing.

▶ **EXAMPLE 2**

The French teacher gave the class a quiz.

She returned the quiz the next day.

Practice B

Write each sentence on your paper. Then underline the subject. Ask yourself who or what the sentence is about.

1. The students wrote an essay about summer.

2. Summer is their favorite season.

3. They handed in the essay today.

4. The teacher will grade the papers tonight.

5. The whole class did the assignment.

The Predicate

The **predicate** is another part of a sentence. It tells something about the subject. It can be one word or many words. It always contains a **verb.** A verb does one of three things:

- A verb can express action.
- A verb can express a state of being.
- A verb can link ideas.

You will learn more about verbs in Chapters 5 and 6.

▶ **EXAMPLE 3**

Angela swims.

Angela tried out for the swimming team.

She is a very fast swimmer.

Practice C

Write each sentence on your paper. Underline each predicate.

1. Swim practice begins at 3:00 PM.

2. Angela practices every day.

3. She has a job at the YMCA.

4. She is a lifeguard at the pool.

5. The lifeguards had a picnic last week.

Reading Strategy:
Summarizing

Write a summary of this lesson using the words *subject* and *predicate*.

Practice D

These sentence fragments have subjects. Write each one on your paper. Add a predicate so each group of words expresses a whole thought. Add end punctuation.

1. Every summer I
2. The book on the table
3. The first football game
4. My best friend
5. My breakfast

Practice E

Here is a list of sentence predicates. Write each one on your paper. Add a subject so each group of words expresses a complete thought. Add end punctuation.

1. go to the beach
2. moved here from another town
3. went to the movies
4. got ruined in the wash
5. was late

REVIEW

Write each sentence on your paper. Underline the subject.

1. Rosa is an old friend of mine.

2. Her birthday is on August 7.

3. I will give her a CD.

Write each sentence on your paper. Underline the predicate.

4. Rosa and I met in middle school.

5. We rode the same school bus.

6. She sat next to me.

Each sentence is missing a subject. Add a word or words to make the sentence complete. Write the sentence on your paper.

7. _____ is the most interesting president.

8. _____ begins at 3:00 PM.

9. _____ interests me very much.

10. _____ is playing on the radio.

SPELLING BUILDER

Spelling Words with a Final e

Say the words *hid* and *hide*. When you hear a long vowel sound in a short word, you often see an *e* at the end of the word.

Add a final e to each word below. You will make a word with a long vowel sound. Then write a sentence using the new word.

1. plan   2. not   3. slid   4. fin   5. cub

Purposes of Sentences

**Declarative
sentence**

A sentence that gives
information

**Interrogative
sentence**

A sentence that asks a
question

**Imperative
sentence**

A sentence that gives
a command or makes
a request

**Exclamatory
sentence**

A sentence that
expresses strong
feelings

Reading Strategy:
Summarizing

Write a one-sentence
summary of this page.

There are four kinds of sentences. A statement that gives
information is called a **declarative sentence.** It states a
fact. It ends with a period.

▶ **EXAMPLE 1**

Nathan likes to read.

He is interested in American history.

John Adams was the second president of the United States.

A question is also called an **interrogative sentence.** It ends
with a question mark.

▶ **EXAMPLE 2**

Who was the third president?

What is Nathan reading about today?

Why does Nathan like history?

A command or request is an **imperative sentence.** It tells
someone to do something. It ends with a period.

▶ **EXAMPLE 3**

Give me that book.

Turn to page 200.

Please read out loud.

An exclamation is also called an **exclamatory sentence.**
It expresses strong feelings. It ends with an exclamation
mark.

▶ **EXAMPLE 4**

This book is great!

That was the best story ever!

Practice A

Read each sentence. Decide what kind of sentence it is. Write one of these on your paper: *statement*, *question*, *command*, or *exclamation*.

1. Angela is on the swim team.

2. She will swim in the state finals.

3. I really hope she will win a medal!

4. Will she make the Olympic team someday?

5. Hurry up, Angela.

Practice B

Read each sentence. Decide what kind of sentence it is. Write one of these on your paper: *declarative*, *interrogative*, *imperative*, or *exclamatory*.

1. Who plays shortstop on that baseball team?

2. He bought a new CD player.

3. Just sign the check.

4. What kind of computer is that?

5. The water is too hot!

Practice C

Write three declarative sentences about yourself. Begin each sentence with a different word. Capitalize the first word in each sentence. Put a punctuation mark at the end.

People ask questions to get information. Always put a question mark at the end of a question. The answer to a question is usually a statement. Use a period at the end of an answer.

▶ **EXAMPLE 5**

Question	Who was the fifth president of the United States?
Answer	James Monroe was the fifth president.

Practice D

Write five questions on your paper. Then write the answers. Begin every sentence with a capital letter. End every sentence with a punctuation mark.

Reading Strategy:
Summarizing

Step back and think about Chapter 1. What is the main idea of this chapter?

Angela asked her teacher a question about an assignment.

REVIEW

Read each sentence. Decide what kind of sentence it is. Write one of these on your paper: *statement*, *question*, *command*, or *exclamation*.

1. Practice starts in five minutes.

2. Are you going to be late?

3. I am never late!

4. Are you sure?

5. Stop giving me a hard time.

6. How many days will you be gone?

7. What a silly idea!

8. What a great place this is!

9. I will count them again.

10. Could you carry a million pennies?

PUTTING IT ALL TOGETHER

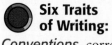

Six Traits of Writing:

Conventions correct grammar, spelling, and mechanics

Write a note to a friend. In the note, talk about something you plan to do together. Use each of the four different kinds of sentences. Be sure that each sentence has a subject and a predicate. Begin each sentence with a capital letter and use correct end punctuation.

Writing a Letter of Complaint

Jamal Jones ordered a music CD from a catalog. When he received the disc, it was damaged. Jamal wrote to complain to the company. He asked for a new disc. In his letter, he is polite but firm. Read Jamal's letter carefully. Then follow the directions below.

17 Windham Place
Charlotte, NC 59121
January 8, 2007

Gateland Music, Inc.
1500 Industry Road
Seattle, WA 20889

Dear Sir or Madam:

   I bought one of your music CDs.
It did not work. The CD must be broken.
I am very disappointed! Can you replace the
CD with one that works? Please mail it to the
address above. Thank you for your help.

Sincerely,

Jamal Jones

Jamal Jones

1. Draw a two-column chart on your paper. Write *subject* at the top of the first column. Write *predicate* at the top of the second column. Read the main paragraph of Jamal's letter. List the subject and predicate of each sentence in the correct columns.

2. List the four kinds of sentences. Find an example of each kind in Jamal's letter.

3. CRITICAL THINKING Why should a business letter be free of all mistakes?

LISTENING AND SPEAKING

Imagine that Jamal makes a phone call of complaint. Work with a partner. One of you can be Jamal. The other can be someone who works for Gateland Music, Inc. Make sure both of you speak in complete sentences.

BUILDING RESEARCH SKILLS

Using a Dictionary

A dictionary lists words in alphabetical order. Each word is followed by information about the word. The word and the information that goes with it are called an entry. Look at this sample entry:

> **jour•nal** \'jėr′nl\ *n* [fr. Middle English, a book containing the hours of the day, fr. Latin diurnus of the day] **1:** a daily record of transactions, for example in a business **2:** a daily record of experiences and thoughts kept for private use **3:** a daily newspaper **4:** a magazine dealing with matters of current interest

The entry tells you:

- how to spell the word
- how to divide the word into syllables
- how to say the word
- the word's history
- all the meanings the word may have

Choose one of these words: *magazine, souvenir, lumber, vegetable.* Look up the word in a dictionary. How many syllables does the word have? What is its history? Write a sentence using the word. Which meaning fits the way you have used it in your sentence?

Use the sample dictionary entry at the left to answer each question below.

1. Suppose your teacher asks you to write about something in your journal. Which definition for *journal* fits the way it is used in the assignment?

2. Write three different kinds of sentences using three different meanings of *journal.*

3. **CRITICAL THINKING** Definitions 1 through 4 describe different kinds of journals. In what way are they all alike?

 ## TECHNOLOGY

In the past, all dictionaries were books. Today, you can find dictionaries on a CD-ROM or the Internet. Electronic dictionaries do not list words in alphabetical order. You just type in the word you are looking for. Choose a word. Find it in a printed dictionary. Then look it up in an electronic dictionary. How are the entries different?

SUMMARY

- Write sentences that contain subjects and predicates.

- The subject tells who or what the sentence is about. The subject contains a noun.

- The predicate tells something about the subject. The predicate contains a verb.

- Begin each sentence with a capital letter.

- Use a declarative statement to give information. End it with a period.

- Use a command or request to tell someone to do something. End this kind of sentence with a period.

- Use an interrogative sentence to ask a question. End it with a question mark.

- Use an exclamation to show strong feelings. End it with an exclamation point.

GROUP ACTIVITY

Work with a small group to write steps for a fire drill at school. What should students do when they hear the alarm? Where should they go? Start each sentence with a capital letter and end it with the correct punctuation mark. Then have each group member read one step. As a group, think of ways to make your writing better.

Word Bank

capital letter

declarative
  sentence

end punctuation

exclamatory
  sentence

imperative sentence

interrogative
  sentence

predicate

sentence

sentence fragment

subject

verb

Part A Write the word or phrase from the Word Bank that completes each sentence.

1. An _____ shows strong feelings.

2. A _____ is the uppercase form of a letter.

3. A _____ is a group of words that expresses a complete thought.

4. A sentence that gives information is a _____.

5. An _____ gives a command.

6. The _____ of a sentence tells who or what the sentence is about.

7. A _____ does not express a complete thought.

8. A question is also called an ___.

9. The _____ in a sentence tells something about the subject.

10. A period, a question mark, and an exclamation mark are all _____ marks.

11. A _____ expresses action or state of being or links ideas.

Part B Write each sentence. Draw a line under each subject. Draw two lines under each predicate.

12. My favorite sweater is blue.

13. The school bus got a flat tire today.

14. My friends and I went skiing last weekend.

15. The field trip to the museum was fun.

16. The map of the city confuses me.

17. We celebrated our team's Homecoming victory.

Part C Find the sentences in the paragraph below. List them on your paper. Start each sentence with a capital letter. End each sentence with an end punctuation mark.

18.   it is almost Thanksgiving david is busy in his kitchen he is cooking a turkey he has made cranberry sauce and a pumpkin pie david invited six people to his Thanksgiving dinner

Part D Write *sentence* if the group of words is a sentence. Write *fragment* if the group of words is a fragment.

19. During October, students celebrate Homecoming.

20. A Homecoming King and Queen.

21. Some of the teachers.

22. Homecoming was a huge success.

Part E Write the letter of your answer.

23. Which of these is a declarative sentence?
   A Is Thanksgiving on your birthday?
   B Thanksgiving is always on Thursday.
   C What a wonderful meal!
   D Put the dirty dishes here.

24. Which of these is an interrogative sentence?
   A Excuse me!   **C** Wash your hands.
   B I have a cold.   **D** Are you feeling better?

25. Which of these is an imperative sentence?
   A Is this your room?   **C** I hate cleaning!
   B Make your bed.   **D** My closet is small.

Test Tip

To study for a test, write your own test questions. Trade your questions with another student. Answer each other's questions. Check your answers.

Using Nouns in Sentences

N ouns are words that name people, places, things, events, and ideas. It is hard to write or talk about anything without using a noun. Look around and you will see thousands of nouns.

Look at the photo of the market. Name what you see. There are tomatoes, cucumbers, and radishes. There are apples, apricots, and mushrooms. All of the names you use are nouns.

In Chapter 2, you will learn about nouns. Each lesson tells about different kinds of nouns. You will learn how they are used in everyday speech and writing.

GOALS FOR LEARNING

- To recognize nouns in sentences, and to identify and use compound and collective nouns
- To identify and use common and proper nouns, and to capitalize proper nouns
- To identify and use abstract and concrete nouns
- To identify nouns as singular or plural, and to spell plural nouns
- To spell plural nouns that have irregular forms, and to spell the plural forms of proper nouns, numbers, dates, and letters
- To tell the difference between plural nouns and possessive nouns

Reading Strategy: Questioning

Asking questions as you read will help you understand what you are reading. Asking questions will also help you remember what you read. Questioning makes you a more active reader. As you read, ask yourself:

- Why am I reading this?
- What can I decide about the facts and details?
- What links can I make between what I am reading and my life?

Key Vocabulary Words

Noun A word that names a person, place, thing, event, or idea

Collective noun The name of a group of people, places, or things

Compound noun Two or more words that work together to name one thing

Common noun The name of any person, place, thing, event, or idea

Proper noun The name of one particular person, place, thing, event, or idea

Abbreviation A short form of a word

Concrete noun A word that names something you can see or touch

Abstract noun A word that names something you cannot see or touch

Singular noun The name of one person, place, thing, event, or idea

Plural noun The name of more than one person, place, thing, event, or idea

Irregular plural noun A plural that does not follow the normal rules

Possessive noun A word that shows ownership or a relationship between two things

Apostrophe (') A punctuation mark that you use to show that a noun is possessive

What Is a Noun?

Noun
A word that names a person, place, thing, event, or idea

Reading Strategy:
Questioning

What nouns are part of your conversations? What nouns do you see each day?

A **noun** is a word that names a person, place, thing, event, or idea.

▶ **EXAMPLE 1**

Persons	teacher, agent, aunt, worker, Carmela
Places	state, theater, town, Washington
Things	book, dish, apple, Empire State Building
Ideas	choice, thought, belief, happiness

Practice A

Write three more nouns that belong in each group. Use the examples as a guide.

1. sound   noise, whisper
2. event   dance, party
3. person   nurse, neighbor
4. place   kitchen, city
5. feeling   joy, sadness

A noun can be the name of a part of something.

▶ **EXAMPLE 2**

A hand is part of a clock.

A mane is part of a horse.

Collective noun

The name of a group of people, places, or things

Compound noun

Two or more words that work together to name one thing

Practice B

For each noun, write four other nouns that name parts of the noun.

Example: house
Answer: roof, window, wall, porch

1. kitchen

2. tree

3. ship

4. car

5. bicycle

A **collective noun** is the name of a group of people, places, or things.

▶ **EXAMPLE 3**

Groups of People	group, audience, crowd, team
Groups of Places	nation, United States, country
Groups of Animals	herd, flock, swarm, pack
Groups of Things	collection, set, series

Practice C

Read the paragraph below. Which nouns name a group of people or things? Write each one on your paper.

The swim team practices every day. Angela's swim club meets weekly. The whole group went to the meet. The audience cheered for the athletes.

A **compound noun** is two or more words that work together to name one thing. Some compound nouns are written as one word.

▶ **EXAMPLE 4**

fire + fighter = firefighter

back + yard = backyard

Reading Strategy:
Questioning

Ask yourself: Did I understand what I just read? If not, read it again.

Practice D

Use each pair of words to make a new word. Write a sentence using each new compound noun. Start each sentence with a capital letter. End each sentence with correct punctuation. Underline the compound noun in each sentence.

1. earth + quake

2. moon + light

3. thunder + storm

4. tooth + paste

5. water + melon

Some compound nouns use a hyphen between the words. A hyphen is a short dash between parts of a word.

▶ **EXAMPLE 5**

mid-July

mother-in-law

Some compound nouns look like two words. In these compound nouns, the words work together to name one person, place, thing, event, or idea.

▶ **EXAMPLE 6**

White House   Thomas Jefferson

ice cream   swim team

Writing Tip

You cannot tell how to spell a compound noun from its sound. Some are one word. Others are more than one word. Others use hyphens. A dictionary will show you how to spell compound nouns.

Practice E

Find 10 nouns in the paragraph. Write each noun on your paper. If the noun is collective, write *collective* next to it. If the noun is compound, write *compound* next to it.

Tanya thinks that a lily of the valley is a beautiful flower. She brought a bouquet to her sister-in-law who was in the hospital. "These flowers smell so sweet," said Julie. "You are a good friend. I will ask someone to put them in water."

REVIEW

List all of the nouns in each sentence. If a noun is collective, write *collective* beside it. If a noun is compound, write *compound* beside it.

1. The United States has many parks.

2. Yellowstone Park has thousands of springs that throw jets of hot water into the air.

3. The most famous is Old Faithful.

4. The park also has beautiful waterfalls.

5. Visitors arrive by the thousands.

VOCABULARY BUILDER

Using a Variety of Nouns

Sometimes two words have meanings that are close. A synonym is a word that has almost the same meaning as another word. Many nouns have synonyms. For example:

road—street
freedom—liberty

When you write, use different nouns instead of repeating the same ones. You can often find synonyms in a dictionary. Using a variety of nouns will make your writing more interesting.

Write these sentences on your paper. Replace each bold noun with a synonym that you think is more interesting.

1. Angela would like to take a **trip** this **fall**.
2. She wants to go to the **beach**.
3. Her best **friend** Emily will go with her.
4. On this **vacation**, the friends will stay in a **motel**.

Common and Proper Nouns

Common noun
The name of any person, place, thing, event, or idea

Proper noun
The name of one particular person, place, thing, event, or idea

A **common noun** is the name of a general type of person, place, thing, event or idea. Most of the nouns you use are common nouns. Common nouns begin with lower case letters. A **proper noun** is the name of one particular person, place, thing, event, or idea. When you write, always begin proper nouns with capital letters.

▶ **EXAMPLE 1**

Common Noun	Proper Noun
mountain	Mount Everest
holiday	Thanksgiving
magazine	*Garden Design*

Practice A

Write each common noun on your paper. Write a proper noun next to each common noun.

1. country
2. state
3. movie
4. TV show
5. month

My favorite restaurant is Tony's Cafe.

Reading Strategy:
Questioning

What do you already know about using capital letters?

Practice B

Write each sentence on your paper. Capitalize each proper noun. Each sentence has at least one proper noun.

1. My friend angela loves to swim.

2. Her favorite swimmer is janet evans.

3. Janet won three gold medals in the 1988 summer olympics.

4. Those games took place in seoul, korea.

5. Janet also won a gold medal at the 1992 olympics in barcelona, spain.

Parts of the Country or World

The names of parts of the country or world are proper nouns. When compass directions are used as nouns, they are common nouns.

▶ **EXAMPLE 2**

Part of the Country   Darnell visited the East with his family.

Direction   The plane flew toward the east.

Practice C

Write each sentence on your paper. Capitalize each proper noun. Not every sentence has a proper noun.

1. jennifer took a trip to the south.

2. On the first day, she drove 200 miles southeast.

3. She began in springfield and went to tennessee.

4. The next day she headed south toward alabama.

5. She liked the south very much.

Abbreviation

A short form of a word

Languages, Courses, and Subjects

The name of a language is a proper noun. The name of a certain course in school is a proper noun. The name of a subject is a common noun.

▶ **EXAMPLE 3**

Proper Noun	Common Noun
Spanish	language
Algebra II	math

Practice D

Read each pair of sentences. Write the letter of the sentence with the correct capitalization.

1. **A** Celia is in the Band.
   B Celia took Beginning Band this year.

2. **A** Next year Carlos is taking a history class.
   B Next year Carlos is taking a History class.

3. **A** Angela enjoys all physical education classes.
   B Angela enjoys all Physical Education classes.

4. **A** All of the students take english.
   B All of the students take English.

5. **A** Yoko plans to study french next year.
   B Yoko plans to study French next year.

Reading Strategy:
Questioning

When do you use abbreviations in your daily life?

Abbreviations of Proper Nouns

An **abbreviation** is a short form of a word. If the word is a proper noun, capitalize its abbreviation. Titles like Doctor and Mister are proper nouns. They are usually abbreviated.

▶ **EXAMPLE 4**

Proper Noun	Abbreviation
Maryland	MD
Doctor Turner	Dr. Turner
Franklin Street	Franklin St.

Most of the words in an address are proper nouns.

Practice E

Write each address on your paper. Capitalize each proper noun. Capitalize each abbreviation of a proper noun.

1. ms. julie choy
2760 west 86th ave., apt. 9
westminister, co 80030

2. mr. dan connell
923 barnett drive
starkville, mississippi 39759

3. doctor aziza alam
nassau professional building
nassau, delaware 19969

4. mrs. lenora gomez
2138 whitehall court
crofton, md 21114

5. mr. hak lee
6884 johnson way
lanham, md 20706

Titles

Capitalize the first word of a title. Also capitalize each important word. Underline the title of a movie, book, magazine, opera, or play. If you are using a computer to write, use italics instead of underlining. Put quotation marks around the title of a song, poem, or short story.

▶ **EXAMPLE 5**

Song	"America, the Beautiful"
Book	The Red Pony or *The Red Pony*
Short Story	"To Build a Fire"

Practice F

Write each title. Capitalize the first word and each important word. Then underline or add quotation marks.

1. romeo and juliet (play)

2. the wizard of oz (movie)

3. the perfect storm (book)

4. yellow submarine (song)

5. the raven (poem)

REVIEW

Write each noun on your paper. Capitalize each proper noun.

1. donald jacobsen

2. england

3. river

Read each sentence. If the sentence is correct, write *correct* on your paper. If the sentence has a capitalization mistake, write the sentence correctly.

4. Emily enjoys her classes at Wilson High School.

5. Armando's favorite holiday is halloween.

6. We have relatives who live in west virginia.

Write each sentence on your paper. Capitalize each proper noun. Underline or use quotation marks for the titles.

7. Evita is doing her book report on the invisible man, a novel by ralph ellison.

8. One of the most popular short stories is the lady, or the tiger? by frank stockton.

9. Home alone was a hit movie in 1990.

10. Our dentist's name is dr. richard harp.

Abstract and Concrete Nouns

Concrete noun

A word that names something you can see or touch

Abstract noun

A word that names something you cannot see or touch

Reading Strategy:
Questioning

Do you use more concrete nouns or abstract nouns in your daily life?

NOTE

Words about time and numbers are usually abstract. People talk about time and numbers as though they were real. Still, you cannot see or touch time or numbers.

Nouns can be abstract or concrete. A **concrete noun** is a word that names something you can see or touch. An **abstract noun** is a word that names something you cannot see or touch. You can think about it or talk about it.

▶ **EXAMPLE 1**

Concrete Noun	Abstract Noun
money	price
clock	minute
college	education
sports car	type
paper	assignment

Practice A

Read the pairs of nouns. Write each abstract noun.

1. day, sun
2. winter, ice
3. rain, weather
4. opinion, judge
5. bedroom, comfort

Abstract nouns can be difficult to identify. If a noun names something you cannot see or touch, it is an abstract noun.

Practice B

List the nouns in each sentence. Identify each as *abstract* or *concrete*.

1. Nathan wants to buy a car.
2. What kind would Nathan like?
3. Nathan saw an ad in the newspaper.
4. He liked the car, but the price was not right.
5. Maybe next time his luck will be better.

REVIEW

Write a sentence using each abstract noun. Then underline each noun you use.

1. year

2. happiness

3. bravery

4. springtime

5. energy

Find the nouns in each sentence. Write each noun on your paper. Identify each noun as *abstract* or *concrete*.

6. Bill received a medal for his courage.

7. The soldiers fought for peace.

8. Christina has a good idea for our book.

9. The cheering fans expressed their pleasure with the concert.

10. In her happiness, Martha jumped for joy.

Singular and Plural Nouns

Objectives

■ To identify and use singular and plural nouns

■ To spell the plural form of nouns ending in *s, z, x, ch, sh, y, o, f,* and *fe*

Singular noun

The name of one person, place, thing, event, or idea

Plural noun

The name of more than one person, place, thing, event, or idea

 Writing Tip

Check the spelling of a plural noun in a dictionary. If no plural is shown, form the plural by adding -*s*. All other plural forms will appear in the dictionary entry.

A **singular noun** is the name of one person, place, thing, event, or idea. A **plural noun** is the name of more than one person, place, thing, event, or idea. Most plural nouns end in -*s*.

▶ **EXAMPLE 1**

Singular Noun	Plural Noun
flower	flowers
tree	trees
mouth	mouths

Practice A

Write the plural of each noun on your paper.

1. apple

2. boy

3. toe

4. desk

5. computer

Nouns That End with *s, z, x, ch,* or *sh*

Add -*es* to nouns that end in *s, z, x, ch,* or *sh* to form the plural.

▶ **EXAMPLE 2**

Singular Noun	Plural Noun
pass	passes
quiz	quizzes
wish	wishes

Write the plurals of each of these singular nouns on your paper. Add either *-s* or *-es*. Say the plural out loud. You will hear the extra syllable when the plural noun ends in *-es*.

1. tax

2. path

3. peach

4. printer

5. dish

Nouns That End with *y*

Some nouns that end with *y* become plural by changing the *y* to *-ies*.

Some nouns that end with *y* become plural by adding *-s*. Study the two examples. What is the difference between the two groups of words? Say the plural forms in both groups out loud.

▶ **EXAMPLE 3**

	Change *y* to *-ies*		Add *-s*
city	cities	key	keys
lady	ladies	alley	alleys
spy	spies	boy	boys

Here are the rules for making the plural forms of nouns that end with *y*.

Rule 1 The letter before the *y* in *key, alley,* and *boy* is a vowel. You make these nouns plural by adding *-s*.

Rule 2 The letter before the *y* in *city, lady,* and *spy* is a consonant. You make these nouns plural by changing the *y* to *-ies*.

Reading Strategy:
Questioning

Ask yourself: Did I understand what I just read? If not, read it again.

Practice C

Write each word on your paper. Write the plural form of each word next to it. Use the rules on page 35 to guide you.

1. baby
2. toy
3. penny
4. turkey
5. country

Nouns That End with *o*

Some nouns end with a vowel and an *o*. Make the plural form of these nouns by adding *-s*.

▶ **EXAMPLE 4**

Singular Noun	Plural Noun
radio	radios
studio	studios
trio	trios

Some nouns end with a consonant and an *o*. Make the plurals of these nouns by adding *-es*.

▶ **EXAMPLE 5**

Singular Noun	Plural Noun
potato	potatoes
echo	echoes

Practice D

Complete each sentence. Use the plural form of the noun that follows the sentence. Write the plural noun on your paper.

1. Do you know much about _____? (volcano)
2. The farmer raises _____ for meat. (buffalo)
3. Javier likes to cook with fresh _____. (tomato)
4. There are a million _____ in here! (mosquito)
5. Janet Evans is one of Angela's _____. (hero)

NOTE
Some words do not follow these rules. Use a dictionary to check the plural of these words: *photo, zero, cargo,* and *auto.*

Nouns That End with *f, ff,* or *fe*

Some nouns that end with *f, ff,* or *fe* sound different in their plural forms. Say these words out loud. Listen to how they sound.

cliff   cliffs

roof   roofs

You form the plural of some nouns that end with *f, ff,* or *fe* by adding -*s*. Form the plural of others by changing the *f* to *v* and adding -*es*.

▶ **EXAMPLE 7**

Singular Noun	Plural Noun
safe	safes
life	lives
belief	beliefs
leaf	leaves

Practice E

Say each word in the list out loud. Then write its plural form on your paper. Use a dictionary if you are not sure.

1. calf
2. thief
3. chef
4. knife
5. chief

REVIEW

Write the plural form of each noun on your paper.

1. address

2. pony

3. monkey

4. lady

5. wife

6. hero

Each sentence has one mistake. Find the mistake. Then write the sentence correctly.

7. Evans won four gold medales in the Olympics.

8. Mrs. Langston says we will have to make two speechs next term.

9. One of her beliefes is that students should speak in front of an audience.

10. Correta sings with the altoes in the choir.

SPELLING BUILDER

Words with Irregular Spelling
Rules for spelling are useful. They help you make spelling choices when you write. For example, you just learned about nouns that end with a consonant and *o*. You make them plural by adding *-es*. However, some plural nouns do not follow this rule. The plural of *taco* is *tacos*. The plural of *piano* is *pianos*. It is important to learn the rules. It is also important to learn the exceptions.

More About Plural Nouns

- To spell irregular plural nouns
- To form plural proper nouns
- To form plural numbers, dates, and letters

Irregular plural noun

a plural noun that does not follow the normal rules

Reading Strategy: Questioning

What do you think you will learn in this lesson?

Irregular Plural Nouns

Some plural nouns do not follow the regular rules. They are called **irregular plural nouns.** For example, in very few cases the singular and plural forms of a noun are the same.

▶ **EXAMPLE 1**

Singular Noun	Plural Noun
one deer	a herd of deer
one sheep	many sheep
a trout	a school of trout

Practice A

Find the spelling mistakes in these sentences. Write the correct spellings of the words on your paper.

Armando and his family drove out to the country. They went past a field of deers. They saw several farms with flocks of sheeps and herds of cows. They stopped at a lake in a state park to fish. Armando caught three trouts. Everyone enjoyed the day.

To make some nouns plural, you change or add letters.

▶ **EXAMPLE 2**

Singular Noun	Plural Noun
child	children
foot	feet
ox	oxen
mouse	mice
man	men

Practice B

Write the plural form of each singular noun. Then use the plural noun in a sentence.

1. child

2. woman

3. goose

4. tooth

5. mouse

Plural Proper Nouns

You form the plurals of most proper nouns by adding -s. If a proper noun ends in s or z, add -es to make it plural.

▶ **EXAMPLE 3**

Singular Proper Noun	Plural Proper Noun
the Jones family	the Joneses
the Hernandez family	the Hernandezes

Practice C

Write the plural form of each family name. Then use the plural name in a sentence.

1. Williams

2. Martinez

3. Choy

4. Weiss

5. Okada

Plural Forms of Numbers, Dates, and Letters

Make a number, date, or letter plural by adding -*s*. No apostrophe is needed.

▶ **EXAMPLE 4**

The 1990s were years of great changes in technology.

Inez got two As on her report card.

Several papers got scores in the 90s.

Practice D

Find the mistake in each sentence. Write the correct word on your paper.

1. In the 1960's the Beatles were popular.
2. Meg got two C's on her report card.
3. All the students' scores were in the 70's or higher.
4. Put all of the B's and C's in a column.
5. I know my ABCS.

Brandon was happy to get two Bs on his report card.

REVIEW

Rewrite each sentence. Change each bold noun to its plural form.

1. We saw five **fish** near the pier.

2. Several **woman** joined the committee.

3. The **child** saw several dogs in the yard.

Find the mistake in each sentence. Write the sentence correctly on your paper.

4. Armando and Nathan are both hoping for A's on their report cards.

5. The music teacher is teaching them songs from the 1960's.

6. They met the O'Hara's at the pond.

Write the plural form of each of these words in a sentence.

7. 1920

8. Hudson

9. Williams

10. ABC

Possessive Nouns

A **possessive noun** is a word that shows ownership or a relationship between two things. A possessive noun uses an **apostrophe** ('). An apostrophe is a punctuation mark.

▶ **EXAMPLE 1**

Where are Dante's shoes? (The shoes belong to Dante.)

Dante's swim team won. (Dante is part of the team.)

The team's score is 2. (The team has a score of 2.)

To make a noun possessive, follow these rules:

Rule 1 Make a singular noun possessive by adding an apostrophe and -s ('s).

▶ **EXAMPLE 2**

Dante's team   the computer's keyboard

Rule 2 When a singular noun ends in s, add an apostrophe and -s ('s).

▶ **EXAMPLE 3**

the boss's day off   Gail Russ's book

Possessive noun

A word that shows ownership or a relationship between two things

Apostrophe (')

A punctuation mark that you use to show that a noun is possessive

Rule 3 Make a plural noun possessive by adding only an apostrophe (').

▶ **EXAMPLE 4**

the trains' routes   the trumpets' sounds

Rule 4 If a plural noun does not end in s, add an apostrophe and -s ('s).

▶ **EXAMPLE 5**

the children's toys   the men's locker room

Reading Strategy:
Questioning

What do you already know about possessive nouns?

Reading Strategy:
Questioning

Ask yourself: Do I
understand what I just
read? If not, read it
again.

Practice A

Write each bold word on your paper. Add an apostrophe
if the word shows possession. If the word is a plural noun,
write *plural* next to it.

1. All of the teams met at the **citys** new stadium.

2. The **swimmers** were there for the meet.

3. Everyone on **Dantes** team was ready for the
   competition.

4. The **coachs** last words were to try their best.

5. The winner of the meet will go to the state **finals**.

Practice B

Write the possessive form of each noun. Some of the nouns
are singular and some are plural.

1. team

2. wolves

3. man

4. Jones

5. cities

Use an apostrophe in phrases such as *one dollar's worth* or
a week's vacation. If the word is plural and ends in *s*, add
only an apostrophe.

▶ **EXAMPLE 6**

Singular	Plural
one cent's worth	ten cents' worth
a month's vacation	two months' vacation

Practice C

Read each pair of sentences. Choose the correct sentence in each pair. Write it on your paper.

1. **A** Anthony likes to put in his two cents' worth.
   B Anthony likes to put in his two cent's worth.

2. **A** Please give me two dollar's worth of stamps.
   B Please give me two dollars' worth of stamps.

3. **A** You will only have a minute's wait.
   B You will only have a minutes' wait.

4. **A** The week's classes were posted on the board.
   B The weeks classes were posted on the board.

5. **A** The snow caused an hours delay.
   B The snow caused an hour's delay.

To decide whether to use a plural or possessive noun, think about what each one means. Look at the blue words in Example 7. How are they different? What does each word mean?

▶ **EXAMPLE 7**

Plural   There were six teams at the meet.

Possessive   The team's prize was a trophy.

Practice D

Read each sentence. Write whether the bold word is *plural* or *possessive*.

1. I have three **uncles.**

2. One **uncle's** name is Irving.

3. All three have cell **phones.**

4. The **phones'** numbers are all alike.

5. I often make a mistake when I dial their **numbers.**

REVIEW

Read each pair of sentences. Choose the correct one and write it on your paper.

1. **A** Where are Armando's running shoes?
   B Where are Armandos running shoes?

2. **A** All of the team's were ready for the swim meet.
   B All of the teams were ready for the swim meet.

3. **A** My neighbor's dog ran away.
   B My neighbors dog ran away.

4. **A** Mrs. Avila looked everywhere for her car keys'.
   B Mrs. Avila looked everywhere for her car keys.

5. **A** Everyone had high hopes at the swim meet.
   B Everyone had high hope's at the swim meet.

Add a possessive noun to complete each sentence.

6. What is your _____ name?

7. Randy met the _____ father.

8. The _____ crops are blackberries and potatoes.

9. The _____ notebook was in her locker.

10. There were many items on the _____ menu.

PUTTING IT ALL TOGETHER

Imagine you have been left alone on an island. Write a paragraph about it. Name three items you wish you had with you. Explain why you wish you had each item. Describe your thoughts and feelings. Use at least one abstract noun. Include both singular and plural nouns in your paragraph. Use at least one possessive noun.

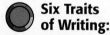

Six Traits of Writing:

Ideas message, details, and purpose

Police Officer

Shara Doli is a police officer. As part of her job, she writes police reports. These reports are about thefts, car accidents, and other problems. When Officer Doli writes a report, she must give clear and correct information. She has to explain things clearly, but she must use few words. Officer Doli wrote the following report. Read her police report. Then follow the directions below.

> On January 28, at 5:15 PM, a woman saw a man running from her car. He was carrying several items. She said that the man's hair was brown. He was wearing black pants and boots. The woman's purse, keys, and watch were missing from her car.

1. List the nouns in the report. Next to each one, write *singular* or *plural*.

2. List the possessive nouns in the report.

3. **CRITICAL THINKING** Why do you think many theft reports include concrete nouns?

⋃ VIEWING

Work with a partner. Imagine that you and your partner are at a crowded place. Your partner gets lost and you want to describe him or her to someone. Look carefully at your partner's clothing. Write a short description of him or her. Think about the words that you use. Are any of them concrete nouns? Are any of them abstract nouns? Are any of them proper nouns? Are any of them possessive nouns?

Finding Facts About a Topic

A research project always starts with a topic. Use the topic to think of questions to ask. Then look for details to answer the questions.

For example, suppose your teacher asks you to write a report about using wind as a source of power. Start by asking yourself questions. Use the words *who, what, when, where, why,* and *how.* Make a list of questions. You might use a graphic organizer like the one at the right.

- Who uses wind power?
- How do people use wind power?
- What are its good points?
- What are its bad points?
- How much does it cost?

1. Write three more questions about wind power.

2. Choose the question that interests you most. Where would you look to find answers to this question?

3. **CRITICAL THINKING** Asking an expert is a good way to find information. Who might be an expert on wind power?

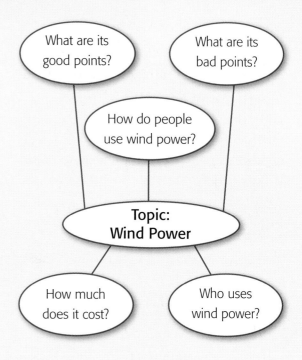

TECHNOLOGY

Use the Internet to help you find answers to research questions. Make a list of keywords to help you. Suppose you want to find facts to answer "How do people use wind power?" You might search for information using the keywords *wind + power + use.* Keep track of the Web sites you visit. How did each one help you?

SUMMARY

- Use nouns to name people, places, things, events, or ideas.

- Use common nouns to name general kinds of people, places, things, events, or ideas.

- Use proper nouns to name particular persons, places, things, events, or ideas.

- Use a capital letter to start each proper noun.

- Use concrete nouns to name things you can see or touch.

- Use abstract nouns to name things you cannot see or touch.

- Make most nouns plural by adding -s. Add -es to nouns that end in s, z, x, ch, or sh.

- Make some nouns that end in -y plural by changing the y to -ies.

- To make a number, date, or letter plural, add an -s. Do not use an apostrophe.

- The singular and plural forms of some nouns are the same.

- Use a possessive noun to show ownership or relationship. Always use an apostrophe with a possessive noun.

GROUP ACTIVITY

Work in a small group to write directions from your classroom to another place in your school. Decide where you want to go. Use both common and proper nouns.

Trade papers with another group. Check the other group's directions for errors. Suggest ways to improve their directions.

Word Bank

abbreviation

abstract noun

apostrophe

collective noun

common noun

compound noun

concrete noun

irregular plural noun

noun

plural noun

possessive noun

proper noun

singular noun

Part A Write the word or words from the Word Bank that complete each sentence.

1. A _____ is a word that names a person, place, thing, or idea.

2. A _____ is the name of a particular person, place, thing, or idea and is always capitalized.

3. An _____ is the short form of a word.

4. A _____ names only one person, place, thing, or idea.

5. An _____ names something you cannot see or touch but can think or talk about.

6. The name of more than one person, place, thing, or idea is a _____.

7. A _____ is made from two words.

8. A _____ is the name of a general type of person, place, thing, or idea.

9. An _____ shows that a noun is possessive.

10. A _____ names a group of people, places, or things.

11. A _____ names something you can see or touch.

12. A _____ shows ownership or relationship and needs an apostrophe.

13. A plural noun that does not follow the normal rules is an _____.

Part B Write the nouns in each sentence.

14. Emily bought a new pair of wheels for her bike.

15. Emily wants to ride her bike.

16. Emily decides to take a friend along.

17. Angela says she will meet Emily at her house.

Part C Write each sentence. Capitalize the proper nouns.

18. On saturday annie visits aunt edna.

19. She just moved to town from houston, texas.

20. She used to teach at the university of florida.

21. She was a professor of american history.

Part D Write the letter of the answer.

22. Which of these is an abbreviation?
   A Doctor   **C** Louisiana
   B Mr.   **D** Boston's

23. Which of these is a possessive noun?
   A dogs   **C** turkeys
   B cat's   **D** Smiths

24. Which of these is a plural noun?
   A Cassie's   **C** geese
   B Davis   **D** group

25. Which of these is a concrete noun?
   A candle   **C** happiness
   B difference   **D** time

Test Tip
To study definitions of words, write each word on a card. Write the word's definition on the other side of the card. Use the cards to test yourself.

Using Pronouns in Sentences

When you write or speak, you name people and things. The words you use to name people and things are nouns. After you write or say a noun, you do not have to repeat it again and again. You can use a pronoun in its place.

Look at this photo. What is the worker doing? She has removed one billboard. She is replacing it with a new one. That is what pronouns do, too. They replace nouns. For example, the word *she* is a pronoun. In the sentences above, can you see two places where *she* replaced the noun *worker*?

In Chapter 3, you will learn about kinds of pronouns and how to use them in sentences.

GOALS FOR LEARNING

- To understand how pronouns and antecedents work together
- To identify and use personal pronouns
- To identify and use relative pronouns
- To identify and use interrogative pronouns
- To identify and use demonstrative pronouns
- To identify and use indefinite pronouns
- To write contractions that use pronouns

Reading Strategy: Predicting

When you preview a text, you take a quick look through it. Previewing a text helps you think about what you already know about the subject. It also helps you predict what will come next. To predict means to make a smart guess about what lies ahead. Do these things as you preview and predict:

- Make your best guess about what might follow.
- Use what you already know to predict meaning or order.
- Ask yourself why you think certain things will follow.

Key Vocabulary Words

Pronoun A word that takes the place of one or more nouns

Antecedent The noun or nouns that a pronoun replaces

Personal pronoun A pronoun that refers to a person or a thing

First-person pronoun A pronoun that refers to the speaker

Second-person pronoun A pronoun that refers to the person who is being spoken to

Third-person pronoun A pronoun that refers to the person or thing that is being talked about

Reflexive pronoun A pronoun that ends in *-self* or *-selves*

Possessive pronoun A pronoun that shows that something belongs to someone or something

Relative pronoun One of these pronouns: *who, whom, whose, that,* and *which*

Compound relative pronoun One of these pronouns: *whoever, whomever, whichever,* and *whatever*

Interrogative pronoun A pronoun that asks a question

Demonstrative pronoun A pronoun that points out a particular person or thing

Indefinite pronoun A pronoun that does not refer to a specific person or thing

Contraction Two words made into one by replacing one or more letters with an apostrophe

What Is a Pronoun?

Objectives

- To identify a pronoun and its antecedent
- To understand how a pronoun and its antecedent agree

Pronoun

A word that takes the place of one or more nouns

Antecedent

The noun or nouns that a pronoun replaces

Reading Strategy:
Predicting

Preview the lesson title. Predict what you will learn in this lesson.

NOTE

The word *antecedent* comes from two Latin words that mean "to go before or in front." The antecedent of a pronoun usually comes before or in front of the pronoun.

A **pronoun** is a word that takes the place of one or more nouns. Pronouns can replace either common nouns or proper nouns.

▶ **EXAMPLE 1**

Armando is a senior. He writes for the school newspaper. One of his stories appears in every issue.

The pronoun *he* takes the place of the proper noun *Armando*. The pronoun *his* takes the place of the possessive noun *Armando's*. The **antecedent** is the noun that a pronoun replaces.

Practice A

List each bold pronoun. After it, write its antecedent.

Armando and Joe are both seniors. **They** are friends. Mrs. Benson is one of **their** teachers. **She** teaches history. Tanya Johnson is also in the class. Joe has known **her** for years. **They** went to the same elementary school.

Why are pronouns useful? Without them, you would have to repeat the same nouns over and over again.

▶ **EXAMPLE 2**

Nathan said that Nathan was going to call Nathan's mother.

Nathan said that he was going to call his mother.

List each word or phrase in bold. After it, write a pronoun to replace it.

Armando looked for **Armando's** history class. To **Armando**, history is fun. **Armando** hurried to the second floor. Near the door, an old friend waved hello. "I'm in this class, too," **the friend** said. **Armando and Armando's friend** walked in together.

Pronoun-Antecedent Agreement

A pronoun must agree with its antecedent. This means:

- The antecedent and pronoun must be the *same in number*. If the antecedent is singular, the pronoun must be singular. If the antecedent is plural, the pronoun must be plural.

- Some singular antecedents have a gender (masculine or feminine). The singular pronoun must have the *same gender* as the antecedent.

▶ **EXAMPLE 3**

Robin will wash the floor and wax it. (singular, no gender)

Grace and Jake know that they will be late. (plural)

Sam goes fishing whenever he can. (singular, masculine)

Sandra will help if she is not working. (singular, feminine)

Practice C

Write the pronoun that goes in the blank. It must agree with the number and gender of its antecedent.

1. Lauren, did ____ put the dog outside?
2. Tyrone and I got lost as ____ explored the woods.
3. When he finished the book, he put ____ on the table.
4. The deer came near, so Tomás took a picture of ____.
5. David and I loved the gifts you bought for ____.

NOTE

Some nouns and pronouns have a gender. *Gender* is either masculine or feminine. *Masculine* refers to males, and *feminine* refers to females.

Reading Strategy:
Predicting

Think about what you predicted this lesson would be about. Was your prediction correct?

REVIEW

Write each bold pronoun. Next to each pronoun, write its antecedent.

1. Emily and Angela like school, and **they** enjoy history class.

2. Emily was glad that **she** had studied for the test.

3. Angela and I studied hard, so **we** were well prepared.

4. Because Mr. Thomas just gave a test, **he** will start a new unit next week.

5. Emily, Angela, and I are excited to get **our** tests back.

Number your paper from 6 to 10. Write the five pronouns in the paragraph. Write the antecedent next to each one.

> Armando is on the soccer team. He asked Angela and Nathan to come to his game on Tuesday. They both came and cheered loudly for Armando. He scored one goal. After the game, they all went to Tony's to celebrate.

VOCABULARY BUILDER

Understanding Root Words

The root word *tele* comes from a Greek word that means "far away." Here are five words that contain the root word *tele: telegram, telegraph, telephone, telescope, television.* Write your own definition of each word. Then use a dictionary to check your definitions.

Study the dictionary pages where you found these words. Find two other words that contain the root word *tele.* What do these words mean? How are they related to the meaning "far away"?

Personal Pronouns

Objectives

- To understand and use first-, second-, and third-person pronouns
- To understand and use possessive pronouns
- To understand and use reflexive pronouns

Personal pronoun

A pronoun that refers to a person or a thing

First-person pronoun

A pronoun that refers to the speaker

Second-person pronoun

A pronoun that refers to the person who is being spoken to

Third-person pronoun

A pronoun that refers to the person or thing that is being talked about

Personal pronouns refer to people or things. A **first-person pronoun** refers to the person speaking. A **second-person pronoun** refers to the person being spoken to. A **third-person pronoun** refers to the person or thing being talked about. Personal pronouns can be singular or plural. A singular pronoun refers to one person or thing. A plural pronoun refers to more than one person or thing.

▶ **EXAMPLE 1**

I am ready. (first person, singular)

You are ready. (second person, singular)

He is ready. She is ready. It is ready. (third person, singular)

We are ready. (first person, plural)

You are ready. (second person, plural)

They are ready. (third person, plural)

Here is a chart showing personal pronouns. Personal pronouns can be used in different ways in sentences—as the *subject*, or as the *object* of a verb or preposition.

	Subject	Object
Singular		
First Person	I	me
Second Person	you	you
Third Person	he, she, it	him, her, it
Plural		
First Person	we	us
Second Person	you	you
Third Person	they	them

Reading Strategy:
Predicting

What do you already know about the word *personal*? Use it to predict what you will learn in this lesson.

Practice A

Use the pronoun chart. Write the person (*first, second,* or *third*) of each bold pronoun. Then decide whether each pronoun is singular or plural. Write *singular* or *plural*.

1. Alicia and Juan gave **us** their seats at the lunch table.

2. **They** were going back to class early.

3. "Are **you** really hungry?" Alicia asked me.

4. **I** could tell that Alicia wanted my sandwich.

5. She was staring at **it**.

Practice B

Decide whether each bold pronoun is a subject or an object in the sentence. Write *subject* or *object*.

1. **I** offered Alicia part of my sandwich.

2. She had a small bite of **it**.

3. She told **me** that it was delicious.

4. We waved goodbye to **them**.

5. **They** went back to class.

Rachel, Megan, and Brenna were happy to finally sit down and eat. They were so hungry!

Possessive Pronouns

A **possessive pronoun** is a personal pronoun that takes the place of a possessive noun. It shows ownership. Sometimes, a noun follows a possessive pronoun.

Singular possessive pronouns: my, your, his, her, its

Plural possessive pronouns: our, your, their

▶ **EXAMPLE 2**

This is Jill's book.

This is her book.

The Smiths' dog is very playful.

Their dog is very playful.

At other times, possessive pronouns are used alone.

Singular possessive pronouns: mine, yours, his, hers, its

Plural possessive pronouns: ours, yours, theirs

▶ **EXAMPLE 3**

This book is Jill's.

This book is hers.

The playful dog is the Smiths'.

The playful dog is theirs.

Practice C

Write the possessive pronoun in each sentence.

1. Their guitars came from Spain.

2. Mine has a red sticker on it.

3. How old is her brother?

4. That tree lost all of its leaves.

5. I told him that your house is for sale.

Reflexive Pronouns

A **reflexive pronoun** is a personal pronoun that ends in *-self* or *-selves*.

Reflexive Pronouns

Singular	
First Person	myself
Second Person	yourself
Third Person	himself, herself, itself
Plural	
First Person	ourselves
Second Person	yourselves
Third Person	themselves

▶ **EXAMPLE 4**

Jon prides himself on his manners. (third person, singular)

We helped ourselves to more potatoes. (first person, plural)

Practice D

On your paper, write the reflexive pronoun in each sentence. Identify each as *singular* or *plural*.

1. Jim scheduled himself to open the swimming pool on Wednesdays.

2. He jokes, "The pool can't open itself!"

3. Angela's students push themselves to swim better and faster.

4. The students say, "If we challenge ourselves, maybe we can be as good as Angela!"

5. When they say that, Angela feels proud of herself.

REVIEW

Write the possessive pronoun that completes each sentence.

1. (My, Mine) homework is almost finished.

2. Jan said that (her, hers) is broken.

3. Is that car (their, theirs)?

4. The dog wagged (it, its) tail.

5. I like my bike, but I like (your, yours) better.

Write each sentence. Add the reflexive pronoun that fits.

6. I like to walk home by _____.

7. Ari and Babette let _____ in the front door.

8. Did you buy _____ a birthday gift?

9. Eduardo reminded _____ by writing a note.

10. We promised _____ that we would do it, and we did.

Relative Pronouns

Objectives

■ To understand how relative pronouns are used

■ To identify and use relative pronouns

Relative pronoun

One of these pronouns: *who, whom, whose, that,* and *which*

Reading Strategy: Predicting

The lessons in this book are written in a certain pattern. You can predict that Examples are followed by Practices.

The **relative pronouns** are *who, whom, whose, that,* and *which*. In a sentence, a relative pronoun follows its antecedent.

Who and *whom* refer to a person or people. *Whose* shows that something belongs to or with someone.

▶ **EXAMPLE 1**

The woman who is speaking is my aunt. (antecedent: woman)

The man to whom I spoke is my uncle. (antecedent: man)

The boy whose dog is lost gave a reward. (antecedent: boy)

That and *which* refer to places or things. When a phrase starts with *which*, it usually needs a comma before and after it.

▶ **EXAMPLE 2**

The bread that Ned baked is delicious. (antecedent: bread)

The book, which has a red cover, is hers. (antecedent: book)

Practice A

Write the relative pronoun in each sentence. Next to it, write the antecedent.

1. The man who owns the music store sells CDs and cassettes.

2. There is the customer whom Emily met last week.

3. Emily wants the book that is on the table.

4. Emily's dog, which is a poodle, likes to eat noodles.

5. Her dog prefers Thai noodles, which are very spicy.

Reading Strategy:

Predicting

Based on the practices in this lesson, what do you think the Lesson 3-3 Review will be like?

Practice B

Write each sentence on your paper. Add the relative pronoun that fits.

1. Ted has a voice _____ carries far.

2. The woman _____ came to the door did not live there.

3. The CDs, _____ are old and scratched, belong to him.

4. The girl _____ ticket got lost was very sad.

5. The story _____ he told was unbelievable.

The **compound relative pronouns** are *whoever, whomever, whichever,* and *whatever*. They are compound because they combine two words. *Whoever* and *whomever* take the place of the names of people. *Whichever* and *whatever* take the place of the names of things.

▶ **EXAMPLE 3**

"Whoever wants to read this book may borrow it," said the teacher.

"Blue shoes or black shoes," said Emily's mother. "Choose whichever you want."

Practice C

Write each compound relative pronoun on your paper.

1. Here are several books. Choose whichever you want for your book report.

2. Do whatever you think should be done.

3. Invite whomever you want to the party.

4. I have lots of CDs. Take whichever you like best.

5. Whoever wants this sandwich can have it.

REVIEW

Write the relative pronoun in each sentence. Next to it, write its antecedent.

1. Nathan wants the new stamps that the post office just issued.

2. The bandleader is Mr. Jackson, who played the trumpet in college.

3. Emily went to the library, which is next to the post office.

4. Angela, whose book bag is on the table, is late for school.

5. Carol is whom I talked to in the office.

Write the compound relative pronoun that completes each sentence.

6. (Whoever, Whatever) made that mess should clean it up.

7. Please do (whichever, whatever) you can to help us.

8. We will ask (whomever, whichever) we want to the concert.

9. You may have (whichever, whoever) of the desserts you like.

10. (Whatever, Whoever) answered the phone sounded excited.

Pronouns That Ask Questions

Interrogative pronoun

A pronoun that asks a question

Reading Strategy: Predicting

Think back to your study of kinds of sentences. Why do you think *who, whom, whose, which,* and *what* are called interrogative pronouns?

The **interrogative pronouns** are *who, whom, whose, which,* and *what.* They are used to ask a question.

▶ **EXAMPLE 1**

Who is planning the party?

Whom did you call?

Whose is this hat?

Which of these movies do you like?

What is your telephone number?

You can use an interrogative pronoun to ask a question directly or indirectly.

▶ **EXAMPLE 2**

Direct	Who is going to be there?
Indirect	Tell me who is going to be there.
Direct	Which of these shirts is on sale?
Indirect	She asked which of these shirts is on sale.

Practice A

Write the interrogative pronoun in each sentence.

1. With whom did you go to dinner?
2. I do not know which one to choose!
3. Who came to the office?
4. Whose dog was lost?
5. Tell me what caused the argument.

NOTE

To *interrogate* means to examine by asking questions. After a crime, police officers interrogate possible suspects.

Reading Strategy:
Predicting

Was the prediction you made on page 66 correct?

The words *who, whom, whose, which,* and *what* are interrogative pronouns only when they ask a question. Sometimes these words are used as relative pronouns. Relative pronouns do not ask a question.

▶ **EXAMPLE 3**

Interrogative   Who is planning the party?

Relative   Greg helped the student who missed class.

An interrogative pronoun is different from a personal or relative pronoun. It does not have an antecedent that can be stated. Its "antecedent" is the answer to the question it asks.

Who refers to a person or persons. *What* refers to things, places, or ideas.

▶ **EXAMPLE 4**

Who is your swimming coach?

What is the name of your town?

Which can refer to people or things. Use *which* when there is a choice between two or more things. *Whose* is a possessive pronoun. Use it to show belonging.

▶ **EXAMPLE 5**

Which team will win the game?

Whose car is this?

Practice B

Write the pronoun that completes each sentence.

1. (Which, Who) of the students asked for directions?
2. (Who, Whose) homework is this?
3. (What, Which) is the process for making a cake?
4. Next to (who, whom) do you want to sit?
5. I cannot remember (who, whom) borrowed my notes.

REVIEW

Write the interrogative pronoun in each sentence.

1. What does Angela do after school on Fridays?

2. Who said, "I have a dream"?

3. Whose was the big blue boat?

4. What did Mr. Thomas just say?

5. Which of the fruits is your favorite?

Number your paper from 6 to 10. List the five pronouns in these sentences. Next to each pronoun, write whether it is *personal*, *relative*, or *interrogative*.

Neeru is a new student who goes to Wilson High School.

Which is her hometown—Bombay or Calcutta?

She lived in Calcutta, which is in India.

Demonstrative Pronouns

Objectives

- To identify demonstrative pronouns
- To understand how demonstrative pronouns are used

Demonstrative pronoun

A pronoun that points out a particular person or thing

Reading Strategy:
Predicting

What do you already know about the word *demonstrate*? Based on this knowledge, predict what a demonstrative pronoun might be.

A **demonstrative pronoun** points out a particular person or thing. The four demonstrative pronouns are *this*, *these*, *that*, and *those*.

This and *that* are singular. They refer to one person or thing. *These* and *those* are plural. They refer to more than one person or thing.

▶ **EXAMPLE 1**

This is my house. (singular)

That is my high school. (singular)

These are my pencils. (plural)

Those are my cousins. (plural)

Practice A

Write the demonstrative pronoun in each sentence. Next to it, write whether it is *singular* or *plural*.

1. Is this the right assignment?
2. These are roses from Mrs. Choy's garden.
3. Is that the shirt Armando wore to practice yesterday?
4. This is the auditorium where the Drama Club performs.
5. Are those Emily's clarinet reeds?

Reading Strategy:
Predicting

How close was
your prediction
of the definition
of demonstrative
pronoun?

This and *these* point out people and things that are close by.
That and *those* point out people and things that are farther
away.

▶ **EXAMPLE 2**

This is a pen I have in my hand. (near)

These are new shoes I have on my feet. (near)

That is my friend Angela standing over there. (far)

Those are my books by the door. (far)

Practice B

Write the pronoun that completes the sentence.

1. Was (this, that) a shooting star that I saw?

2. Is (this, that) your sheet music that I have, Emily?

3. (These, Those) are my favorite rings. I wear them all
the time.

4. Here are your notebooks. (These, Those) over there
are mine.

5. I found a pen. Was Nathan looking for (this, that)?

*This playing field is
better than that one
over there.*

REVIEW

Write the demonstrative pronoun in each sentence.

1. Whose paper is this?
2. That is a very ugly car.
3. These are the football team's new uniforms.
4. Do you know if this is Angela's jacket?
5. Those are my parents standing by the door.

Find the pronouns in the sentences below. Next to each pronoun, write whether it is *personal*, *relative*, *interrogative*, or *demonstrative*.

6. Which lane will Angela be swimming in?
7. Ms. Benson, who teaches math, lives near school.
8. This is Nathan's book.
9. Mr. Santos is our advisor.
10. Have you seen those pens I bought yesterday?

SPELLING BUILDER

Doubling Consonants

Read these words: *hottest, hopping.* Notice the double consonants before the -*est* and -*ing* endings. The endings -*est* and -*ing* begin with vowels. Sometimes you add an ending that begins with a vowel to a consonant-vowel-consonant (CVC) word. You must double the final consonant of that word. Then add the ending.

1. Add -*est* to *wet* and to *red*.
2. Add -*ed* and -*ing* to *tap* and to *jog*.
3. Make a list of four more CVC words. Then add one of these endings to each word: -*ed*, -*est*, or -*ing*.

Indefinite Pronouns

Objectives

- To identify indefinite pronouns
- To understand agreement between an indefinite pronoun and one or more possessive pronouns that refer to it
- To use indefinite pronouns in sentences

Indefinite pronoun

A pronoun that does not refer to a specific person or thing

Reading Strategy:
Predicting

What do you already know about the word *definite*? Predict what an indefinite pronoun might be.

Indefinite pronouns do not refer to specific people or things. Because of this, they do not have clear antecedents. Most indefinite pronouns are singular. Very few are plural.

Singular Indefinite Pronouns

anybody	either	neither	one
anyone	everybody	nobody	somebody
anything	everyone	no one	someone
each	everything	nothing	something

Plural Indefinite Pronouns

both	few	many	several	some

An indefinite pronoun can be the antecedent for another pronoun.

▶ **EXAMPLE 1**

Both brought their books. (plural)

Each of the girls has her book. (singular)

Practice A

Write the indefinite pronoun in each sentence. After it, write whether the pronoun is *singular* or *plural*.

1. Many want to come.

2. Nobody feels ready.

3. Both speak Spanish well.

4. Neither like broccoli.

5. Either is a fine choice.

Use plural possessive pronouns with plural indefinite pronouns. Use singular possessive pronouns with singular indefinite pronouns. Sometimes you do not know whether a singular indefinite pronoun names a male or female. Sometimes, the pronoun names a group of people, but it is still singular. You can use *his* or *her,* as in the first sentence of Example 2. You can also rewrite the sentence with a plural subject, as in the second sentence in Example 2.

▶ **EXAMPLE 2**

Everyone played his or her own instrument. (singular)

All of the students played their own instruments. (plural)

Practice B

Write the pronoun on your paper that completes the sentence.

1. Everyone should turn in (his or her, their) paper.

2. Several gave (his or her, their) parents the newsletter.

3. Everyone must take off (his or her, their) shoes.

4. Few could identify (his or her, their) bags.

5. Someone left (his or her, their) lights on.

REVIEW

Write the indefinite pronoun in each sentence. Tell whether each pronoun is *singular* or *plural*.

1. There is nothing I like more than a good movie.

2. Somebody is at the door.

3. Is anyone listening to me?

4. Neither knows the answer.

5. None is cheap.

Number your paper from 6 to 10. List each pronoun in the paragraph. Next to each pronoun, write whether it is *personal*, *relative*, or *indefinite*.

After school, everyone likes to go to Tony's Cafe. Emily enjoys seeing her friends who meet there. They think Tony's Cafe has the best food in town. Everything tastes great!

Pronouns in Contractions

Contraction

Two words made into one by replacing one or more letters with an apostrophe

Reading Strategy:
Predicting

Preview the lesson title. Predict what you will learn in this lesson.

 Writing Tip

You probably use contractions when you speak. You may also use contractions in informal writing. Avoid using contractions in formal writing such as an assignment or a business letter.

In Chapter 2, you learned that a possessive noun, such as *student's*, has an apostrophe ('). You also use an apostrophe in a **contraction**. A contraction is two words made into one by replacing one or more letters with an apostrophe.

▶ **EXAMPLE 1**

I will go. (two words)

I'll go. (contraction)

These contractions are made from a pronoun and a verb.

Common Contractions

I'd = I would, I had	who's = who is
I'll = I will	we'll = we will
I'm = I am	we're = we are
I've = I have	we'd = we would, we had
you'll = you will	we've = we have
you're = you are	they'd = they would, they had
you've = you have	they're = they are
he's = he is, he has	they've = they have
she's = she is, she has	that's = that is
it's = it is, it has	that's = that is
let's = let us	

Practice A

Write each contraction in the paragraph as two words.

I'd like to tell you a story about the invention of the radio. We'd not have a radio without the invention of the microphone and the Audion tube. You're probably asking, "What's an Audion tube?" It's a tube that makes electrical impulses louder and sends them through the air.

REVIEW

Number your paper from 1 to 5. List each contraction in the paragraph. After each one, write the two words used to make it.

You've probably heard people talk about yoga. It's something people have been doing for three thousand years. If you took a yoga class, you'd find that yoga is more than exercise. It's helpful for the mind and body. The yoga student's first job is to learn how to breathe. "I know how to breathe," you'll probably say. But yoga breathing is very different.

Number your paper from 6 to 10. List each contraction in the paragraph. After each one, write the two words used to make it.

What do you know about Robert Frost? He's one of America's most famous poets. If you've read "The Road Not Taken," you'll know why he's so popular. President John F. Kennedy asked Frost to read a poem. It was read on the day when Kennedy became president. What's the name of the poem Frost read? Its title is "The Gift Outright." During his lifetime, Robert Frost won the Pulitzer Prize for poetry four times.

PUTTING IT ALL TOGETHER

Create a web diagram for pronouns. Draw a circle. Write the word *Pronouns* in the center. Then draw five lines that extend out from the circle. Draw a circle at the end of each line. Write these words in the new circles: *Personal, Reflexive, Possessive, Demonstrative,* and *Indefinite.* In each circle, write three examples of that kind of pronoun.

Six Traits of Writing:
Conventions correct grammar, spelling, and mechanics

Writing a Thank-You Letter

Jordan Perez and Peggy Ormand are best friends. Both are hockey fans. Jordan's father bought them two tickets for last Saturday night's hockey game. Here is the thank-you letter Peggy sent to Jordan's father after the game. Read Peggy's letter carefully. Then follow the directions.

> September 2, 2006
>
> Dear Mr. Perez,
>
> Thank you very much for the hockey ticket for last Saturday's game. Jordan and I had a great time. We cheered so loudly that we lost our voices in the third period. Nobody enjoyed the game more than I did! Thanks again.
>
> Sincerely,
>
> Peggy

1. Write the antecedent for the pronoun *you* in the first sentence.

2. List all of the pronouns that appear in the letter. After each one, write the kind of pronoun it is.

3. CRITICAL THINKING Why is it important to use pronouns correctly in a letter?

SPEAKING AND LISTENING

Write a thank-you letter to someone who has helped you or given you a gift. Use pronouns to avoid repetition. Then get together with a partner. Read each other's letters aloud. Suggest ways that your partner might improve his or her letter.

BUILDING RESEARCH SKILLS

Using a Book of Quotations

Sometimes you may want to copy someone's exact words. Those words, called a quotation, are always placed in quotation marks. One place to find interesting quotations is in a book of quotations. A popular one is *Bartlett's Familiar Quotations*. You can find it in your library. There are two ways to search for quotations in *Bartlett's*.

First, you can look up a person by his or her last name in the author index. This index is at the front of the book. If you want a quotation by John F. Kennedy, look up *Kennedy* in the index.

Second, you can search for a quotation on a certain subject. Look for the subject in the keyword index. This index is at the back of the book. Each entry gives a few words from a quotation. It also gives the page number on which the quotation is found. See the index entry for *weather* below. The entry uses *w.* for *weather*.

Index

Weather, always fair w., 589:3
appeared when w. cleared, 545:3
both with anxiety about w., 589:3
clear w. spreads cloudless, 53:9
cloudy was the w., 792:17
come wind come w., 272:29

Write your answer to each question.

1. Suppose your teacher asks you to find a quotation by W. C. Fields. Where in *Bartlett's* would you look?

2. Use a book of quotations to find a quotation by a famous person. Next, find a quotation on a subject that interests you. Write each quotation and its author on your paper. Include the page number where each quotation is found in the book.

3. **CRITICAL THINKING** Why is it important to write down information about where a quotation can be found?

TECHNOLOGY

You can use a search engine on a computer to find quotations on the Internet. To use a search engine, log onto the Internet. A Web browser contains a search box. In this box, type in one or more keywords plus the word *quotation.* Then click on the search button. Your search results will appear. What would you type in the search box to find a quotation by Robert Frost about snow?

SUMMARY

- Use pronouns to replace nouns or other pronouns.

- Make sure a pronoun agrees with its antecedent in number and gender.

- Personal pronouns can be first-, second-, or third-person.

- Recognize that reflexive pronouns end in *-self* or *-selves*.

- Use possessive pronouns to show that something belongs to someone or something.

- Use relative pronouns to connect groups of words to nouns or pronouns.

- A compound relative pronoun refers to an antecedent not stated in the sentence.

- Use an interrogative pronoun to ask a question directly or indirectly.

- Use a demonstrative pronoun to point out a person or thing.

- Use an indefinite pronoun to refer to an unknown person or thing.

- Do not use contractions in formal writing. A contraction is two words made into one by replacing letters with an apostrophe.

GROUP ACTIVITY

Jamie planned a surprise party for her brother. The invitation she sent is at the right. Work in a small group to write an invitation to the rest of the class. Invite them to an imaginary event, such as a party, a meeting, or a fair. Use the headings *What*, *When*, *Where*, and *Given By*. Write a note at the bottom like Jamie did. Use pronouns in the note.

> ### YOU ARE INVITED!
> What: It is a surprise party for Juan!
> When: 8:00 PM on July 3
> Where: Bruno's Italian Restaurant
> Given By: Jamie
> Call Jamie at (555) 123-4567 by June 25.
> Remember, Juan does not know about the party. Don't tell him!

Word Bank

antecedent

compound relative
  pronoun

contraction

demonstrative
  pronoun

first-person
  pronoun

indefinite pronoun

interrogative
  pronoun

personal pronoun

possessive pronoun

pronoun

reflexive pronoun

relative pronoun

second-person
  pronoun

third-person
  pronoun

Part A Write the word or words from the Word Bank that complete each sentence.

1. A _____ makes two words into one by replacing letters with an apostrophe.

2. An _____ asks a question.

3. A _____ is a pronoun such as *whoever*, *whomever*, *whichever*, and *whatever*.

4. A _____ refers to the person who is speaking.

5. A _____ refers to a person or thing.

6. An _____ does not refer to a specific person or thing.

7. A _____ refers to the person or thing being talked about.

8. A _____ ends in *-self* or *-selves*.

9. An _____ is a noun that a pronoun replaces.

10. A _____ points out a particular person or thing.

11. A _____ refers to the person who is spoken to.

12. A _____ is a word that takes the place of a noun.

13. A _____ is a pronoun such as *who*, *whom*, *whose*, *that*, and *which*.

14. A _____ shows ownership.

Part B Write the pronoun in each sentence. Write the antecedent next to each pronoun.

15. Angela was glad she went to the game.

16. Michelle left her notebook here.

17. Emily played a song she really likes.

Part C Write the pronoun(s) in each sentence. Next to each pronoun, write whether it is *personal*, *relative*, *interrogative*, *demonstrative*, or *indefinite*.

18. I don't like people who interrupt.

19. Everybody in the class likes math because it challenges them.

20. Which classes do you like most?

Part D Write the letter of the correct answer.

21. Armando went to see a trainer _____ he had met through a friend.

    A which   **B** whom   **C** whoever   **D** whenever

22. "I want to make _____ arms stronger," he said.

    A my   **B** mine   **C** their   **D** whose

23. Looking at the machines, Armando asked, "What do _____ do?"

    A this   **B** these   **C** any   **D** many

Part E Write each contraction as two words.

24. I'll let you know when we're ready to go.

25. That's the only route they've taken.

Test Tip

When studying for a test, review earlier assignments and quizzes that cover the same information.

4

Using Adjectives in Sentences

Sometimes just naming a person, place, or thing is not enough. You want to tell more about it. You may want to talk about its size, its color, or your feelings about it. You may want to compare it to something else. This is the time to use an adjective. Adjectives are words that describe nouns and pronouns.

Look at the photo of the city. See the shorter, old buildings in the front? See the new, taller buildings in the back? See the green leaves? The words *shorter*, *old*, *new*, *taller*, and *green* are adjectives.

In Chapter 4, you will learn about adjectives and how to use them in sentences. By choosing good adjectives, you can change dull writing into interesting writing.

GOALS FOR LEARNING

- To recognize adjectives in sentences, and to identify the nouns they describe
- To recognize and use definite and indefinite articles
- To use proper adjectives
- To use possessive nouns and pronouns as adjectives
- To use numbers as adjectives
- To use demonstrative pronouns as adjectives
- To use adjectives that compare

Reading Strategy: Text Structure

Information in a book or chapter comes in a certain order. Knowing that order can help you decide what information is most important. It can also help you see how the different parts fit together. This order and fit is called structure.

Before you begin reading this chapter, take a few minutes to look at the structure. Look at the chapter and lesson titles. Their focus is adjectives. Notice the Lesson Reviews and the Chapter Review.

Ask yourself: What are the parts of each lesson? Notice the bold vocabulary words. Examples show how to use adjectives. Practice sets are activities that will help you use adjectives.

Summarize the text by thinking about its structure.

Key Vocabulary Words

Adjective A word that describes or tells about a noun or pronoun

Predicate adjective An adjective that follows a verb and describes the subject of the sentence

Definite article The word *the*; it means a particular person or thing

Indefinite article The word *a* or *an*; it means any one of a group of people or things

Proper adjective A proper noun used as an adjective, or an adjective made from a proper noun

Demonstrative adjective The word *this*, *that*, *these*, or *those* used as an adjective

Positive form The form of an adjective used to describe people or things

Comparative form The form of an adjective used to compare two people or things

Superlative form The form of an adjective used to compare more than two people or things

What Is an Adjective?

Objectives

- To identify an adjective that comes before a noun
- To identify an adjective that comes after a noun
- To identify the noun or pronoun that an adjective describes
- To use adjectives to describe nouns and pronouns

Adjective

A word that describes or tells about a noun or pronoun

Reading Strategy:
Text Structure

Before you read a lesson, read the list of Objectives. They are your learning goals for the lesson.

An **adjective** is a word that describes a noun or pronoun. An adjective may tell what kind, which one, how many, or how much. Usually, an adjective comes before the noun it is describing.

▶ **EXAMPLE 1**

What kind?	Ana likes winter weather.
Which one?	I saw the new pony.
How many?	We planted two trees.
How much?	The dress cost thirty dollars.

Practice A

The words in bold are adjectives. List each adjective on your paper. After each one, write the noun it describes.

1. The suit matches her **new** robe.

2. She dives into the **chilly** pool.

3. Angela takes an **old** towel to swim meets for **good** luck.

4. She swims in **two** races.

5. Angela wins a **blue** ribbon for **first** place.

You can use more than one adjective to describe a noun.

▶ **EXAMPLE 2**

Wednesday was a cool, windy day.

(*Cool* and *windy* describe the day.)

Practice B

Write each sentence on your paper. Add one or more adjectives to describe each noun in bold.

1. Emily sits on the **couch.**

2. Nathan's family took a **trip.**

3. Franco played a **game.**

4. Nora wore **clothes** from Spain.

5. We all drank mugs of **cocoa**.

Most adjectives come in front of the nouns they describe. Sometimes adjectives come after the noun. Then they are set off with commas.

▶ **EXAMPLE 3**

The eager and excited players took the field.

The players, eager and excited, took the field.

Some adjectives follow the verb in a sentence. They come in the predicate of the sentence. These adjectives are called **predicate adjectives.** A predicate adjective tells about the noun or pronoun that is the subject of the sentence.

Reading Strategy:
Text Structure

Why is the term *predicate adjectives* in bold in this paragraph?

▶ **EXAMPLE 4**

The students were happy. (*Happy* describes the students.)

Practice C

Write the adjective or adjectives in each sentence. Next to each one, write the noun or pronoun it describes.

1. Mr. Jackson is the band teacher.

2. He is great at playing the trumpet.

3. The band plays many songs, popular and classical.

4. Mr. Jackson is eager to get large audiences.

5. He stands, tall and patient, until the class is ready.

REVIEW

Write each adjective in bold on your paper. Next to each adjective, write the noun it describes.

1. Angela is **excited**.

2. She has **strong** arms and legs from **swim** practice.

3. Neeru is **tiny**.

4. She has **long, black** hair.

5. Nathan is **stocky** and **strong**.

6. He has **wavy** hair and a **nice** smile.

Write each sentence. Add an adjective to describe each noun in the sentence. Underline each adjective you use.

7. The coat is on the chair.

8. We bought it at a sale.

9. Her brother wore it to a game.

10. The gym was packed with fans.

The Articles *A*, *An*, and *The*

Objectives

- To recognize and use definite articles
- To recognize and use indefinite articles

Definite article

The word *the*; it means a particular person or thing

Indefinite article

The word *a* or *an*; it means any one of a group of people or things

The words *a*, *an*, and *the* are special adjectives called articles. An article always comes before the noun it describes. Use the **definite article** *the* when you are talking about a particular person or thing. Use an **indefinite article** when you are talking about any one of a group of people or things. *A* and *an* are indefinite articles.

▶ **EXAMPLE 1**

Emily wants the book about frogs.

(Emily wants a particular book. It is the book about frogs.)

Nathan was looking for a book.

(Nathan does not want a particular book. Any book will do.)

Practice A

Write each sentence on your paper. Underline each article.

1. Jackie saw a show about the making of a movie.
2. The special effects were amazing.
3. A model ship was used for part of the movie.
4. It was an effect that was needed.
5. The ship is now in a museum.

Runi heard that this movie features an unusual ship.

Reading Strategy:
Text Structure

In this book, Examples are followed by Practices.

Use the article *a* before a word that begins with a consonant sound. Use the article *an* before a word that begins with a vowel sound.

▶ **EXAMPLE 2**

a book   a math problem

an apple   an easy problem

Practice B

Write the article that completes each sentence.

1. Yesterday was (a, an) unusual day.
2. I need (a, an) explanation.
3. The student raised her hand to give (a, an) answer.
4. The new television was (a, an) big bargain.
5. Michelle wanted (a, an) new pair of shoes.

Use the articles *a* and *an* only with singular nouns. You can use the article *the* with singular and plural nouns.

▶ **EXAMPLE 3**

Angela bought a swimsuit. (*Swimsuit* is singular.)

She wore it to the practice. (*Practice* is singular.)

She talked to the swimmers. (*Swimmers* is plural.)

Practice C

Write each sentence. Fill in each blank with *a* or *an*.

1. José took _____ trip to _____ island.
2. He found _____ starfish and _____ oyster shell.
3. José built _____ huge sand castle on the beach.
4. _____ exciting tour of the island lasted _____ hour.
5. _____ person in the group asked _____ question.

REVIEW

Write the article that belongs in each sentence.

1. Emily has (a, the) pear in her lunch.

2. She sat on (a, an) bench near the door.

3. Mr. Thomas gave (a, the) assignments for tomorrow.

4. Andy and (a, the) soccer team played a great game.

5. We waited for more than (a, an) hour.

Number your paper from 6 to 10. Write five sentences about today's weather. Use at least five articles in your sentences. Underline each article.

SPELLING BUILDER

Contraction or Possessive Pronoun?
Read this sentence:

This is (you're, your) book.

Which word do you use: *your*, the possessive pronoun, or *you're*, the contraction? Find out by changing *you're* into the words that form the contraction: *you are*. Does the sentence make sense when you use *you are* in it? If not, use *your*.

Write a sentence using each word below:

1. they're   2. their   3. who's   4. whose

Proper Adjectives

Objectives

■ To recognize and use proper adjectives

■ To capitalize proper adjectives

Proper adjective

A proper noun used as an adjective, or an adjective made from a proper noun

A **proper adjective** is a proper noun that you use as an adjective. A proper adjective refers to the name of a particular person, place, thing, event, or idea. Capitalize a proper adjective.

▶ **EXAMPLE 1**

| Proper Noun | Emily speaks English. |
| Proper Adjective | Emily speaks the English language. |

Sometimes you must change the spelling of a proper noun to make it into an adjective.

▶ **EXAMPLE 2**

| Proper Noun | Nathan would like to visit Spain someday. |
| Proper Adjective | Nathan would like to see the Spanish countryside. |

Practice A

Write the proper adjective in each sentence. Next to each adjective, write the noun it describes.

1. Italian cooking is very popular in this country.

2. They saw Canada geese flying overhead.

3. There is nothing like a California sunset.

4. My mother's family is German.

5. We bought some Florida oranges.

Practice B

Write a sentence using each proper adjective. Underline the word that the proper adjective describes.

1. American
2. Spanish
3. French
4. African
5. Chinese

Noun or Adjective?

A proper noun and a proper adjective may be spelled exactly the same way. How do you tell if the word is a noun or an adjective? You must look carefully at how the word is used in its sentence.

▶ **EXAMPLE 3**

| Proper Noun | Jeong Chang lives in Hollywood. (a particular place) |
| Proper Adjective | Curtis enjoys Hollywood movies. (a kind of movie) |

Practice C

Write each word in bold. How is the word used in the sentence? If it is used as an adjective, write *adjective* next to it. If it is used as a noun, write *noun*.

1. The poetry has made me a **Shakespeare** fan.
2. I drive an **American** car.
3. This coat was made in **Canada.**
4. Mr. Thomas visited **Egypt** last summer.
5. Mrs. Young made **French** toast.

REVIEW

Write each sentence on your paper. Capitalize each proper adjective. Then underline the noun it describes.

1. Suzi bought towels at the january sale.

2. One of the tallest trees is the california redwood.

3. The waitress brought us our canadian bacon.

4. I ordered a swiss cheese sandwich.

5. The tuesday meeting was three hours long.

Write a sentence using each proper noun as a proper adjective. Underline the noun that the proper adjective describes.

6. German

7. Paris

8. June

9. Asian

10. Texas

Possessive Nouns and Pronouns as Adjectives

Objectives

- To use possessive nouns as adjectives
- To use possessive pronouns as adjectives

Do you remember learning about possessive nouns in Chapter 2? How about possessive pronouns in Chapter 3? Both show belonging. They have something else in common. Both describe nouns. This means that they are adjectives.

Possessive Nouns

Both common nouns and proper nouns can be turned into possessive adjectives.

▶ **EXAMPLE 1**

This is my sister's bedroom.

Sister's is a possessive adjective made from the common noun *sister*. It is used to describe the noun *bedroom*.

▶ **EXAMPLE 2**

Roxanne's dog is huge!

Roxanne's is a possessive adjective made from the proper noun *Roxanne*. It is used to describe the noun *dog*.

Practice A

Write each possessive adjective in bold. Next to it, write the noun it describes.

1. My **friend's** rabbit has smooth fur.
2. Emily likes **Angela's** jokes.
3. My **mother's** ring is missing.
4. Where is **Armando's** soccer ball?
5. The **band's** CD quickly became popular.

Practice B

Write a sentence using each possessive adjective. Underline the noun that the adjective describes.

1. Mandy's
2. teacher's
3. team's
4. Javier's
5. city's

Possessive Pronouns

Possessive pronouns act as both pronouns and adjectives.

▶ **EXAMPLE 3**

Anne is excited. Her team is competing today.

The word *her* is a possessive pronoun. It works as an adjective to describe the noun *team*. It also has an antecedent: *Anne.*

Reading Strategy:
Text Structure

In the Example 3, the word *her* appears in blue. Why are certain words shown this way?

Practice C

Write each possessive adjective in bold. Next to it, write the noun that it describes.

1. **Our** puppy likes to play.
2. **My** car is red and white.
3. **His** plan was a success.
4. Michelle likes **her** new computer.
5. The students were proud of **their** effort.

Its and It's

Many writers confuse these two little words. They sound alike, but they are not the same word. *Its* is a possessive pronoun that you use as an adjective. *It's* is a contraction of the two words *it* and *is*.

▶ **EXAMPLE 4**

Its bark is too loud. (Whose bark? Its bark.)

It's a nice day. (It is a nice day.)

Reading Strategy:
Text Structure

If you need help with a Practice activity, look at the Example before it. Use this Example as a guide.

Practice D

Write the word that completes each sentence.

1. The cat lost (its, it's) collar.
2. The printer is beeping. (Its, It's) out of paper.
3. The show was popular because of (its, it's) actors.
4. The book lost (its, it's) importance after the discovery.
5. The puppy is barking. I think (its, it's) hungry.

Angela's final project is a vase. Its shape will be tall and thin.

REVIEW

Number your paper from 1 to 10. Find the 10 possessive adjectives in these sentences. List them in order. Next to each one, write the noun it describes.

Nathan and his older brother David went to hear the new mayor give a speech. David drove them into town in his car. He had to fill the car's gas tank, so they stopped at a gas station. Then they went to their father's office to pick up their tickets. They had a great view from their seats in the third row. After the mayor's speech, Nathan and David went exploring. Soon, Nathan's stomach was growling. He and his brother had a quick meal before driving back to their house.

VOCABULARY BUILDER

Choosing Mighty Words

You can say a lot with just one word. Read the sentence below. Try each of the four choices in the blank. Which one provides the most information?

The bear let out a _____ roar. It frightened the campers.

  A fierce   **B** small   **C** savage   **D** big

The word *fierce* or *savage* gives more detail than the word *big*. Use a thesaurus to find three words that mean strong. Write a sentence using each one. Read your sentences to a partner.

Numbers as Adjectives

Objectives

■ To recognize and use numbers as adjectives

■ To recognize and use indefinite pronouns as adjectives

You can use numbers as adjectives. A number decribes a noun by telling how many. Spell out numbers one through nine. Numbers 10 and above are often shown as numerals.

▶ **EXAMPLE 1**

Sam drove 112 miles. It took him two hours.

Do you remember learning about indefinite pronouns in Chapter 3? They are words such as *many, both, some,* and *neither.* You can also use indefinite pronouns as adjectives. Like numbers, indefinite pronouns tell how many, but the exact number is unknown.

▶ **EXAMPLE 2**

Several people wanted to go to the concert.

Few students were able to go.

Practice A

Write the number or indefinite pronoun used as an adjective in each sentence.

1. The concert was three hours long.

2. Many people got there early.

3. There were a few songs Sam had heard before.

4. There were 30 people in the band.

5. The drive home took Sam's family 15 minutes.

Practice B

Use each word as an adjective in a sentence. Underline the noun each adjective describes.

1. nine   **2.** few   **3.** several   **4.** six   **5.** one

Pronoun or Adjective?

The same word may be an indefinite pronoun or an adjective. To tell the difference, you must think carefully about how the word works in the sentence. Remember that a pronoun takes the place of a noun. It acts like a noun. It names something or someone. An adjective describes a person, place, thing, or idea.

▶ **EXAMPLE 3**

Pronoun   Many people clapped, and several cheered.

(The antecedent of *several* is *people*.)

Adjective   Several families were there.

(*Several* describes *families*. It tells how many.)

Practice C

Write each bold word. Next to it, write *adjective* or *pronoun*.

1. **Everyone** was happy at the dance.
2. When the band played, **most** people danced.
3. When the dance was over, **no one** wanted to go home.
4. **Some** people went to Tony's Cafe afterwards.
5. **Others** went bowling.

Practice D

Write each word used as an adjective in the paragraph. After each one, write the noun or pronoun it describes.

Summer picnics at Kai's house are fun. Most of her family comes. Nine people crowd into one small house! Kai's mom cooks the chicken, and it is hot and tasty. Kai's aunt makes a potato salad. Everyone loves the sweet lemonade.

REVIEW

Write the number or indefinite pronoun used as an adjective in each sentence. After it, write the noun or pronoun it describes.

1. Most people enjoy going to the movies.

2. Tony's Cafe has several kinds of sandwiches.

3. Track season lasts three months.

4. Math class is forty-eight minutes long.

5. My room is two doors down on the right.

Write each sentence on your paper. Add a number or indefinite pronoun to complete each sentence. Underline the word you added.

6. The rain fell for _____ hours.

7. He asked for _____ eggs.

8. The speed limit is _____ miles per hour.

9. I saw _____ of my friends.

10. _____ students go to Wilson High School.

Demonstrative Adjectives

Demonstrative adjective

The word *this*, *that*, *these*, or *those* used as an adjective

Reading Strategy:
Text Structure

What part of this page helps you remember what demonstrative adjectives are?

Do you remember learning about demonstrative pronouns in Chapter 3? You can also use these pronouns as adjectives. The four **demonstrative adjectives** are *this*, *that*, *these*, and *those*. They point to a particular thing or things.

▶ **EXAMPLE 1**

Pronoun	That is a long book.
Adjective	That book is long. (Which book?)
Pronoun	These are my favorite CDs.
Adjective	These CDs are my favorite. (Which CDs?)

Practice A

Write each word in bold. After each one, write *adjective* or *pronoun*.

1. **Those** are good boots.

2. I like the way **these** pens write.

3. **This** book is very funny.

4. **Those** are Andy's poems.

5. Did you hear **that** duck?

Practice B

Write five sentences describing things in your classroom. Use a demonstrative adjective in each sentence. Underline each one.

Example: Light streams through <u>that</u> window.

REVIEW

Write the demonstrative adjective in each sentence. Next to it, write the noun that it describes.

1. We had a very strange day this week.

2. That Wednesday is one I will remember.

3. First, those new bells rang several times each hour.

4. No one knew whether a bell meant to leave that class or not.

5. Then the cafeteria served those odd sandwiches.

Choose a demonstrative adjective for each blank. Write the sentence on your paper.

6. Did you draw _____ pictures?

7. This car is mine, and _____ one is my brother's.

8. Look at _____ mountains!

9. _____ cut is healing.

10. Please read _____ words to me.

Adjectives That Compare

Objectives

- To recognize adjectives that compare
- To use the positive, comparative, and superlative forms of adjectives

Positive form

The form of an adjective used to describe people or things

Comparative form

The form of an adjective used to compare two people or things

Superlative form

The form of an adjective used to compare more than two people or things

Reading Strategy:
Text Structure

Study the Examples in this book. They will help you understand the lessons.

You use adjectives to describe people or things. You can also use adjectives to compare people or things. Adjectives have three forms—**positive, comparative,** and **superlative.**

▶ **EXAMPLE 1**

Positive	Comparative	Superlative
pretty	prettier	prettiest
new	newer	newest

Rule 1 Use the positive form to describe one thing.

Rule 2 Use the comparative form to compare two things. This form often ends in *-er*.

Rule 3 Use the superlative form to compare more than two things. This form often ends in *-est*.

▶ **EXAMPLE 2**

Positive	That computer is fast.
Comparative	That computer is faster than this computer.
Superlative	Of all the computers, this one is the fastest.

Practice A

Write the correct form of the adjective for each sentence.

1. Nina's hair is (longer, longest) than Carrie's.
2. This room is the (bigger, biggest) in the house.
3. This is a very (hard, harder) job.
4. My uncle is (older, oldest) than my mother.
5. She told the (funny, funniest) story!

Reading Strategy:
Text Structure

How does each
Practice set relate to
the Example before it?

NOTE

Some adjectives do
not have comparative
and superlative forms.
For example, an object
cannot be the *most
square*. Something is
either square or it is not.

Doubling the Final Consonant

To make the comparative and superlative forms of some
adjectives, you must double the final consonant. Then you
add *-er* or *-est*. Double the final consonant in these cases:

- The word has one syllable.
- The word ends in one consonant.
- The word has one vowel before the final consonant.

▶ **EXAMPLE 3**

big + -er = bigger   big + -est = biggest

sad + -er = sadder   sad + -est = saddest

Practice B

Write the adjective that belongs in each blank. Use the
comparative or superlative form of the word at the end of
each sentence.

1. Nathan is _____ than Tom. (thin)

2. I was the _____ one of all! (mad)

3. Nathan's hair is _____ than mine. (red)

4. She was the _____ person on the beach. (tan)

5. All three dogs were wet, but the _____ was Duke. (wet)

Using *More* and *Less*, *Most* and *Least*

For longer adjectives, you use the words *more* and *less* to
make the comparative form. You use *most* or *least* to make
the superlative form.

▶ **EXAMPLE 4**

Positive	Comparative	Superlative
delicious	more delicious	most delicious
wonderful	less helpful	least helpful
exciting	less exciting	least exciting

Write each adjective on your paper. Next to each one, write its comparative and superlative forms.

1. timid
2. amazing
3. graceful

4. popular
5. rugged

Irregular Adjectives

Remember that an *irregular* word does not follow usual rules or patterns. Some adjectives have completely different words for their comparative and superlative forms. You need to remember these words or look them up in a dictionary to be sure.

▶ **EXAMPLE 5**

Positive	Comparative	Superlative
good	better	best
bad	worse	worst
little	less	least
many	more	most

Practice D

Write the correct form of the adjective for each sentence.

1. Jesse thinks Amy Tan is a (good, best) writer.
2. Nathan is watching (less, least) TV lately.
3. He is doing (more, most) reading.
4. The writer I like (better, best) is Anne Tyler.
5. This is the (worse, worst) movie I have ever seen!

REVIEW

Write the letter of the correct sentence.

1. **A** Old Pew is one of the meanest men around.
   B Old Pew is one of the most mean men around.

2. **A** Which of those two ships can sail faster?
   B Which of those two ships can sail fastest?

3. **A** Long John Silver hopes to be richer soon.
   B Long John Silver hopes to be more rich soon.

4. **A** *Treasure Island* is the goodest book I have read.
   B *Treasure Island* is the best book I have read.

5. **A** I have fewer CDs than Armando.
   B I have fewest CDs than Armando.

Number your paper from 6 to 10. Write each bold adjective in the paragraph. After each one, write *positive*, *comparative*, or *superlative*.

Many readers think *Treasure Island* is the **most exciting** story of all. They love its **colorful** characters. Old Pew is a scary fellow, but even **more frightening** is Long John Silver. Have you read the book? Which character do you think is the **most unforgettable** one? Why do the characters seem **more real** than those in other books?

PUTTING IT ALL TOGETHER

Write several sentences that tell how you and a friend are alike and different. Use possessive nouns and pronouns. Use adjectives in both their positive and comparative forms. Use both definite and indefinite articles. Try to use at least one proper adjective.

Six Traits of Writing:

Word Choice vivid words that "show, not tell"

COMMUNICATING ON THE JOB

Veterinary Assistant

A veterinarian is a doctor who cares for animals. Megan Green works as a veterinary assistant in an animal hospital. She feeds, washes, and cares for sick animals. She also listens while owners describe their pet's problems. She writes down what the owners say for Dr. Santiago, the veterinarian.

Ed Allen brought his dog Fritz to the animal hospital. Something was wrong with Fritz's paw. Megan wrote a description for Dr. Santiago. Read Megan's description. Then answer the questions.

Note to the Doctor

Fritz's front paw is red and puffy. Fritz will not walk on it. It is puffier than it was yesterday. He may have cut it on a sharp fence.

1. What adjectives are used in this note?

2. Which adjective in the note is used to compare?

3. CRITICAL THINKING How do adjectives make written and spoken messages better?

SPEAKING AND LISTENING

Work with a partner to do some role-playing. One of you will play a veterinary assistant. The other will play a cat owner. The owner should describe a sick cat's problems. The veterinary assistant should listen carefully and write a description of the problem. Work together to add adjectives to the description.

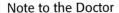

Getting Information from Several Sources

Imagine that your teacher asks you to write a report. You choose Susan B. Anthony for your topic. You begin by looking for information in a book on American history. You learn how Anthony helped women get the right to vote. Don't stop there. A good report uses information from more than one source.

You might look in an encyclopedia to find facts about Anthony's life. You also might check *The Book of Distinguished American Women*. Keep looking. Talk to a history teacher. Search the Internet. You might find one of the speeches that Anthony gave.

The more sources you find and use, the better your report will be. Each new source will offer new facts and a fresh point of view. When you have information from many sources, you will be ready to write your report. Combine the information you have collected. Put it into your own words.

A bibliography is a list of the sources used to write a report. The sample bibliography above lists three sources about Susan B. Anthony. It lists a movie, a newspaper article, and a book.

Biography: Susan B. Anthony. Videotape. A & E Home Video, 1999.

"Miss Susan B. Anthony Died This Morning," *The New York Times*, March 13, 1906.

Wilson, Vincent, and Gale S. McClung. *The Book of Distinguished American Women*. Brookville, MD: American History Research Associates, 2003.

1. Find another source that has information about Susan B. Anthony. Write it down.

2. Write two adjectives to describe a report that only uses one source. Write two adjectives that describe a report that uses several sources.

3. **CRITICAL THINKING** Think about all the places you can find information. Make a list of as many different types of sources as you can.

 MEDIA

A library catalog is a list of everything the library contains. You can use this catalog to find information about a topic. Sometimes, libraries loan materials to each other. If your library has a loan program, you can borrow materials from other libraries. Ask your librarian for help.

- Use adjectives to describe nouns and pronouns. Most adjectives appear before the nouns they describe.

- Use predicate adjectives after certain verbs to describe subjects.

- Use the definite article *the* with a particular person or thing.

- Use the indefinite articles *a* or *an* with any one of a group of people or things.

- Make proper adjectives from proper nouns. Always begin a proper adjective with a capital letter.

- Possessive nouns and pronouns are adjectives. They describe nouns by saying to whom or to what they belong.

- Use numbers as adjectives to tell how many.

- Use indefinite pronouns to tell how many when the exact number is unknown.

- Use demonstrative pronouns to point to a particular thing or things. The demonstrative pronouns are *this*, *that*, *these*, and *those*.

- Use adjectives to compare. Use all three adjective forms: positive, comparative, and superlative.

GROUP ACTIVITY

A carnival is coming to town! Work with a group to write a flyer. Your flyer should convince visitors to try new carnival rides. Use your imagination. Describe each ride.

Use strong adjectives to make your writing interesting. Trade flyers with another group. Suggest ways to make that group's writing even stronger.

Word Bank

adjective

comparative form

definite article

demonstrative
  adjective

indefinite article

positive form

predicate adjective

proper adjective

superlative form

Part A Write the word or words from the Word Bank that complete each sentence.

1. The word *the* is a _____. It is used to talk about a specific person or thing.

2. A _____ is a proper noun that is used as an adjective.

3. The _____ of an adjective compares two people or things.

4. A _____ is an adjective that comes after the noun or pronoun it describes.

5. The _____ of an adjective is used to describe people or things.

6. The word *a* or *an* is an _____.

7. The _____ of an adjective compares more than two people or things.

8. A word that describes or tells about a noun or pronoun is an _____.

9. A _____ is the word *this*, *that*, *these*, or *those* used as an adjective.

Part B Write the word that completes each sentence.

10. Last Monday was (a, an) awful day.

11. (Its, It's) three days until the big game.

12. Jesse is (more helpful, more helpfuler) than Jan.

13. This book is the (better, best) one in the library.

14. Craig's joke was (funnier, more funny) than Sam's.

15. He missed the (february, February) event.

Part C List each adjective in bold. Next to each one, write the noun it describes.

16. **The** floor was as bright as a **new** penny.

17. He went to a **good** school when he was **young.**

18. The teacher, **alert** and **quiet,** watched us.

19. **One** man ran through the **thick** grass.

20. We had **a** long day of **hard** work ahead of us.

Part D

21. List the 16 adjectives in this description of Long John Silver, a character in *Treasure Island* by Robert Louis Stevenson. Include articles and possessive pronouns.

Long John Silver was a tall, strong man. His messy hair fell down the back of his blue coat. His hands were bruised, with black fingernails. The knife cut across his chin was a dirty, ugly white.

Part E Write the letter of the answer.

22. Which word is an adjective in the superlative form?
A cleaner   **B** pest   **C** good   **D** boldest

23. Which word is an adjective in the comparative form?
A newest   **B** that   **C** younger   **D** loud

24. Which phrase contains an indefinite pronouns used as an adjective?
A some friends   **C** the friends
B new friends   **D** two friends

25. Which phrase contains a proper adjective?
A green tea   **C** Roman ruin
B larger size   **D** perfect game

Using Action Verbs in Sentences

E very sentence must have a verb. Verbs express action or state of being. Verbs can make your writing lively and exciting. Choose them carefully.

Study the photo on the opposite page. What do you see? There is so much movement that the photo is blurry! People skate, hold hands, and glide. Other people spin, fall, and laugh. Some people are still. All of these words—*skate*, *hold*, *glide*, *spin*, *fall*, *laugh*, *are*—are verbs.

In Chapter 5, you will learn about action verbs. Verbs have many different forms. You will learn how to use the different verb forms in sentences.

GOALS FOR LEARNING

- To identify and use action verbs
- To identify and use simple and perfect tenses
- To identify and use regular and irregular verb forms
- To identify and use progressive verb phrases
- To make a subject and a verb agree
- To use the verb *do* as a helping verb and as a main verb
- To use conditional verbs to show action that is possible or necessary

Reading Strategy: Visualizing

To visualize means to imagine what something looks like. Visualizing can help you understand what you are reading. It is like making a movie in your mind. As you read:

- Look at the photos, tables, and lists in a text.
- Pay attention to words that describe. Imagine all five senses: sight, sound, smell, taste, and touch.
- Build pictures in your mind of what you are reading. Think about related things in your own life.
- Notice the order in which things are happening. Think about what might happen next.

Key Vocabulary Words

Action verb A word that tells what someone or something did, does, or will do

Tense The time when an action takes place

Simple tense The present, past, or future form of a verb

Perfect tense The present perfect, past perfect, or future perfect form of a verb

Helping verb A verb that combines with a main verb to form a verb phrase

Verb phrase A main verb plus a helping verb

Past participle The verb form used to form the perfect tenses

Infinitive The word *to* plus the present tense of a verb

Regular verb A verb whose past tense and past participle end with *-ed* or *-d*

Irregular verb A verb whose past tense and past participle are formed in different ways

Present participle The form of a verb that ends in *-ing*

Progressive verb phrase A form of *be* plus the present participle of a verb

Compound Two or more sentences or sentence parts that are connected with a conjunction

Conditional verb A verb that shows that the action is possible or necessary

What Is an Action Verb?

Action verb

A word that tells what someone or something did, does, or will do

An **action verb** tells what someone or something did, does, or will do. Find the action verb in a sentence by asking yourself two questions:

- Who or what is doing something? The answer is the subject of the sentence.

- What are they doing? The answer is the verb.

▶ **EXAMPLE 1**

Every morning Mr. Choy makes coffee.

Who is doing something? *Mr. Choy* is the subject. What does Mr. Choy do? The verb is *makes*.

Practice A

Write the verb in each sentence on your paper.

1. Wilson High School students keep reading logs.

2. They read every day for 30 minutes.

3. Angela enjoys short stories.

4. She discovered a collection by S.E. Hinton.

5. Nathan gobbles up history books.

A sentence can have more than one verb.

▶ **EXAMPLE 2**

Mrs. Choy cooks breakfast and packs lunches.

Practice B

Write the two verbs in each sentence.

1. The students hurry to the cafeteria and form a line.

2. Each student takes a tray and puts a plate on it.

3. Angela chooses an apple and asks for a hamburger.

4. Armando buys a carton of milk and then grabs a straw.

5. Angela and Armando pay for their lunches and search for a table.

A verb can tell about action you can see. You can see someone cooking breakfast or packing a lunch. A verb can also tell about action you cannot see. It can tell about a thought or feeling.

▶ **EXAMPLE 3**

Mr. Choy likes coffee.

Practice C

Write the verb in each sentence.

1. Nadia and I wanted a salad for lunch.

2. Julio misses his brother.

3. Miguel dreamed about alligators.

4. Mr. Ruben thought about the problem.

5. Everyone on the team wished for a home run.

Reading Strategy:
Visualizing

As you do Practice B, picture the trays, the apple, the hamburger, and the milk. Imagine the sights, sounds, and smells of the cafeteria.

 Writing Tip

Using lively action verbs adds interest to your writing. Substitute specific verbs for ordinary verbs. For example, use *stroll* instead of *walk*. Use *dash* instead of *run*.

REVIEW

Write the action verb in each sentence.

1. Angela wandered down the crowded hallway.
2. She gazed at the artwork on the walls.
3. She noticed a large, colorful poster.
4. Angela admired the poster.
5. Sasha designed that poster.

Complete each sentence with an action verb of your own. Write the new sentence.

6. Vito _____ a new stereo.
7. We _____ a big surprise for Lauren.
8. Lupe _____ into the room.
9. Melissa _____ a new car.
10. I _____ until midnight.

Simple and Perfect Tenses

The verb in a sentence can describe action. The verb can also express **tense**, or time. A verb tense tells when an action takes place. Verbs use endings, helping verbs, or both to express tense.

Simple Tenses

There are three **simple tenses**: present, past, and future. Use the present tense when the action is happening now or is generally happening all the time. Use the past tense when the action has already happened. Use the future tense when the action will happen in the future.

Tense
The time when an action takes place

Simple tense
The present, past, or future form of a verb

▶ **EXAMPLE 1**

Present Tense	He fishes in that lake often. (Use the verb or the verb plus -s or -es.)
Past Tense	He fished in that lake last week. (Add -ed or -d to the present form.)
Future Tense	He will fish there tomorrow. (Add the helping verb will or shall.)

Practice A

Reading Strategy:
Visualizing

As you do Practice A, think about the time that the events happened or will happen.

Write the verbs in bold on your paper. Identify the tense of each verb as *present*, *past*, or *future*.

1. The band **marched** onto the field.
2. They **will play** the school song at the rally.
3. The students **gathered** for the rally.
4. The players **look** forward to this game.
5. The students **will support** their team.

Perfect tense

The present perfect, past perfect, or future perfect form of a verb

Helping verb

A verb that combines with a main verb to form a verb phrase

Reading Strategy:
Visualizing

As you read Example 2, think about when each event happened.

Perfect Tenses

There are three **perfect tenses** of a verb. They are present perfect, past perfect, and future perfect.

A **helping verb** combines with a main verb to express a perfect tense. The perfect tenses use the helping verb *have* with the past tense of a verb.

▶ **EXAMPLE 2**

Present Perfect
Neeru has joined the school choir.
(The action took place in the past and continues in the present.)

Past Perfect
Neeru had belonged to a choir before she moved here.
(One action was complete before another action began.)

Future Perfect
By May, she will have belonged to the choir for a month.
(The action will be completed before a certain time in the future.)

Use the different forms of *have* to form the perfect tenses.

Verb Forms of *Have*

Present	Armando's team **has** the ball. (singular) They **have** three goals so far. (plural)
Past	The team **had** the lead a minute ago.
Future	They **will have** practice tomorrow.
Present Perfect	Armando **has had** a good game so far. (singular) The players **have had** chances to score. (plural)
Past Perfect	They **had had** many victories before today.
Future Perfect	They **will have had** a winning season.

Verb Phrases

A **verb phrase** is a main verb and one or more helping verbs. The main verb tells what happens. The helping verb helps the main verb express tense.

▶ **EXAMPLE 3**

Present Perfect	Jim has talked to the team about practice.
Future	Emily will take a vacation with her family.

Practice B

Find the verb phrase in each sentence. Write it on your paper.

1. Neeru has performed in choirs before.

2. Neeru will travel with the choir.

3. The choir has toured before.

4. The singers had recorded their last concert.

5. They will sell their new CD.

Practice C

Write each verb or verb phrase in bold on your paper. Next to each one, write the tense of the verb.

1. Emily **enjoys** the school band.

2. She **had joined** the band a year ago.

3. The other flute players in the band **welcomed** Emily.

4. The band **had held** a concert in the spring.

5. Emily **will practice** every day.

REVIEW

Write the bold verb or verb phrase. Identify the tense of the verb as *present, past, future, present perfect, past perfect,* or *future perfect*.

1. Nathan and his friends **had planned** a special trip.

2. They **will report** on the trip in the school newspaper.

3. They **will have traveled** to three different caves this year.

4. They **explored** a system of caves during the trip.

5. Their safety gear **includes** helmets and headlamps.

6. Nathan **has replaced** his old helmet with a better one.

Write the past and future tenses of each of these present tense verbs.

7. move

8. look

9. ask

10. clean

Regular and Irregular Verbs

Infinitive
The word *to* plus the present tense of a verb

Past participle
The verb form used to form the perfect tenses

Regular verb
A verb whose past tense and past participle end with *-ed* or *-d*

Irregular verb
A verb whose past tense and past participle are formed in different ways

 NOTE

The verbs *be, have,* and *do* are irregular verbs. You use them as helping verbs and as main verbs.

Verbs have three main forms. These are **infinitive** (present), **past**, and **past participle**. The past participle is the verb form you use to make the perfect tenses. **Regular verbs** form their past and past participles by adding *-ed* or *-d*. You studied regular verbs in Lesson 5-2.

▶ **EXAMPLE 1**

Infinitive	Present	Past	Past Participle
to look	look, looks	looked	(has) looked
to jump	jump, jumps	jumped	(has) jumped

Irregular verbs do not follow the usual rules. Sometimes the past and past participles are different. In a few cases, the present tense has different forms.

Some Irregular Verbs

Infinitive	Present	Past	Past Participle
to be	am, is, are	was, were	(has) been
to have	has, have	had	(has) had
to do	do, does	did	(has) done
to eat	eat	ate	(has) eaten
to go	go	went	(has) gone

Practice A

Complete each sentence with the correct form of the verb in parentheses. Write the correct form verb.

1. Ms. Roy _____ the science teacher for two years. (be)
2. The students have already _____ their dinner. (eat)
3. Emily has _____ her job for nearly a year. (have)
4. They already _____ their homework. (do)
5. Armando has _____ to soccer practice. (go)

For some irregular verbs, the past tense and past participle are the same.

Some Irregular Verbs with Same Past Tense and Past Participle

Present	Past	Past Participle
bring(s)	brought	(has) brought
buy(s)	bought	(has) bought
catch(es)	caught	(has) caught
dig(s)	dug	(has) dug
feed(s)	fed	(has) fed
get(s)	got	(has) got (gotten)
hear(s)	heard	(has) heard
keep(s)	kept	(has) kept
lead(s)	led	(has) led
leave(s)	left	(has) left
lose(s)	lost	(has) lost
make(s)	made	(has) made
send(s)	sent	(has) sent
swing(s)	swung	(has) swung
teach(es)	taught	(has) taught
think(s)	thought	(has) thought
win(s)	won	(has) won

Practice B

Change each bold verb to either the past tense or the past participle. Write the new sentence on your paper. Next to the sentence, write *past tense* or *past participle*.

Reading Strategy:
Visualizing

Imagine a picture that could go with each sentence in Practice B.

1. Neeru **think** about joining the basketball team.

2. Mrs. Benson has **teach** journalism for several years.

3. Has the soccer team **win** its game yet?

4. Has Armando **buy** the paint he needs?

5. Nathan **catch** trout at his favorite stream.

For some irregular verbs, the past tense and past participle are different. Study the irregular verbs in this table.

Some Irregular Verbs with Different Past Tense and Past Participle

Present	Past	Past Participle
begin(s)	began	(has) begun
break(s)	broke	(has) broken
choose(s)	chose	(has) chosen
drive(s)	drove	(has) driven
fall(s)	fell	(has) fallen
fly (flies)	flew	(has) flown
forget(s)	forgot	(has) forgotten
give(s)	gave	(has) given
grow(s)	grew	(has) grown
know(s)	knew	(has) known
ride(s)	rode	(has) ridden
ring(s)	rang	(has) rung
see(s)	saw	(has) seen
swim(s)	swam	(has) swum
take(s)	took	(has) taken
wear(s)	wore	(has) worn
write(s)	wrote	(has) written

Practice C

Write the form of the verb in parentheses that correctly completes each sentence.

Reading Strategy:
Visualizing

As you read the sentences in Practice C, let each one make a new picture in your mind. Imagine when each action took place.

1. Armando has _____ Nathan for many years. (know)
2. Angela _____ in the state meet. (swim)
3. Neeru has _____ her cousin in India a letter. (write)
4. The cup _____ when it fell off the shelf. (break)
5. Nathan has _____ that movie twice. (see)

For some irregular verbs, the past tense and past participle are the same as their present tense.

More Irregular Verbs

Present	Past	Past Participle
burst(s)	burst	(has) burst
cost(s)	cost	(has) cost
cut(s)	cut	(has) cut
hit(s)	hit	(has) hit
put(s)	put	(has) put
read(s)	read	(has) read
set(s)	set	(has) set

Practice D

Read each sentence. Decide whether the bold verb is present, past, or future tense. Write the verb tense on your paper.

1. I **will read** that book next week.

2. We **cut** our grass once a week in the summer.

3. Emily **put** a napkin on her lap at the restaurant.

4. Armando **hit** a home run during the last inning.

5. Last year, a side salad **cost** two dollars at Tony's Cafe.

I usually cut the grass every Wednesday.
However, last week I cut the grass on Thursday.

REVIEW

The bold verb in each sentence is incorrect. Write the correct form of the verb on your paper.

1. Emily **bringed** a board game to the party.

2. The teacher **beginned** to speak.

3. The bottle in the freezer **bursted**.

4. I **buyed** these shoes a week ago.

5. This is the first time Jon has **flew** in an airplane.

Use each of the verbs or verb phrases in a sentence. Pay careful attention to the tense.

6. have grown

7. took

8. ring

9. fly

10. has imagined

Progressive Tenses

A **present participle** shows action that continues. Add -*ing* to the present tense of the verb to form the present participle. The helping verb *be* plus the present participle forms a **progressive verb phrase**.

▶ **EXAMPLE 1**

Present	Emily practices her flute every day.
Present Progressive	Emily is practicing her flute right now.

The verb *be* is the most common verb in English. It is used in many ways. This verb changes when it is used with different subjects. It changes in different tenses. It changes when it is used with other verbs. Study the table below to see how different forms of *be* are used in sentences.

Verb Tense Forms of Be

Present	I **am** on the team with Armando. (singular)
	Armando's team **is** on the field. (singular)
	They **are** in the lead. (plural)
Past	The team **was** in the lead a minute ago. (singular)
	The players **were** near the goal. (plural)
Future	We think they **will be** the winners.
Present Perfect	It **has been** a good game so far. (singular)
	The players **have been** eager to score. (plural)
Past Perfect	They **had been** the winners before.
Future Perfect	They **will have been** on the field for an hour.

Practice A

Write the progressive verb phrase in each sentence.

1. Armando is designing a poster.
2. "I am working at the music store," said Emily.
3. Angela is swimming in the pool.
4. They are going to the library.
5. Neeru is singing her favorite song.

The word *progress* means "to move through time." Read the examples below. Think about how the different progressive verb phrases move an action through time. Notice how the verbs *be* and *have* form different tenses in these verb phrases.

▶ **EXAMPLE 2**

Present Progressive	She is running.
Past Progressive	She was running.
Future Progressive	She will be running.
Present Perfect Progressive	She has been running.
Past Perfect Progressive	She had been running.
Future Perfect Progressive	She will have been running.

Practice B

Write the tense of each bold verb.

1. Nathan **is going** to the library.
2. Emily **will be meeting** him there.
3. They **have been looking** for a book.
4. They **will have been looking** for this book for a week.
5. Nathan **had been expecting** to find it.

REVIEW

Write the progressive verb phrase in each sentence.

1. Armando has been playing soccer for many years.

2. They have been thinking about a new car.

3. Nathan was looking for a book about caves.

4. Emily is planning a visit to an art gallery.

5. Are you going to the gallery this weekend?

Write the tense of each progressive verb phrase in bold.

6. Mrs. Watson **is enjoying** music.

7. She **was listening** to a CD player.

8. Ty's mother **had been waiting** for him to come home.

9. Mrs. Watson **has been wondering** where Emily is.

10. Emily **will be working** at the music store all day.

VOCABULARY BUILDER

Choosing Specific Verbs

Good writers think about the verbs they use. When a verb is ordinary or dull, they look for a more specific verb. If they use one verb too often, they search for new ones. Specific verbs help readers visualize what the writer imagined. They pull you into the sentence by creating a picture in your mind.

Ordinary Verb	Specific Verb
get	snag
eat	gobble
walk	stagger

Use each specific verb listed above in a sentence. Notice how much interest they add to your sentences.

Subject-Verb Agreement

Objectives

- To understand subject-verb agreement in a sentence
- To change the form of a verb to agree with the subject

Reading Strategy: Visualizing

Picture a subject and its verb as two hands shaking in agreement.

The subject of a sentence can be either singular or plural. The verb must agree in number with the subject. The present tense of a regular verb has two forms. Use the singular verb form with a singular subject. Use the plural verb form with a plural subject.

Add -s or -es to the present tense of a verb when the subject is a singular noun. When the subject is plural, the verb does not end in s.

▶ **EXAMPLE 1**

| Singular Subject | Emily's dog barks for its dinner. |
| Plural Subject | Both dogs bark for their dinner. |

When the subject is *I, you, we,* or *they,* use the plural form of the verb (no -s). When the subject is *he, she,* or *it,* use the singular form of the verb.

▶ **EXAMPLE 2**

I enjoy eating on Thanksgiving.

He enjoys Thanksgiving, too.

We always enjoy our Thanksgiving meal.

They enjoy being together on Thanksgiving.

Practice A

Write the verb that correctly completes each sentence.

1. Glen (hope, hopes) to win the contest.
2. The three friends (enjoy, enjoys) art class.
3. I (want, wants) a new set of paints.
4. Neeru (watch, watches) TV after school.
5. The bird (fly, flies) to its nest.

Subject-Verb Agreement with Indefinite Pronouns

You have learned about indefinite pronouns in Chapter 3. They include words such as *everyone, nobody,* and *anything.* Most indefinite pronouns are singular even if their meaning seems to be plural. They take a singular form of the verb.

▶ **EXAMPLE 3**

| Correct | Everyone goes to the beach in the summer. |
| Incorrect | Everyone go to the beach in the summer. |

A few indefinite pronouns may be singular or plural. This depends on how they are used in a sentence. These pronouns are *all, any, most,* and *none.*

Reading Strategy:
Visualizing

In Example 4, picture *all of the money* as one pile or one amount.

▶ **EXAMPLE 4**

| Singular | All of the money is safe in the bank. |
| Plural | All of the boys are going to the concert. |

Practice B

Write the verb that correctly completes each sentence.

1. All of the fruit (look, looks) fresh.
2. Anyone (is, are) welcome at the concert.
3. Most of the students (go, goes) to Tony's for snacks.
4. All of the students (attend, attends) the band concert.
5. None of us (are, is) going.

Writing Tip

Reading a sentence aloud can help you decide on the correct verb form.

Some indefinite pronouns are always plural: *both*, *many*, *few*, *some*, and *several*. A plural indefinite pronoun takes a plural form of the verb.

▶ **EXAMPLE 5**

Several of the people want fruit for dessert.

Practice C

Write the verb that correctly completes each sentence.

1. Everyone (is, are) coming to the dance.

2. Both of the girls (seem, seems) happy to help.

3. Few of them (was, were) prepared for the test.

4. Nothing (sound, sounds) as noisy as a basketball game.

5. Several teachers (decorate, decorates) the gym.

Almost everybody in the stands cheers and claps. Some watch quietly.

Subject-Verb Agreement with Compound Subjects

A sentence may have a **compound** subject. When two or more subjects are joined by a conjunction, they form a compound subject. When the subjects are joined by *and*, use a plural verb form.

▶ **EXAMPLE 6**

The paper and the pencil are on the table.

Sometimes, the subjects are joined by *or* or *nor*. In this case, the verb agrees with the last noun or pronoun.

▶ **EXAMPLE 7**

Plural   Either the paper or the pencils are on the table.

Singular   Neither the papers nor the pencil is on the table.

Practice D

Write each sentence using the correct form of the verb in parentheses.

1. The Library Association _____ to raise money. (plan)

2. The United States _____ to sign that agreement. (want)

3. *The Canterbury Tales* _____ a book by Geoffrey Chaucer. (be)

4. The Bahamas _____ an island country south of Florida. (be)

5. The Red Cross _____ people when disaster strikes. (help)

REVIEW

Write the verb that correctly completes each sentence.

1. Car accidents (causes, cause) many injuries.

2. Some people (injures, injure) themselves in falls.

3. Most people who ski (is, are) daring and fit.

4. A council on safety (records, record) these facts.

5. Everyone (needs, need) ways to find information.

Write the correct form of the verb in parentheses.

6. The blue or red shirt best _____ those pants. (match)

7. Jake, Leslie, and their parents _____ a Labor Day party every year. (throw)

8. *War and Peace* _____ the longest book I ever read. (be)

9. Honduras _____ bananas to other countries. (sell)

10. A quarter of the projects _____ completed. (be)

SPELLING BUILDER

Understanding Syllables

A syllable is a part of a word that has one vowel sound. A word can have one syllable or many syllables. Clapping as you say a word will help you hear the syllables.

　　teach (one syllable)　　teaching (two syllables)

The vowels are *a, e, i, o,* and *u. Y* can also be a vowel when it sounds like *e* or *i.*

　　young, yet (*y* as a consonant)

　　baby, cry (*y* as a vowel)

Count the syllables in each of these words: *explore, listening, hug, napkin, messenger.* Write the numbers on your paper.

The Verb *Do*

A form of the verb *do* can be used as a helping verb in verb phrases. The main verb *do* means "to perform an action."

▶ **EXAMPLE 1**

Neeru does her chores on the weekends. (main verb)

She did vacuum the bedrooms. (helping verb)

Practice A

A form of the verb *do* is in bold in each sentence. Write it on your paper. Decide if it is the main verb or a helping verb. Then write *main* or *helping*.

1. Neeru **does** her homework in the evening.

2. On weekends, the family **does** housework.

3. They **do** the work together.

4. Her brother **did** not want his salad.

5. "You **do** like tomatoes, don't you?" he asked.

The helping verb *do* has three main uses. It is used in questions. It is used with the word *not*. It is also used for emphasis—to make a statement stronger. In Example 2, the main verb is *like*.

▶ **EXAMPLE 2**

Do you like baseball? (helping verb in a question)

I do not like baseball. (helping verb with the word *not*)

I do like baseball. (helping verb for emphasis)

Practice B

Change each question to a statement. Use the same words. Write the statement. Underline the verb phrase.

1. Do they like spicy food?

2. Did Alec send the e-mail message?

3. Does Stephen play the guitar?

4. Did Sandra have a good time on her vacation?

5. Does Elliot know how to drive?

Verb Forms of *Do*

Present	Michelle **does** her homework after school. (singular)
	The students **do** their research in the library. (plural)
Past	Michelle **did** her report on César Chávez.
Future	She **will do** another report on farm workers.
Present Perfect	Armando **has done** three reports. (singular)
	The students **have done** several reports this year. (plural)
Past Perfect	They **had done** research on the Internet.
Future Perfect	They **will have done** a total of six reports by May.

Practice C

Write the verb in each sentence on your paper. Write the tense of the verb next to it.

1. Efran does his research at the library and on the Internet.

2. He did his last report on Neil Armstrong.

3. He has done two reports on the space program.

4. Emily had done her first report on Mozart.

5. She will do her next report on Beyoncé Knowles.

REVIEW

Write the verb or verb phrase in each sentence. Next to each verb or verb phrase, write its tense.

1. Did Columbus land in the Americas in 1492?

2. Yes, he did explore the Americas then.

3. Do you know the exact date?

4. No, I do not know.

5. According to the almanac, Columbus's crew did sight land on October 12.

Use each verb or verb phrase in a sentence. Write the sentence. You may split up a verb phrase to form a question.

6. will have done

7. did go

8. will do

9. does play

10. do

LESSON 5-7

Conditional Verbs

Objectives

■ To identify helping verbs that put a condition on an action
■ To form conditional verb phrases with helping verbs

Conditional verb

A verb that shows that the action is possible or necessary

Reading Strategy: Visualizing

As you read each sentence in Example 1, think about the situation when the action is possible.

Helping verbs change the meaning of a sentence. For example, **conditional verbs** show when a verb's action is possible or necessary. They show that the action happens under a certain condition. The helping verbs used to make conditional verbs are *may, might, can, could, shall, should, will, would,* and *must*. In Example 1, each verb phrase is in blue.

▶ **EXAMPLE 1**

May—Might	Armando may visit Mammoth Cave. Nathan might get a job.
Can—Could	Neeru can sing very well. Angela could win a gold medal.
Shall—Should	We shall succeed. Mrs. Choy should finish her work.
Will—Would	The team will practice after school. They would like to win their next game.
Must	Sally must return her book.

Practice A

Write the verb phrase in each sentence on your paper.

1. Emily can play the flute quite well.
2. They must get to class on time.
3. Would you like some carrots?
4. Neeru will sing a solo in the spring concert.
5. *Jane Eyre* may be my favorite book.

A conditional verb can be formed from a helping verb and a perfect tense verb.

▶ **EXAMPLE 2**

Present Perfect   The band may have gone.

Past Perfect   The band could have gone.

Present Progressive   The band may be going.

Past Progressive   The band would be going.

Practice B

Write the verb phrase in each sentence. After it, write its tense.

1. Miguel's poster might win the contest.

2. He could have won last year.

3. The teacher may hang the poster in the art room.

4. Miguel could have used brighter colors.

5. Should he try again?

May and *can* have slightly different meanings. Do you know the difference? *Can* shows the ability to do something. *May* asks for permission.

▶ **EXAMPLE 3**

I can swim a mile in 30 minutes. (I am able to swim.)

May I go swimming now? (Do I have permission to swim?)

Practice C

Write the word that correctly completes each sentence.

1. Neeru wondered, "(Can, May) I hit those high notes?"

2. Nathan asked, "(Can, May) I check out this book?"

3. Mia said that she (can, may) kick a soccer ball a mile.

4. Emily asked the teacher, "(Can, May) I switch seats?"

5. "(May, Can) I have your attention?" asked Mr. Lee.

REVIEW

Write the verb phrase in each sentence.

1. I could wear my purple socks.

2. We should eat a more balanced diet.

3. Singers must breathe properly.

4. The dynamite might explode!

5. Bats can hang upside down.

Write the verb or verb phrase that correctly completes each sentence.

6. Emily (should have, should of) practiced her flute longer.

7. "(Can, May) I play the solo in this piece?" asked Emily.

8. The students played popular songs when they (could, can).

9. Miguel visits the art gallery whenever he (could, can).

10. If he (would have, had) gone Friday, he would have seen Armando.

PUTTING IT ALL TOGETHER

Suggest a theme for a school celebration. Put your suggestion in writing. Use at least one verb in a simple tense. Use at least one verb in a perfect tense. Use at least one verb in a progressive tense. Make sure each verb agrees with the subject of the sentence.

● Six Traits of Writing:
Sentence Fluency
smooth rhythm and flow

Writing a Résumé

Philip Franco wants to be a home health aide. He sees an ad in a newspaper that offers a job that he wants. The ad asks people to send a letter and a résumé.

A résumé begins with a person's name, address, phone number, and e-mail address. It lists a person's skills and work experience. It also tells about the person's education. Some résumés include a career goal. Philip's goal is to find a job as a home health aide.

Here is part of Philip's résumé. It describes his work as a volunteer. Read it, and then follow the directions.

```
Work Experience
I volunteer at the Chelmsford
Nursing Home.
• I help residents with daily tasks.
• I walk residents to the cafeteria.
• I serve meals to residents.
• I play checkers with residents.
• I change bed linens.
```

1. Write the six present tense action verbs in Philip's résumé.

2. Imagine that Philip no longer volunteers at the nursing home. Change the present tense verbs to past tense verbs.

3. CRITICAL THINKING Why should you use clear, specific verbs in a résumé?

LISTENING AND SPEAKING

After you send a résumé to an employer, you might have an interview. Practice your interview skills ahead of time. Role-play a job interview with a partner. Write five questions you might be asked in an interview. Take turns asking and answering the questions. How does your partner present himself or herself? Pay attention to eye contact, tone of voice, and posture.

Reading a Newspaper

The newspaper is a rich source of information. In newspapers, you can find almost anything. You can find sports scores. You can find daily movie listings. You can find ads for jobs, cars, and homes. You can find articles on recent national and local events.

Most libraries have indexes of newspapers. You can also read many newspapers online.

Read the newspaper article at the right. Then follow the directions below.

1. Write these verbs from the article: *marked, will live, set, had thought.* Next to each one, write the verb's tense. Identify whether the verb is regular or irregular.

2. Find a different newspaper article that is written in past tense. Choose one paragraph from it. Rewrite the paragraph in present tense.

3. **CRITICAL THINKING** Different newspapers report the same news in different ways. Find an article in two different papers about the same event. How are the two articles similar? How are they different?

Schools Show Olympic Spirit

Last night at Wilson High School, there was a giant party. It marked the end of two weeks of Olympic-style competition among 12 high schools. Star athletes thrilled fans. Others claimed surprise wins. Some suffered defeat. Athletes broke records in the water and on land. The memory of their victories will live on forever.

During the first week, the most exciting action happened in the pool. Regional champ Brian Linn, a senior at Springfield High, set three freestyle records. During the second week, success was especially sweet for sprinter Laura Orrico, a junior at Central High. When she sprained her ankle last month, she had thought her chance to compete was over. She surprised everyone by competing and winning the gold medal in the 100-meter race.

TECHNOLOGY

How can you find newspaper articles on a special topic? Try an online database. Data means information. A database is a set of information. Find a database of newspaper articles online. Choose a topic you want to learn about. Use the database to find three newspaper articles on the topic.

SUMMARY

- Find an action verb in a sentence by asking what the subject is doing.

- Identify verb tense to know when the action happens.

- Use the present tense when the action is happening now. Use the past tense if the action has already happened. Use the future tense when the action will happen in the future.

- Form verb phrases by using a helping verb with a main verb.

- Form the past and past participle of regular verbs by adding *-d* or *-ed*.

- Use the past participle and the helping verb *have* to form the perfect tenses.

- Learn the tense forms of irregular verbs. These are verbs that do not follow normal rules for past tense and past participle.

- Form the present participle of a verb by adding *-ing* to the present tense.

- Use the present participle and the helping verbs *be* and *have* to form the six progressive tenses.

- Make sure that the subject and verb in a sentence agree.

- Check that an indefinite pronoun or a compound subject agrees with the verb.

- Use the verb *do* as a main verb or as a helping verb.

- Use *do* as a helping verb in questions, with the word *not*, and for emphasis.

- Use conditional verbs to show that an action is possible or necessary. The helping verbs used to make conditional verbs are *may*, *might*, *can*, *could*, *shall*, *should*, *will*, *would*, and *must*.

GROUP ACTIVITY

Work in a small group. Write a short description of your English class. Tell what the class is about. Tell what students learn from the class. Tell what past students have gained from taking the class. Use action verbs in the present and past tenses. Trade your writing with another group. Suggest ways to improve the other group's writing.

Word Bank

action verb

conditional verb

helping verb

infinitive

irregular verb

past participle

perfect tenses

present participle

progressive verb
  phrase

regular verb

simple tenses

tense

verb phrase

Part A Write the word or words from the Word Bank that complete each sentence.

1. A _____ is a verb whose past tense and past participle end in -*ed* or -*d*.

2. The _____ is used to form the perfect tenses.

3. An _____ tells what someone or something did, does, or will do.

4. A _____ is a main verb plus a helping verb.

5. A _____ is the form of a verb that ends in -*ing*.

6. A _____ combines with a main verb to form a verb phrase.

7. A verb's _____ tells the time when the action takes place.

8. The three _____ are present perfect, past perfect, and future perfect.

9. An _____ has a past tense and past participle formed in different ways.

10. Verbs can express three kinds of _____: present, past, and future.

11. A _____ is a form of *be* plus the present participle of a verb.

12. An _____ is the word *to* plus the present tense of a verb.

13. A _____ shows that the action is possible or necessary.

Part B Write the verb form that completes each sentence.

14. The temperatures this winter (have breaked, have broken) many records.

15. Where has Neeru (went, gone)?

16. She (has took, has taken) the letter to the post office.

Part C Write the verb or verb phrase in each sentence. Then write its tense.

17. Neeru is singing in the concert.

18. She has sung in many concerts.

19. Brooke could have played her flute.

20. She practices her music every day.

21. Brooke will miss the concert.

Part D Write the letter of the answer to each question.

22. Which verb or verb phrase is in the present progressive tense?
    A goes   **C** will be moving
    B is learning   **D** has been playing

23. Which sentence has a verb phrase in it?
    A Martha has been jogging every day.
    B Lisa shops on Tuesdays.
    C Joseph won a prize.
    D The Ravens play on Sunday.

24. Which verb phrase is in the present perfect tense?
    A has won   **C** had been winning
    B will perform   **D** had run

25. Which of these is an irregular verb?
    A kiss   **C** walk
    B sing   **D** study

Test Tip

You can study tenses by making flash cards. Write a sentence on the front of the card. On the back, write the tense of the verb in the sentence. Use the flash cards to test your knowledge.

Using State-of-Being Verbs in Sentences

S ome verbs do not show action. They show a state of being. A state of being is the way something is. A state of being can be the way someone looks or feels. It can also express what something is.

Look at the photo on the opposite page. How would you describe this place? *This place is beautiful. The flowers are pink. The path becomes invisible. The air smells clean.* These sentences use state-of-being verbs to express what you see, hear, taste, touch, or smell. You can also use state-of-being verbs to express how you feel: *I feel calm.*

In Chapter 6, you will learn about state-of-being verbs. Each lesson tells about how state-of-being verbs are used in everyday speech and writing.

GOALS FOR LEARNING

- To identify state-of-being verbs and verb phrases
- To use the correct form of state-of-being verbs in sentences
- To tell the difference between a state-of-being verb and an action verb

Reading Strategy: Inferencing

Sometimes the meaning of what you read is not directly stated in the words. The writer hints at the meaning, but does not directly say it. You have to make an inference to figure out the meaning. An inference is a conclusion based on what you already know and on what you read.

What You Know + What You Read = Inference

To make inferences, you have to think "outside" the words you read. Predicting what will happen can help you make inferences. Making connections between the things you read about can also help.

Key Vocabulary Word

State-of-being verb A verb that links the subject of a sentence to a word or phrase that tells something about it

What Is a State-of-Being Verb?

A **state-of-being verb** links the subject of a sentence to words that tell about it. State-of-being verbs can show the condition of the subject. They also can show that the subject is (or equals) something or someone else.

▶ **EXAMPLE 1**

Juan is in the band. (state-of-being verb)

Juan plays the drums. (action verb)

The first sentence in Example 1 tells you something about Juan. The second sentence tells you about something Juan does. A state-of-being verb tells about *being*. An action verb tells about *doing*.

The most common state-of-being verb is *be*. *To be* means "to exist, to live, or to happen."

Verb Forms of *Be*

	Singular	Plural
Present	(I) am (he, she, it) is	are
Past	was	were
Future	will be	will be
Present Perfect	has been	have been
Past Perfect	had been	had been
Future Perfect	will have been	will have been
Present Progressive	(I) am being (he, she, it) is being	are being
Past Progressive	was being	were being
Future Progressive	will be being	will be being

NOTE

Think about the state-of-being verbs *look*, *sound*, *feel*, *taste*, and *smell*. They will help you describe subjects in your writing.

Practice A

Write the verb or verb phrase in each sentence. Next to it, write the tense.

1. Amanda and Emily have been at the mall.

2. Neeru was at home.

3. She is at the library once a week.

4. Neeru has been in the school band since fourth grade.

5. She will be the lead clarinet player this year.

Here are some other state-of-being verbs. Many of them are about the five senses. Others are about change.

Some State-of-Being Verbs

act	feel	keep	seem	stay
appear	get	look	smell	taste
become	grow	remain	sound	turn

▶ **EXAMPLE 2**

The class stayed quiet during the speech.

The flowers still look fresh.

Practice B

Write the verb or verb phrase in each sentence. Next to it, write the tense.

1. This piano sounds out of tune.

2. The art teacher has remained Jill's friend.

3. The tea tastes bitter.

4. Will everything turn out all right?

5. Nate appeared tired after his long trip.

REVIEW

Write the verb or verb phrase in each sentence.

1. The summer seems hotter than usual.

2. The sun gets warmer in the afternoon.

3. The family is staying cool inside.

4. Cool water would feel great.

5. The pool at the park looked very busy.

Add a different state-of-being verb to each sentence. Write the sentences on your paper.

6. Nathan _____ like a friendly person.

7. Armando _____ an artist.

8. The sky _____ stormy.

9. That fresh bread _____ delicious.

10. We _____ friends for many years.

VOCABULARY BUILDER

Building a Word Family

Suffixes and prefixes are word parts that are added to root words. A suffix is added at the end of a word. A prefix is added at the beginning. When you add a suffix or prefix, you change the root word's meaning.

The root word *port* means "to carry." The suffix *-able* means "able to be." Can you guess what *portable* means? Here are some other words in the *port* family: *export, important, reporter, transport, report, support.* What do you think the word *porter* means? Check your guess in a dictionary.

Tenses of State-of-Being Verbs

You learned that an action verb must agree with its subject. Subject-verb agreement for state-of-being verbs is the same. You use one verb form with a singular subject. You use another verb form with a plural subject.

When the subject is singular, add -*s* or -*es* to the present tense of regular verbs. Do the same for most irregular verbs.

▶ **EXAMPLE 1**

George seems happy. (singular subject)

His friends seem happy too. (plural subject)

Practice A

Write the correct verb form for each sentence. Be sure that the subject and the verb agree.

1. Steve (feel) sure that his answer is correct.
2. The girls (appear) pleased with their sign.
3. Pat (look) sad.
4. The pasta sauce (smell) delicious.
5. The sandwiches (taste) good.

The past tense of regular verbs is the same for singular and plural subjects. The past tense of verbs that end in -*e* is usually formed by adding -*d*. The past tense of verbs that end in a consonant is usually formed by adding -*ed*.

▶ **EXAMPLE 2**

Ralph sounded excited about the game. (singular subject)

His friends sounded excited, too. (plural subject)

Reading Strategy:
Inferencing

What do you already know about irregular verbs? Add your knowledge to the information in this lesson.

Writing Tip

Use clear, specific nouns and adjectives with state-of-being verbs. *The roses were deep red.* This helps the reader imagine what you are describing.

Practice B

Write the past tense of each verb in parentheses.

1. John _____ hopeful that his answer was correct. (remain)

2. The students _____ pleased with their test results. (appear)

3. Barbara _____ sad. (look)

4. The pasta sauce cooking on the stove _____ delicious. (smell)

5. The sandwiches _____ good. (taste)

The verb *be* is an irregular verb. Its form changes when it is used with a singular or plural subject. Its form also changes when the subject is first, second, or third person.

Present and Past Forms of the Irregular Verb *Be*

	Present	Past
Singular		
First Person	(I) am	(I) was
Second Person	(you) are	(you) were
Third Person	(he, she, it) is	(he, she, it) was
Plural		
First Person	(we) are	(we) were
Second Person	(you) are	(you) were
Third Person	(they) are	(they) were

The pronoun *you* can be singular or plural. Use the same form of *be* with *you* when it is singular and when it is plural.

▶ **EXAMPLE 3**

You are a kind person. (singular subject)

You are kind people. (plural subject)

Practice C

Complete each sentence with a form of the verb *be*. Write the verb on your paper.

1. Joanna _____ now a student at Wilson High School.

2. Joanna's mother _____ a student there years ago.

3. Ramon and Chris _____ in history class this year.

4. _____ you in the class too?

5. I _____ on the school newspaper staff this year.

I am on the newspaper staff. Rom and Emily are on it, too.

Some verbs can be used as state-of-being verbs *or* action verbs. State-of-being verbs have the same verb tenses as action verbs.

Different Forms and Uses of the Verb *Look*

	State-of-Being Verb	Action Verb
Present	Mia **looks** sad.	Mia **looks** at a book.
Past	Mia **looked** sad.	Mia **looked** at a book.
Future	Mia **will look** sad.	Mia **will look** at a book.
Present Perfect	Mia **has looked** sad.	Mia **has looked** at a book.
Past Perfect	Mia **had looked** sad.	Mia **had looked** at a book.
Future Perfect	Mia **will have looked** sad.	Mia **will have looked** at a book.

Practice D

Write the verb form. Then write a sentence using that verb form as a state-of-being verb.

1. the present tense of *smell*
2. the future tense of *appear*
3. the present perfect tense of *grow*
4. the past perfect tense of *be*
5. the future perfect tense of *feel*

REVIEW

Write the form of the verb that agrees with the subject.

1. The hiker (was, were) cold and tired.

2. Frances (look, looks) restless.

3. The cats (appear, appears) bored.

4. Where (is, are) your jacket?

5. Armando and Joe (feel, feels) good about the game.

Write the verb or verb phrase in each sentence. Next to it, write the tense.

6. In the last decade, computers have grown more popular.

7. For many years, computers have been tools for scientists.

8. Some people seem helpless without their computers.

9. Many students have become expert computer users.

10. Computers will remain an important tool in schools.

SPELLING BUILDER

Using Homophones

Sometimes two words sound alike but are spelled differently. These words are called homophones. You need to hear these words in a sentence to spell them correctly.

clothes	things made of cloth that you wear (noun)
close	to shut or shut down (verb)
past	time gone by (noun) or relating to a time gone by (adjective)
passed	the past tense of pass (verb)

Write four sentences. In each one, use a state-of-being verb and one of the words above.

Action or State of Being?

Reading Strategy:
Inferencing

Think about the meaning of a verb to decide if it is an action verb or a state-of-being verb.

Forms of the verb *be* are always state-of-being verbs when they are alone. The verb *seem* is never an action verb. It is always a state-of-being verb.

▶ **EXAMPLE 1**

The sky is dark and stormy.

The snow on the ground was deep.

This lesson seems easy.

Other state-of-being verbs can also be action verbs. How can you tell if these verbs show action or state of being? You must think about their meaning in a sentence. Ask yourself these questions:

- Is the subject doing something? If the answer is yes, the verb is an action verb.

- Is the sentence telling about the condition of the subject? If the answer is yes, the verb is a state-of-being verb.

▶ **EXAMPLE 2**

Mrs. Choy grew roses in her yard. (action)

Armando grew strong from exercise. (state of being)

I can smell the onions. (action)

These potatoes smell rotten. (state of being)

Writing Tip

Use specific state-of-being verbs when you write. Do not always use forms of *be*. This will make your writing more lively.

Practice A

Write the verb in each sentence. Next to each verb, write *action* or *state of being*.

1. The weather today is cold and windy.

2. The temperature remains below freezing.

3. Angela tasted the hot chocolate.

4. In case of fire, sound the alarm.

5. The wind feels very biting.

Verbs often have more than one meaning. Some meanings express action, and some express state of being. Remember to think about the way the verb is used in the sentence.

▶ **EXAMPLE 3**

Appear   The storm appeared suddenly. (action)

         The storm appears to be dangerous. (state of being)

Feel   Neeru felt the warmth of the fire. (action)

         She felt that she would be safe. (state of being)

         Neeru felt warm. (state of being)

Smell   Jamar smelled the bread. (action)

         The bread smells good. (state of being)

Look   Neeru looked out of the window. (action)

         Neeru looks cold. (state of being)

Taste   Mrs. Choy tasted the tea. (action)

         The tea tasted bitter. (state of being)

Get   The package got to India on time. (action)

         It gets cold after dark. (state of being)

Reading Strategy:
Inferencing

After reading this lesson, what conclusion can you make about the uses of verbs?

Practice B

Decide whether each bold verb expresses action or state of being. For each pair of sentences, write *action* and *state of being* in the order in which the verbs are used.

Example: Jon **is getting** nervous. He **is getting** his jacket.
Answer: state of being, action

1. Emily **felt** sick. Her father **felt** her forehead.

2. Ms. Wilson **looked** for her keys. She **looked** worried.

3. Emily **appeared** better. Ms. Wilson's keys **appeared**!

4. Jamar **tasted** the apple cider. It **tasted** sweet.

5. The air **smelled** fresh. Angela **smelled** the flowers.

Angela smelled the flowers. They smelled wonderful!

REVIEW

Word Bank

got

has tasted

seemed

will appear

Write the verb or verb phrase from the Word Bank that completes each sentence. Use each verb or verb phrase only once. Then decide if it is an action or state-of-being verb. Write *action* or *state of being*.

1. Salvador _____ sleepy while doing his math homework.

2. Yesterday, Hanna _____ to be thinking about something.

3. At some point, the sun _____ above the horizon.

4. Reshma _____ cotton candy before.

Number your paper from 5 to 10. Find the six verbs or verb phrases in the paragraph. Write each one on your paper. Then write *action* or *state of being* next to each one.

Some people become fans of baseball at a very early age. Fans often share information and bits of history with each other. Who hit the first home run on Wrigley Field? At the ballpark, the air smells like popcorn. The children sound excited. Everyone appears very focused on the game.

PUTTING IT ALL TOGETHER

Write a description of an object in your classroom. Choose something that is not alive. Use at least three state-of-being verbs. Use at least three action verbs. Then trade descriptions with a partner. Underline the verbs in your partner's description. Tell which verbs show action and which verbs show state of being.

Six Traits of Writing:

Ideas message, details, and purpose

COMMUNICATING ON THE JOB

Construction Crew Worker

This summer, Marc Young is working on a construction crew. The crew is building a house. Today is Marc's first day on the job. His boss could not be there on Marc's first morning. His boss left this note for Marc. Read the note. Then follow the directions below.

> Dear Marc,
>
> Welcome to the crew! I'm sorry I cannot be here for your first morning of work. Barb will be in charge. She will start you on a project. She will work right beside you. She does excellent work and is a great teacher. I like workers to do jobs in pairs. It is safer! I will return this afternoon. I hope to talk with you then. I'm happy to answer any questions you might have. Remember that everyone learns on the job—even when it is not the first day.
>
> Mr. Martinez

1. Write three action verbs used in the note.

2. Describe the construction boss in one sentence. Use a state-of-being verb in your sentence.

3. CRITICAL THINKING The note contains many state-of-being verbs. Explain why this is true.

SPEAKING AND LISTENING

Work with a partner on a "construction project." The task is to cover a book. One student gives instructions. The other listens carefully and follows the instructions. Trade roles. Cover a second book. How does a good boss speak? How does a good worker listen?

BUILDING RESEARCH SKILLS

Finding Information You Can Trust

You will find all sorts of information on the Internet. It is written by all kinds of people. When you search for facts, you need to find information you can trust. You cannot trust everything you find on a Web site.

For example, imagine you are searching for facts about Mars. You can usually trust facts on a government Web site or an online encyclopedia. However, only use up-to-date information. Something written in 1990 will not include recent discoveries. Also, only use information that names the author of the article or Web site.

Here are three questions that will help you decide what you can trust:

- Who wrote this? Is the person an expert?

- Was this written within the past five years?

- Does the author identify or explain where the information came from?

If the answer to all three questions is yes, then you can probably trust the information.

Write the answers to these questions.

1. How can you tell when something was written?

2. Write a one-sentence summary of this page using a state-of-being verb.

3. **CRITICAL THINKING** Below are two places to find facts about Mars. Which one probably has better information? Why?

   NASA. "NASA's Mars Exploration Program." http://mars.jpl.nasa.gov

   Martin, Lisa. "Mars: The Red Planet," *Science Magazine*, May 5, 1982

 TECHNOLOGY

Most Web site addresses have a three-letter ending. These letters show you the kind of Web site it is. These letters will help you decide whether it is a site you can trust.

.gov	a state or national government
.org	an organization
.edu	a college or university
.net	a network
.com	a business

Avoid using Web sites with addresses that end in *.net* or *.com*.

SUMMARY

- Use a state-of-being verb to link the subject of a sentence to words that tell about it.

- Use state-of-being verbs that add interest to your writing.

- Make sure that the subject and the state-of-being verb agree.

- Form the plural present tense of most regular verbs by adding -*s* or -*es*.

- Form the plural past tense of most regular verbs by adding -*d* or -*ed*.

- The verb *be* is irregular. Its different forms do not look alike.

- Notice how you use state-of-being verbs in your sentences. Most state-of-being verbs can also work as action verbs. Only the verbs *be* and *seem* do not work as action verbs.

GROUP ACTIVITY

Work with a small group to write a paragraph describing your school. Tell how many students attend. Describe the special features of the building. Describe the programs, clubs, and people. Tell what you like best and least about your school.

Then circle the action verbs and underline the state-of-being verbs. Read your paragraph to the class. After hearing the descriptions of other groups, how would you rewrite your group's description?

Part A Write the verb or verb phrase in each sentence.

1. Neeru has never been in a snowstorm.
2. The sky appears darker than usual.
3. The air even smells like snow.
4. Everyone gets excited.
5. The air is growing colder.
6. The sleds are in the garage.

Part B Complete each sentence with a form of *be* or another state-of-being verb. Write the sentence.

7. Gina's clothes never _____ wrinkled.
8. The phone call _____ for Denis.
9. I never _____ bored.
10. The party guests _____ noisy.
11. You _____ my best friend.
12. These flowers _____ sweet.

Part C Does the bold verb in each sentence express action or state of being? Write *action* or *state of being*.

13. The teacher **appeared** unexpectedly in the room.
14. The classroom **turned** quiet.
15. You **will feel** tired after the long trip.
16. Marie **felt** the soft black cloth.
17. "You **look** worried," Mr. Thomas said.
18. The test **seemed** hard.
19. Bart **remained** calm.
20. He **stayed** in his seat.

Part D Choose the verb that completes each sentence. Write the letter of your answer. Pay attention to whether the subject is singular or plural.

21. Every student there _____ talking.
    - **A** are
    - **B** have been
    - **C** were
    - **D** was

22. Both of these juices _____ tangy.
    - **A** taste
    - **B** tastes
    - **C** have tasted
    - **D** had tasted

23. Now the students _____ quiet as the movie begins.
    - **A** grow
    - **B** grew
    - **C** had grown
    - **D** will have grown

24. This movie _____ my favorite.
    - **A** remain
    - **B** remained
    - **C** remains
    - **D** had remained

25. The pie on the counter _____ fresh.
    - **A** smell
    - **B** smells
    - **C** will smell
    - **D** has smelled

Test Tip

Sometimes a test question is about one part of a sentence, such as the verb. First read the whole sentence to understand the meaning. Then go back and answer the question about the sentence part.

Using Adverbs in Sentences

You have learned about nouns and verbs. You have also learned about pronouns and adjectives. Those parts of speech cover most of the words in English, but not all. In this chapter, you will learn about adverbs. Like adjectives, adverbs give more details about other words.

For example, what is happening in this photo? A dog carries a toy, and the water is moving in waves. However, there is more to say or write. The dog runs happily and quickly. He is very wet. The tide comes and goes daily, but slowly. These words—*happily, quickly, very, daily, slowly*—are adverbs. They show how, where, when, or how many times something happens.

In Chapter 7, you will learn about different kinds of adverbs. You will learn how to use these words to make your writing stronger.

GOALS FOR LEARNING

- To recognize adverbs, and to identify the word in a sentence that an adverb answers questions about
- To recognize and use adverbs of degree
- To recognize and use adverbs that mean "no," and to correct double negatives
- To recognize and use adverbs that compare
- To tell the difference between an adverb and an adjective

Reading Strategy: Metacognition

Metacognition means "thinking about your thinking." You can use metacognition to become a better reader. Here are some steps you can take as you read this chapter:

- Look at the previous two pages. Look at the Key Vocabulary Words below. How do they prepare you to learn about adverbs?
- Look ahead in the chapter and make predictions about what you will learn.
- As you begin each lesson, ask yourself what you already know about the subject.
- Keep track of what you have learned. Write down main ideas and details.
- If something does not make sense, go back and read it again.

Key Vocabulary Words

Adverb A word that tells more about a verb, a verb phrase, an adjective, or another adverb in a sentence

Adverb of degree An adverb that tells how much, how little, or how often something happens or is present

Negative A word or phrase that means "no"

Adverb of negation The adverb *never* or *not*

Double negative A sentence with two negatives

What Is an Adverb?

Adverbs are words that can tell about a verb or a verb phrase. Adverbs can also tell about adjectives or other adverbs. An adverb tells *how, when, how many times,* or *where.* Many adverbs tell about action verbs. Adverbs can also tell about state-of-being verbs such as *be.*

Adverbs That Tell How

Adverbs that answer the question *how* are usually used with action verbs. They tell more about the way the action was done. Some adverbs end in *-ly.*

▶ **EXAMPLE 1**

A rainbow suddenly appeared.

The family ate dinner quickly.

Practice A

Write the adverb in each sentence.

1. Neeru sings beautifully.
2. Emily plays the flute well.
3. The librarian gladly helped Angela find a book.
4. I clumsily dropped the mug.
5. Angela swam her race fast.

Adverbs of Time

Some adverbs are about time. They answer the question *when, how long,* or *how many times.* For example, *yesterday* shows past time. *Later* or *tomorrow* show the future. An adverb about time must agree with the tense of the verb it tells about.

Reading Strategy:
Metacognition

Why do some words
in Examples appear
in blue? Do you pay
closer attention to
these words?

▶ **EXAMPLE 2**

Yesterday we went to school.

Lili worked twice last week.

Practice B

Choose an adverb about time to complete each sentence.
Use the question to help you. Write the adverb.

1. Michael will be home _____. (When?)

2. Joel arrived _____ at the dentist. (When?)

3. Efran sneezed _____. (How many times?)

4. Brush your teeth _____. (How often?)

5. The band played _____. (How long?)

Adverbs of Place

Adverbs can also tell about place. They answer the
question *where* or *in what direction*.

▶ **EXAMPLE 3**

Aim the arrow here.

My bike will be outside.

The hikers headed east.

Practice C

Write the adverb in each sentence. Then write the verb
each one describes.

1. The explorers traveled south.

2. We held the party indoors because of rain.

3. The tree crashed down.

4. The children ran upstairs.

5. The police car sped ahead.

REVIEW

Write the adverb in each sentence.

1. The woman spoke quietly.

2. Some birds can fly backward.

3. Jill held the rope firmly.

4. Robby opened the present slowly.

5. Yesterday, she walked to the post office.

Write the adverb in each sentence. What does it tell you? Next to each adverb, write *how*, *where*, *when*, or *how many times*.

6. Two students stepped forward.

7. Kelly called me twice.

8. Tomorrow Neeru will write a letter to her cousin.

9. She writes to her cousin monthly.

10. They will sleep downstairs.

VOCABULARY BUILDER

Words That Sound Similar

People often confuse pairs of words that sound similar. Read these examples aloud:

> quiet (adjective) means "lacking sound"
> quite (adverb) means "almost"
> probable (adjective) means "likely"
> probably (adverb) means "likely"

Write the word that completes each sentence.

1. I thought the book was (quite, quiet) interesting.
2. Please be (quiet, quite) in the library.
3. Her team will (probable, probably) win the race.
4. It is (probable, probably) that Adam will play.

Adverbs of Degree

Objectives

In Lesson 7-1, you learned about adverbs that tell about verbs. Adverbs can also answer questions about adjectives and other adverbs. **Adverbs of degree** tell *how much*, *how little*, or *how often* something happens or is present.

Adverbs of Degree

almost	extremely	rather
altogether	just	so
awfully	little	somewhat
completely	nearly	too
entirely	partly	unusually
especially	quite	very

Adverb of degree

An adverb that tells how much, how little, or how often something happens or is present

Adverbs that answer questions about adjectives are in front of the adjective.

▶ **EXAMPLE 1**

How Hot?	The coffee was too hot.
How Soft?	That puppy's ears are especially soft.
How Cold?	Today was quite cold.

Reading Strategy:
Metacognition

Remember to ask yourself questions as you read.

Practice A

Find the adjective in each sentence. Then add an adverb of degree to tell *how much*, *how little*, or *how often*. Write the new sentence. Underline the adverb you added.

1. Angie was late for practice.

2. We saw an exciting movie.

3. The rain on the roof is loud.

4. The salsa tastes spicy.

5. Cody is a careful reader.

Adverbs that answer questions about other adverbs are usually in front of the adverb.

▶ **EXAMPLE 2**

How Slowly?   The girls walked rather slowly.

How Quickly?   Emily finished the test so quickly.

Practice B

Find the adverb in each sentence. Add an adverb of degree to tell *how much*, *how little*, or *how often*. Write the new sentence. Underline the adverb you added.

1. The dogs were barking loudly.

2. The wheel turned slowly.

3. She ended the song quickly.

4. He read the letter carefully.

5. Ms. Benson cleared her throat loudly.

Rex was especially dirty after our walk along the river.

REVIEW

Find the adverb in each sentence that tells about an adjective or another adverb. Write the adverb on your paper.

1. Emily almost always reads before going to bed.

2. Neeru was too tired before her game.

3. I walked rather clumsily up the stairs.

4. Stacy was completely happy with her paycheck.

5. Angela climbed the hill very carefully.

The bold words are either adverbs or adjectives. Add an adverb of degree in front of each one. Write the new sentence.

6. Nathan woke up **late** and missed the bus.

7. It was **silent** in the halls when he got to school.

8. He **slowly** opened the door to his classroom.

9. "This is turning out to be a **bad** day!" he said when he realized he forgot a notebook.

10. Because he was **tired**, he fell asleep in class.

Adverbs That Mean "No"

Negative
A word or phrase that means "no"

Adverb of negation
The adverb *never* or *not*

Double negative
A sentence with two negatives

A **negative** is a word or phrase that means "no." Some negative words are adverbs. *Never* and *not* are **adverbs of negation**. Some negative adverbs mean that an action will not happen. Others mean that something is not true.

▶ **EXAMPLE 1**

Armando never misses his art class.

Mrs. Choy is not home today.

Practice A

Write each sentence on your paper. Underline the adverb of negation.

1. Tess has never been to New York.

2. Emily did not bring her shoes to practice.

3. The snow was not deep.

4. I never said this would be easy.

5. This is not Logan's house.

Double Negatives

Read this sentence carefully: *I do not have no clean socks.* The speaker of the sentence means that he or she has no clean socks. But the sentence has two negatives, *not* and *no*. In English, this is incorrect. Be careful to avoid using **double negatives**.

▶ **EXAMPLE 2**

Incorrect	I do not have no money.
Correct	I do not have any money.
Correct	I have no money.

The words *no, nothing, none, no one,* and *nobody* are negatives. They are not adverbs, however.

Practice B

Rewrite each sentence. Correct the double negative.

1. Jason does not know nothing about the game.

2. Rosa did not bring no music with her.

3. He is never not home.

4. I could not do nothing to fix my bike.

5. A picnic in the rain is not no fun.

Not in Contractions

You learned about certain contractions in Chapter 3. Those contractions combined a pronoun and a verb, such as *I'll* and *they're.* Other contractions combine a verb and the adverb *not.* In these contractions, the *o* in *not* is replaced by an apostrophe.

NOTE

The contraction for *will not* is irregular. The contraction for *will not* is *won't.*

▶ **EXAMPLE 3**

I haven't read that book yet. (have not)

Emily can't finish her work today. (cannot)

He won't drink sodas. (will not)

Practice C

In each sentence, find the contraction with an adverb of negation. Write the contraction as two words.

1. Luke didn't watch the news.

2. John's mind wasn't on the game.

3. Nathan couldn't wait to go fishing.

4. You shouldn't have any problems.

5. Emily wasn't on the bus.

Reading Strategy:
Metacognition

Did you understand this lesson? If not, read it again.

REVIEW

Write each sentence on your paper. Underline the adverb of negation. (It might be part of a contraction.)

1. I don't like waiting.

2. Vinny couldn't see the movie.

3. Mr. Thomas never gives homework on weekends.

4. Adam would not stop talking.

Rewrite each sentence to correct the double negative.

5. I didn't get no sleep last night.

6. Adam could not do nothing to stop the noise.

7. There isn't no more paper.

Add an adverb of negation to each sentence. Write the new sentence.

8. There is extra paper in the drawer.

9. I can go to the movies tonight.

10. Angela could find the right answer.

Adverbs That Compare

Objectives

■ To identify and
   use positive,
   comparative, and
   superlative adverbs

■ To use the forms of
   the irregular adverb
   well

Imagine a person running slowly. Then imagine another runner who is even slower. To write about these two runners, you could use an adverb that compares. If a third runner comes along, you could use another adverb to compare all three. Like adjectives, adverbs of comparison can be *positive*, *comparative*, or *superlative*.

▶ **EXAMPLE 1**

Positive	Comparative	Superlative
fast	faster	fastest
slowly	more slowly	most slowly
happily	less happily	least happily
well	better	best

Practice A

Write the adverb in each sentence. Then write whether it is *positive*, *comparative*, or *superlative*.

1. Armando is working harder this year.

2. He writes well.

3. Each week he writes his reports more clearly.

4. Joe contributes stories more often than Armando.

5. Compared to everyone else, Armando writes best.

Comparative adverbs compare two actions. Most adverbs with one syllable form the comparative by adding *-er*. Use *more* or *less* before longer adverbs.

▶ **EXAMPLE 2**

He walks faster than his brother.

He walks more quickly than his brother.

Superlative adverbs compare more than two actions. Most adverbs with one syllable form the superlative by adding *-est*. Use *most* or *least* before longer adverbs.

▶ **EXAMPLE 3**

She spoke the fastest of all the speakers.

She spoke the least clearly of all the speakers.

Practice B

Write the adverb that completes each sentence. Then write whether the adverb is *comparative* or *superlative*.

1. She can sing (higher, highest) than anyone else in choir.

2. Ben drives to school (more often, most often) than Luis.

3. Of all the employees, Emily works (harder, hardest).

4. Angela swam the (faster, fastest) in the third event.

5. Few people like cassette tapes (better, best) than CDs.

A few adverbs, such as *well*, are irregular. The three forms of the adverb *well* are *well*, *better*, and *best*.

▶ **EXAMPLE 4**

He writes well. He writes better than his friend.

Of all the students, who writes best?

Practice C

Write each sentence. Fill in the blank with *well, better,* or *best.*

1. Of the three friends, Javier did _____ on the test.

2. After I had some lunch, I could think _____.

3. Travis danced _____ than Gayle.

4. The band performed _____ at their concert.

5. I can see _____ with these glasses than those ones.

Reading Strategy:
Metacognition

Summarize this lesson to make sure you understand it.

REVIEW

Write the adverb in each sentence. Next to each adverb, write whether it is *positive*, *comparative*, or *superlative*.

1. Nathan quickly finished his lunch.

2. Megan's gift arrived late.

3. Of the three students, Angela swam fastest.

4. Who plays tennis better, Emily or Angela?

5. Can you paint the wall sooner than next week?

Write a sentence using each adverb or adverb phrase.

6. correctly

7. more cheaply

8. most loudly

9. faster

10. best

SPELLING BUILDER

Word Endings That Begin with Consonants
Suppose you want to add one of these endings to a word: *-ly*, *-less*, or *-ful*. Do you change the word's spelling? The answer depends on the word. Use these rules:
• If the word does not end in *y*, just add the ending.
   sad—sadly   *care—careless*   *help—helpful*
• If the word ends in *y*, check the dictionary. For most words with more than one syllable, you change the *y* to *i* and add the ending.
   happy—happily   *penny—penniless*   *play—playful*
Add the ending *-ly* to each of these words:
   1. heavy   **2.** rapid   **3.** entire   **4.** busy

Adjective or Adverb?

Objectives

■ To tell adverbs from adjectives

■ To use *good* and *well* correctly

Reading Strategy:
Metacognition

Think about *how* you read. Before you read this lesson, ask yourself: What can I do to understand it better?

Sometimes, the same word can be used as an adverb and as an adjective. How can you tell the difference? Look closely at how the word is used in the sentence. Remember that adjectives describe nouns and pronouns. Adverbs answer questions about verbs, adjectives, and other adverbs.

▶ **EXAMPLE 1**

Adjective	Angela is a fast swimmer. (What kind of swimmer?)
Adverb	She swims fast. (How does she swim?)
Adjective	He watered the garden last week. (Which week?)
Adverb	He watered the tomato plants last. (When were they watered?)

Practice A

Read each sentence. Think about the word in bold. Decide whether it is an adjective or an adverb. Write *adjective* or *adverb* on your paper.

1. The **next** game is a three-legged race.

2. The sophomore team will go **next**.

3. Students ran **clumsily** to the finish.

4. Ana and Beth won the **first** race.

5. They crossed the finish line **first**.

Many adjectives become adverbs when you add *-ly*.

▶ **EXAMPLE 2**

Adjective	Adverb
That is her usual way.	She usually is late.
The ocean is calm.	The teacher spoke calmly.

Practice B

Choose the word in parentheses that completes each sentence. Write the sentence on your paper.

1. It was a (bitter, bitterly) December day.
2. Several (happy, happily) teenagers climbed up the hill.
3. The hard snow crunched (loud, loudly) under their feet.
4. Carlos ran (swift, swiftly) to join them.
5. They (slow, slowly) dragged their sleds up the hill.

Most words that end in *-ly* are adverbs, but some can be used as adjectives.

▶ **EXAMPLE 3**

Adjective	He wrote a daily report.
Adverb	He wrote the report daily.

Practice C

Write each bold word in the paragraph. Next to each word, write *adjective* or *adverb*.

Armando woke up **early** to do his **weekly** workout. He stretched his legs. Then he went for a **lively** jog. Armando ran on a **narrow** road. He ran **quietly** so he wouldn't wake his neighbors.

Writing Tip

Bad is an adjective. Use it after state-of-being verbs like *be*. *Badly* is an adverb. Use it to tell more about action verbs. *Angela was a bad listener. Angela listened badly.*

Using *Good* and *Well*

Good is always an adjective. *Well* is usually an adverb. The adverb *well* means "in a good way." When *well* is an adjective, it means "healthy."

▶ **EXAMPLE 4**

Adjective	This apple juice is good.
	(*Good* describes the juice.)
Adverb	They worked well together.
	(*Well* describes how they worked.)
Adjective	The boy was not well.
	(*Well* describes his health.)

Practice D

Decide whether to complete each sentence with *good* or *well*. Write your answer on your paper.

1. This is a (good, well) snack!

2. No one plays the tuba as (good, well) as Emily.

3. Miguel cleans his room (good, well) every week.

4. One (good, well) deed deserves another.

5. Armando does not feel (good, well) today.

Ramon is in the marching band. He plays the trombone well.

REVIEW

Write the word that completes each sentence.

1. Ms. Benson needed the telephone (quick, quickly).

2. The (swift, swiftly) river was cold and deep.

3. Henry spoke (soft, softly).

4. Abdul is a (graceful, gracefully) swimmer.

5. Dom can draw horses (perfect, perfectly).

Decide whether to use *good* or *well* to complete each sentence. Write your answer on your paper.

6. Efran mixed the batter (good, well).

7. Everyone said the games were a (good, well) idea.

8. I thought the sweet potatoes tasted (good, well).

9. I could not see (good, well) because of the fog.

10. Everyone worked (good, well) together at the games.

PUTTING IT ALL TOGETHER

Six Traits of Writing:

Word Choice vivid words that "show, not tell"

Write a story about something you did that you are proud of. Then underline every verb you wrote. Add adverbs to give the verbs more meaning. Circle the adverbs you added. Read your story aloud in a small group.

Giving Instructions

It is a Friday evening. Alan Martin is babysitting for his little nephew, Juan. Juan is five months old. Alan's sister told him how to care for the baby before she left. She also wrote down what he should do. However, one sentence in her note contains a mistake. Read her instructions. Then answer the questions below.

> Juan will be ready for a bottle at 7:30. You can give it to him early if he gets too fussy. Run warm water over the bottle to heat it slightly. Rock him gently after his bottle until he falls asleep. Then lay him in his bed. Do not leave no toys in his bed while he sleeps. Check on him often. Call me right away if you need anything. Thank you, Alan, for staying with your nephew. We will enjoy our night out!

1. Write at least four adverbs that are in the note.

2. Which sentence contains the mistake? Rewrite it correctly.

3. **CRITICAL THINKING** How do adverbs make these written instructions clearer?

SPEAKING AND LISTENING

Think about the differences between written and spoken instructions. For example, what if Alan's sister just told him what to do instead of writing a note? In this case, which do you think is better? Why? When are spoken instructions better than written ones?

BUILDING RESEARCH SKILLS

Using a Telephone Book

Imagine that you want to call your Uncle Ned. You have forgotten his phone number. You can find it in your local telephone book. You already know your uncle's name. You will use the *white pages* of the phone book. This section lists people by their last names in alphabetical order.

Now imagine that you want to order flowers for Mother's Day. You do not know the name of a flower shop in town. To find one, use the *yellow pages* of the phone book. This section lists businesses by their type. You can find headings such as "Automobile Repairs," "Dance Instruction," and "Flower Shops." These heading are arranged in alphabetical order. Under each heading is a list of businesses. They are also in alphabetical order. Each business gives its address and phone number.

The yellow pages also contain ads for some of the businesses listed. You might be attracted to this ad:

Yellow page ads can be helpful. Still, you may want to try calling businesses that do not have ads. You may want to compare services and prices.

Write the answers to these questions.

1. What three adverbs appear in the ad for Beautiful Bloom Flowers?

2. Look through your yellow pages. Find an ad that includes at least two adverbs. Write the sentences or phrases that include the adverbs.

3. CRITICAL THINKING Some businesses are listed in the yellow pages, and they also pay for a separate ad. Why would a business do both?

TECHNOLOGY

The Internet has borrowed the idea of yellow page ads. Some Web sites give the same information as ads. Many Web sites contain links to more information. By clicking on the links, you can control how much information comes to you.

Beautiful Bloom Flowers

We arrange flowers creatively and uniquely.
We deliver bouquets on time
to meet your needs.
We use the most freshly cut flowers.

(878)555-2398

- Use adverbs to tell more about verbs, adjectives, and other adverbs. An adverb can answer one of these questions: how, when, how long, how many times, where, or in what direction.

- Make sure that an adverb about time agrees with the tense of the verb it tells about.

- Use adverbs of degree to tell how much, how little, or how often.

- Use adverbs of negation to tell that something will not happen or is not true.

- Do not write double negatives.

- Form contractions with certain verbs and the adverb *not*. Replace the *o* in *not* with an apostrophe.

- Form the comparative and superlative forms of short adverbs by adding *-er* and *-est*.

- Form the comparatives of most longer adverbs by using *more* or *less*.

- Form the superlatives of most longer adverbs by using *most* or *least*.

- The adverb *well* is irregular. Its comparative form is *better*, and its superlative form is *best*.

- Some words can be either an adverb or an adjective. You must look carefully at how the word is used in the sentence.

- You can change some adjectives into adverbs by adding *-ly*.

- Know when to use *well* and when to use *good*.

GROUP ACTIVITY

Think of two adverbs to describe each of these verbs: *write*, *walk*, and *talk*. Write each adverb and verb on an index card. Now form a small group with some other students. Combine your cards. Take turns choosing a card. Act out what is on the card. Have everyone guess which adverb and verb you are acting out.

Word Bank

adverb

adverb of degree

adverb of negation

double negative

negative

Part A Write the word or words from the Word Bank that complete each sentence.

1. A _____ is a word or phrase that means "no."

2. An _____ tells more about a verb, an adjective, or another adverb.

3. An _____ tells that something will not happen or is not true.

4. A sentence with two negatives is a _____.

5. An adverb that tells how much, how little, or how often is an _____.

Part B Write the word that completes each sentence.

6. James learned to use a computer (easy, easily).

7. He can type (fast, faster) than Katie.

8. Of all the students, James types (better, best).

9. He uses a very (good, well) typing program.

10. He did very (good, well) on the typing test.

Part C Write the letter of the answer.

11. Which word is an adverb?
    A merely **B** silly   **C** melody   **D** many

12. Which word is an adverb of negation?
    A nothing **B** no one **C** never   **D** none

13. Which adverb is superlative?
    A fastly   **B** fast   **C** faster   **D** fastest

14. Which word is an adverb of degree?
    A too   **B** twice   **C** twin   **D** twenty

15. Which contraction is written correctly?
    A willn't **B** wouldnt **C** when't   **D** won't

Part D Rewrite each sentence. Correct the double negative.

16. Nathan does not have no interest in computers.

17. He never said he was no computer expert.

18. His friends couldn't teach him nothing about computers.

19. He won't never listen to what they say.

20. Computers don't do no homework for you.

Part E Write the adverb in each sentence. After it, write the word it describes.

21. In the past, people usually used pens to write.

22. Fortunately, C. L. Sholes invented the typewriter in 1868.

23. Soon, typewriters became popular.

24. Students often took typing classes in high school.

25. Recently, computers have taken the place of typewriters.

Test Tip

Carefully read test directions. Pay attention to key words that tell you what to do.

Using Prepositional Phrases

Most prepositions are little words. A preposition shows how a noun or pronoun relates to another part of the sentence. A preposition is always part of a phrase.

Look at the picture on the opposite page. What words come to mind? How about *over, under, around, above, below, through, in, on, off, between,* or *among*? These little words help you see how things relate to each other. In this case, the things are highways, ramps, and traffic.

In Chapter 8, you will learn to use prepositional phrases. Prepositional phrases will help you to express your ideas. They will help you write more clearly and in a more exciting way.

GOALS FOR LEARNING

- To identify prepositional phrases in sentences
- To identify the object of a preposition, and to use the correct form of a pronoun in a prepositional phrase
- To identify prepositional phrases used as adjectives
- To identify prepositional phrases used as adverbs
- To use the correct form of a verb in a sentence with a prepositional phrase

Reading Strategy: Summarizing

Summarizing is an important skill. When you summarize, you retell the most important parts of something you see, hear, or read.

Think of a movie that you enjoyed. When you tell someone what it was about, you are summarizing. You describe the important events in the story. You explain how the events relate to each other. You leave out most of the small details. You describe the big picture.

To summarize, answer questions like these:

- What is the main idea?
- What is each part about?
- When will you use this information?
- How will you use this information?

Key Vocabulary Words

Preposition A word that shows how a noun or pronoun relates to another word or phrase in a sentence

Prepositional phrase A group of words that begins with a preposition and ends with a noun or pronoun

Object of the preposition A noun or pronoun at the end of a prepositional phrase

Prepositions and Prepositional Phrases

A **preposition** shows how a noun or pronoun relates to another word or phrase in a sentence.

Common Prepositions

about	at	by	near	through
above	before	down	of	to
across	behind	during	off	toward
after	below	except	on	under
among	beneath	for	out	until
around	beside	from	over	with

A preposition is always a part of a **prepositional phrase**. A phrase is a group of words. A prepositional phrase begins with a preposition and ends with a noun or pronoun. The noun or pronoun is the **object of the preposition**.

▶ **EXAMPLE 1**

The computer is on the desk.

Prepositional Phrase	on the desk
Preposition	on
Object of the Preposition	desk

The prepositional phrase in Example 1 tells *where* the computer is. It tells how the desk relates to the computer. Each preposition has its own meaning. Often, the meaning is about place.

▶ **EXAMPLE 2**

The computer could be beside the desk.

The computer could be under the desk.

Objectives

■ To identify prepositions and objects of prepositions

■ To recognize adjectives and adverbs in prepositional phrases

■ To write sentences with prepositional phrases

Preposition
A word that shows how a noun or pronoun relates to another word or phrase in a sentence

Prepositional phrase
A group of words that begins with a preposition and ends with a noun or pronoun

Object of the preposition
A noun or pronoun at the end of a prepositional phrase

Reading Strategy:
Summarizing

Read the Objectives listed on page 193. They summarize the goals for this lesson.

Practice A

Add a preposition to complete each sentence. Write the sentence on your paper.

1. Sidney found her keys _____ the sofa.

2. Sidney and Marta left the car _____ the field.

3. The car broke down _____ warning.

4. They had to walk _____ the main road.

5. Several people drove _____ them.

Practice B

Write five sentences using prepositions from the table on page 193. Then underline the prepositional phrase in each sentence.

The students in Mr. Hill's class take turns writing prepositions on the chalkboard.

Reading Strategy:
Summarizing

Write one sentence that gives two facts about the object of a preposition.

Every preposition has an object. The object is a noun or pronoun. The object is related to some other part of the sentence. In Example 3, each object is in blue.

▶ **EXAMPLE 3**

The line stretched around the corner.
(*Around the corner* tells where the line stretched.)

The line for the movie was long.
(*For the movie* tells what kind of line.)

The team waited for an hour.
(*For an hour* tells how long the team waited.)

The team from the city waited.
(*From the city* tells where the team was from.)

Practice C

Identify the prepositional phrase in each sentence. Write the object of each prepositional phrase.

1. London Bridge carries people across the Thames River.

2. The bridge was rebuilt many times over the years.

3. Wooden houses once stood on the bridge.

4. There is a popular song about the bridge.

5. The bridge is important for many reasons.

A prepositional phrase can contain adjectives that tell about the object. A prepositional phrase can also contain adverbs.

▶ **EXAMPLE 4**

on the desk

on the messy desk
(*Messy* is an adjective that describes the desk.)

on the extremely messy desk
(*Extremely* is an adverb that tells how messy the desk is.)

Practice D

Use each prepositional phrase in a sentence. Write the sentence on your paper.

1. around the corner
2. during the cold night
3. in the star-filled sky
4. in my right hand
5. through the wide door

REVIEW

Write the prepositional phrase in each sentence. Then underline the object.

1. Nando was looking for a job.

2. He read the ads in the newspaper.

3. Each ad told about a different job.

4. He hoped to find a job for the summer.

5. During the summer, he likes to save money.

Number your paper from 6 to 10. Write five sentences about a job you enjoy. Use a prepositional phrase in each sentence. Underline each prepositional phrase you use.

VOCABULARY BUILDER

Using Compound Prepositions

Compound prepositions are two or more words.

> Darnell sat down **next to** Celia.

Here are some compound prepositions:

according to	due to	next to
along with	in addition to	instead of
because of	in place of	out of

Choose a compound preposition to complete each sentence. Write the sentence on your paper.

1. Celia became a swimmer _____ Janet Evans, an Olympic athlete.

2. Would you like tea _____ coffee?

3. The flight was delayed _____ bad weather.

4. _____ the great review, the play was a success.

Objects of Prepositions

Objectives

- To identify the object of a preposition as a noun or a pronoun
- To use a pronoun as the object of a preposition
- To use *between* and *among* correctly
- To use *beside* and *besides* correctly

Reading Strategy:
Summarizing

How are the last two Objectives for this lesson alike? How are they different?

You learned that the object of a preposition can be a noun or a pronoun.

▶ **EXAMPLE 1**

Armando kicked the ball into the net. (*Net* is a noun.)

The crowd cheered for him. (*Him* is a pronoun.)

In Chapter 3, you learned that a personal pronoun has three forms: subject, object, and possessive. When a pronoun is the object of a preposition, it is always in the object form.

Forms of Personal Pronouns

	Subject	Object	Possessive
Singular			
First person	I	me	my, mine
Second person	you	you	your, yours
Third person	he, she, it	him, her, it	his, her, hers, its
Plural			
First person	we	us	our, ours
Second person	you	you	your, yours
Third person	they	them	their, theirs

▶ **EXAMPLE 2**

Incorrect	Give the pencil to I.
Correct	Give the pencil to me.
Incorrect	The stranger walked toward Jake and I.
Correct	The stranger walked toward Jake and me.

NOTE

If a pronoun is the subject of a sentence, it is always in the subject form.

Practice A

Write the pronoun that completes each sentence. Then identify its form by writing *subject* or *object*.

1. In class, Brittany sat between Joe and (I, me).
2. I found the pen that (he, him) had lost.
3. (She, Her) and Deb sat in the back.
4. Emily gave the notebook to (he, him).
5. I tried not to look at (they, them).

Practice B

Write each sentence. Add a personal pronoun in the correct form.

1. Len ran beside _____.
2. You may go before _____ if you wish.
3. Lee hid behind _____ the whole time.
4. I did not see him leave with _____.
5. I sat behind _____ during the wedding.

Each preposition has its own meaning. Some pairs of prepositions are often mixed up. For example, use *between* when you are telling about two people, things, or groups. Use *among* when you are telling about three or more people, things, or groups.

▶ **EXAMPLE 3**

Nick is sitting between his two sisters.

Nick is sitting among all his relatives.

Reading Strategy:
Summarizing

Summarize the main ideas of this lesson in two or three sentences.

Practice C

Write the preposition that completes each sentence.

1. (Between, Among) the two swimmers, Angela is the fastest.

2. Let's split the work (between, among) all of us.

3. The five boys divided the sandwiches (between, among) them.

4. Ana eats lunch (between, among) third and fourth periods.

5. (Between, Among) the two of them, they got the job done.

Use *beside* when you mean "next to." Use *besides* when you mean "in addition to" or "except."

▶ **EXAMPLE 4**

She put the papers beside the book.

Besides the book, she bought some stamps and pens.

Practice D

Write the preposition that completes each sentence.

1. (Beside, Besides) Tim, there will be four others.

2. Larry walked (beside, besides) Anita.

3. Nobody (beside, besides) Javier wants to go.

4. Our house is (beside, besides) a lake.

5. I know all the answers (beside, besides) this one.

REVIEW

Write the pronoun that completes each sentence. Then identify its form by writing *subject* or *object*.

1. Nathan ran with Emily and (I, me).

2. (Her, She) walked to school with him.

3. Have you been around (they, them) before?

Write the preposition that completes each sentence.

4. Is Daria (between, among) the people in the hall?

5. She sat (between, among) Celia and Yoko at lunch.

6. Nando put his medals (beside, besides) his pictures.

7. (Beside, Besides) art class, I have two other classes.

Write a preposition to complete each sentence.

8. Joe lives _____ the river.

9. We talked _____ class.

10. The flag hung _____ the door.

SPELLING BUILDER

Adding Suffixes That Begin with a Vowel

How do you add a suffix such as *-able* to a word? The answer depends on the word. The rules below can help you add these suffixes: *-ous, -able, -ible, -y, -ance, -ence.*

- If the word does not end in *y* or *e*, just add the suffix: *rent—rentable.*
- If the word ends in a consonant and a *y*, change the *y* to *i* and add the suffix: *envy—envious.*
- If the word ends in *e*, drop the *e* and add the suffix: *use—usable.*

Add *-able* to each of these words: *value, reason, rely, enjoy.*

Adjective Phrases

Objectives

- To recognize adjective phrases
- To use prepositional phrases as adjectives

Reading Strategy:
Summarizing

What do you already know about adjectives?

You have learned to recognize a prepositional phrase. It begins with a preposition and ends with a noun or pronoun. You can use prepositional phrases for different purposes.

In Chapter 4, you learned that an adjective describes a noun or pronoun. You can use a prepositional phrase as an adjective.

▶ **EXAMPLE 1**

| Adjective | The middle book is mine. |
| Prepositional Phrase | The book in the middle is mine. |

A prepositional phrase used as an adjective is called an adjective phrase. It tells *which one, what kind,* or *how many.* Notice in Example 1 that the adjective comes before the noun it describes. The prepositional phrase comes after the noun.

Practice A

Find the prepositional phrase in each sentence. Write it on your paper. Then write the word that the phrase describes.

1. We read a book about China.
2. The story by Ji-Li Jiang was exciting.
3. An invention by Henry Ford changed the world.
4. The book with the blue cover caught my eye.
5. The computer on the teacher's desk had a word list.

A prepositional phrase can describe the object in another prepositional phrase.

▶ **EXAMPLE 2**

A team from a school in northern New York arrived.

In Example 2, the phrase *from a school* describes the noun *team*. The phrase *in northern New York* describes *school*.

Practice B

Write the prepositional phrase in bold in each sentence. Then write the noun it describes.

1. Mario shopped at the store **in the city.**

2. Darnell swam in the pool **at school.**

3. Nando liked the car on the cover **of the magazine.**

4. Amy used the weights in the gym **at the YMCA.**

5. Corinne visited lakes in national parks **in the West.**

Sometimes, you must decide which is better in a sentence: an adjective or an adjective phrase.

▶ **EXAMPLE 3**

Adjective   Our school's swim team won.

Adjective Phrase   The swim team from our school won.

Practice C

Change the word or words in bold into a prepositional phrase. Write the new sentence on your paper.

1. The **roller coaster** ride thrilled Carl.

2. Annie bought a **China** doll.

3. **Edgar Allen Poe's** story was popular with the students.

4. We bought a **six-room** house.

5. The **joke** book was quite short.

REVIEW

Write the prepositional phrase or phrases in each sentence. After each phrase, write the noun or pronoun that the phrase describes.

1. The girl from Canada liked the food in France.

2. Marion took a snack of nuts and fruit.

3. The water in the pool was warm.

4. Some friends of ours had a party at the pool.

5. The girl with Paolo is his cousin from Brazil.

Add a prepositional phrase after each bold noun or pronoun. Be sure your phrase tells something about the noun or pronoun. Write the new sentence on your paper.

6. **Everyone** watched the games.

7. The student liked the **movie.**

8. The **workers** are on their way here.

9. The horse was standing in the **shade.**

10. Elgin's **postcard** was in the mail.

Adverb Phrases

Objectives

- To recognize adverb phrases
- To use prepositional phrases as adverbs

Reading Strategy:
Summarizing

How are Lessons 8-3 and 8-4 alike? How are they different?

In Chapter 7, you learned that an adverb can answer questions about a verb, an adjective, or another adverb. It can answer *how, when, where, how long,* or *how many.* You can use a prepositional phrase as an adverb. When used in this way, the prepositional phrase is called an adverb phrase.

▶ **EXAMPLE 1**

| Adverb | Neeru sang the song joyfully. |
| Adverb Phrase | She sang with joy. |

An adverb phrase may be in different places in a sentence. Read the two sentences in Example 2.

▶ **EXAMPLE 2**

After dinner, we played cards.

We played cards after dinner.

Notice that both sentences mean the same thing. The adverb phrase *after dinner* answers the question *when.*

Practice A

Write the adverb phrase in bold in each sentence. Then decide which question the adverb phrase answers about the verb. Write one of these: *how, when, where, how long,* or *how many.*

1. The fishing season begins each year **in April.**
2. The coach held tryouts **on three different days.**
3. Sign your name **on this sheet** of paper.
4. Letitia stayed **for two hours.**
5. Eric plays the guitar **with great skill.**

An adverb phrase can also answer the question *why*.

▶ **EXAMPLE 3**

They were tired because of their hard work.
(The adverb phrase tells why they were tired.)

Practice B

In each sentence, find the adverb phrase that answers the question *why*. Write the phrase on your paper.

1. Everyone was worn out because of the long hike.

2. Emily was thirsty from her long walk.

3. Celia missed two days of school because of a cold.

4. The road flooded due to the heavy rain during the night.

5. Because of all the traffic, Mrs. Choy was late.

An adverb phrase can tell about an adjective or another adverb.

▶ **EXAMPLE 4**

Jason was late for lunch.
(The adverb phrase tells about the adjective *late*.)

Practice C

Write the adverb phrase in each sentence. After it, write the question that the phrase answers. Write *why, where, when,* or *how many.*

1. Today, Ana ran faster by five seconds.

2. Jon is sick in bed.

3. The sun shone throughout the morning.

4. Ned's painting was good because of his effort.

5. Angela walked alone for two miles.

REVIEW

Write the adverb phrase in each sentence. After it, write the question that the adverb phrase answers about the verb. Write *how*, *when*, *where*, *why*, or *how long*.

1. The school newspaper printed the scores on Friday.

2. He wrote the story at home.

3. The time went quickly because of his skill.

4. Alan has been writing without any help.

5. He has been a reporter for two years.

Add an adverb phrase to each sentence. The phrase should answer a question about the verb. Write the new sentence on your paper. Then underline the adverb phrase that you added.

6. Mrs. Logan coaches the team.

7. The students left early.

8. Mr. Thomas has taught history.

9. The students brought their books.

10. The history class began.

Prepositional Phrases and Subject-Verb Agreement

Objectives

- To understand that a prepositional phrase can appear between the subject and verb of a sentence
- To use the correct verb form in sentences with prepositional phrases

 Writing Tip

The object of a prepositional phrase does not affect the verb in a sentence. The verb must agree with the subject of the sentence.

In Chapter 5, you learned about subject-verb agreement. The subject and the verb in a sentence must agree in number. A singular subject (one item) needs a singular verb. A plural subject (more than one item) needs a verb in plural form.

▶ **EXAMPLE 1**

Dario sings beautifully. (Both *Dario* and *sings* are singular.)

The students sing well. (Both *students* and *sing* are plural.)

Sometimes, the subject of a sentence is followed by a prepositional phrase. The verb must agree with the subject. The verb does not need to agree with the object of the preposition.

▶ **EXAMPLE 2**

The students in the chorus sing well.
(*Sing* must agree with *students*, not *chorus*.)

In Example 2, *in the chorus* is a prepositional phrase between the subject and the verb. *Students* is the subject. The verb *sing* must agree with *students*, not *chorus*.

Choose the correct verb form. Write the sentence on your paper.

1. The papers on the table (is, are) mine.

2. The games at the park (was, were) listed.

3. A book of photos (makes, make) a good gift.

4. The man with all the boxes (needs, need) help.

5. The people in the airport (watches, watch) the planes leave.

Practice B

Reading Strategy:
Summarizing

What rule did you use to do Practice B?

Choose the verb that agrees with the subject of the sentence. Write the sentence.

1. His list of possible answers (fill, fills) the whole page.

2. The members of the jury (listen, listens) to the lawyers.

3. The table by the windows (are, is) set up for wrapping gifts.

4. The papers on the desk (seem, seems) very important.

5. The coach of the team (run, runs) laps with the players.

Three kinds of wrapping paper are available.

REVIEW

If the subject and verb in the sentence agree, write *correct*. If the subject and verb do not agree, rewrite the sentence correctly.

1. A group of birds flies over the field.

2. The days of December grows shorter and shorter.

3. The people from the island treats us well.

4. The trees in the yard shed leaves.

5. My collection of CDs take time to arrange.

Number your paper from 6 to 10. Find five subject-verb agreement mistakes in the sentences below. Write the subject and the correct form of the verb.

The right kind of shoes make all the difference. Patches of ice is dangerous. Shoes with a ridged sole helps you grip the ground. Boots with a rubber sole keep your feet dry. Also, the weight of your shoes are important. Walking with heavy boots make your legs tired.

PUTTING IT ALL TOGETHER

Think about a place in your neighborhood or town that you enjoy visiting. Think about *when, why,* and *how* you go there. Write five sentences about a visit to this place. Use a prepositional phrase in each sentence to make your writing clear and interesting.

Six Traits of Writing:

Word Choice vivid words that "show, not tell"

Flight Attendant

Joni Bright enjoys her job as a flight attendant. She attends to the needs of passengers on planes. She greets passengers and helps them find their seats. She serves food and beverages. She also carefully explains the safety instructions. This is one of her most important duties. Everyone on the plane must know what to do in an emergency. Read Joni's safety instructions. Then answer the questions below.

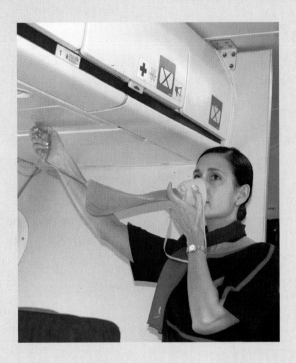

 SAFETY INSTRUCTIONS

In an emergency, a mask may drop down in front of you. The masks on the plane supply oxygen. Slip the strap over your head. Breathe normally. Please help the passengers beside you. Besides oxygen masks, the plane has other safety features. If we land in water, pull the base of your seat loose. It will float and help you to stay on top of the water.

1. What are the three prepositions in the first sentence?

2. Find the last prepositional phrase in the instructions. What is the object in this phrase?

3. CRITICAL THINKING How do prepositional phrases make instructions clearer?

 SPEAKING AND LISTENING

Work with a partner to practice reading Joni's safety instructions aloud. Then read the same instructions without the prepositional phrases. How do prepositional phrases improve written and spoken messages?

Asking an Expert

Suppose you want to find information on a topic. You can go to books, magazines, or the Internet. You can also go to a person. The person you talk to should be an expert. An expert is someone who knows a lot about the topic. An expert is someone you can trust to give you correct information.

For example, to find out about fly fishing, talk to someone who fly fishes. Before the interview, write a list of questions to ask. Here are some sample questions. Notice that they begin with *who, what, where, why, when,* and *how.*

- Who taught you to fly fish?
- What kinds of fish do you catch?
- Where are the best fishing spots?
- Why do people enjoy fly fishing?
- When is the best time to fish?
- How do people learn to fly fish?

If you use information from your interview in a report, you must tell where you got the information. In the report, include the name of the expert. In a bibliography at the end of your report, list the expert's name, your name, and the place and date of the interview. Here is an example:

Bell, Gary. Interview by [your name], Harrison, Maine, April 5, 2007.

Answer the questions below.

1. Invent answers to the six questions about fly fishing. Use a prepositional phrase in each answer.

2. Find a recent newspaper or magazine article that uses words from an expert. What question do the words answer?

3. **CRITICAL THINKING** Would it work to question an expert on the phone? Why or why not?

MEDIA AND TECHNOLOGY

If possible, use a tape recorder or video camera when you talk to an expert. Then you do not have to take as many notes. You can give the person your full attention. Later, you will be able to write what he or she says without missing a word. Work with a partner to practice your interview skills. Choose a topic that your partner knows a lot about. Ask your partner six questions. Take notes as your partner answers them, or use a tape recorder or video camera.

CHAPTER 8

SUMMARY

- Use prepositions to show how a noun or pronoun relates to another part of a sentence.

- To find a prepositional phrase, look for a group of words that begins with a preposition. The phrase ends with a noun or pronoun.

- Use nouns or pronouns as objects of prepositions.

- When a pronoun is the object of a preposition, use its object form.

- Be careful to use prepositions that mean just what you want to say.

- Use *between* when you are discussing two people or things. Use *among* when you are discussing three or more people or things.

- Use *beside* when you mean "next to." Use *besides* when you mean "in addition to" or "except."

- Use prepositional phrases as adjective phrases.

- Use prepositional phrases as adverb phrases.

- Watch for sentences that have a prepositional phrase after the subject. Make sure the verb agrees with the subject, not the object of the preposition.

GROUP ACTIVITY

Work with a small group. Write a set of instructions for something done in steps. Examples are changing a tire, cooking spaghetti, and doing a skateboard trick. Use prepositional phrases to make the instructions clear.

Then trade instructions with another group. Point out the prepositional phrases. Tell the other group how to improve their instructions. Were your instructions clear? Why or why not?

Word Bank

object of
    the preposition

preposition

prepositional
    phrase

Part A Write the word or words from the Word Bank that complete each sentence.

1. A _____ shows how a noun or pronoun relates to another word or phrase in a sentence.

2. A _____ contains a preposition and an object.

3. The noun or pronoun that follows a preposition is the _____.

Part B Find the prepositional phrase in each sentence. Write the object of the preposition.

4. The groceries are still in the car.

5. One of the cats has a short tail.

6. The flowers in the vase are lilacs.

7. In the parking lot, I found a dollar bill.

8. Selana waited at the bus stop.

Part C Write the bold phrase in each sentence. After it, write whether it is an *adjective phrase* or an *adverb phrase*.

9. **During the storm**, the wind blew our old tree down.

10. Mr. Lopez served tacos **on Tuesday.**

11. Andy invited his friends **to his house.**

12. Every one **of his friends** had left by 10:00 PM.

13. The house **by the lake** is built on posts.

Part D Number your paper from 14 to 21. Write the eight prepositional phrases in these sentences.

Eric Carle is one of the most loved creators of children's picture books. He is most famous for *The Very Hungry Caterpillar*. This book has been rewritten in more than 30 languages. It has sold over 22 million copies. It is a fun story for young children. It helps them learn to count. Children around the world love this book.

Part E Write the letter of the answer to each question.

22. Which statement is true about a pronoun that is the object of a preposition?
A It is singular.
B It is plural.
C It is the subject of the sentence.
D It is in the object form.

23. What does an adjective phrase tell about?
A a verb
B a noun
C an adverb
D another adjective

24. Which word is a preposition?
A something
B phrase
C beneath
D beginning

25. Which preposition means "except"?
A beside
B besides
C among
D between

Test Tip

When you answer a multiple-choice item, first cross out the choices you know are wrong. Then choose from the answers that are left.

Using Conjunctions and Interjections

What do you see in this photo? A bridge spans a river. You have to walk across it to get to the other side. In the middle of the bridge, you might stop, look down, and say, "Wow!"

Conjunctions are words that connect parts of sentences. They let readers walk from one idea to another. Words such as *and*, *or*, and *so* are conjunctions. Words like *because*, *since*, and *when* are also conjunctions.

Interjections are words that express strong feelings. They are words such as *Oh no! Hey!* and *Ouch!* Interjections add excitement to your writing.

In Chapter 9, you will learn about conjunctions and interjections. You will learn how to use them in sentences.

GOALS FOR LEARNING

- To recognize and use coordinating conjunctions to connect words in a sentence and to join sentences
- To recognize and use correlative conjunctions, and to use correct verb forms with correlative conjunctions
- To recognize and use subordinating conjunctions in sentences
- To use interjections in sentences, and to correctly punctuate sentences with interjections

Reading Strategy: Questioning

Asking questions as you read will help you understand what you are reading. Asking questions will also help you remember what you read. Questioning makes you a more active reader. As you read, ask yourself:

- Why am I reading this?
- What can I decide about the facts and details?
- What links can I make between what I am reading and my life?

Key Vocabulary Words

Conjunction A word that connects parts of a sentence

Clause A group of words with a subject and a predicate

Coordinating conjunction A word that connects two or more equal parts of a sentence

Series A list of three or more words, phrases, or clauses

Compound subject Two or more subjects that share the same predicate

Compound predicate Two or more predicates that share the same subject

Correlative conjunction Two words that act as a single conjunction connecting words or phrases in a sentence

Independent clause A clause that expresses a complete thought

Dependent clause A clause that does not express a complete thought

Subordinating conjunction A word that begins a dependent clause and connects it to an independent clause

Interjection A word or group of words that expresses a feeling

Coordinating Conjunctions

Objectives

- To identify conjunctions
- To use coordinating conjunctions to connect parts of a sentence
- To use coordinating conjunctions to join sentences

Conjunction

A word that connects parts of a sentence

Clause

A group of words with a subject and a predicate

Coordinating conjunction

A word that connects two or more equal parts of a sentence

Reading Strategy:
Questioning

What do you think you will learn in this lesson?

A **conjunction** is a word that connects parts of a sentence. A conjunction can connect words, phrases, or clauses. A **clause** is a group of words with a subject and a predicate.

▶ **EXAMPLE 1**

Connecting Words	Maurice is a good hitter and fielder.
Connecting Phrases	Give the book to me or to her.
Connecting Clauses	They would play golf, but it is raining.

A **coordinating conjunction** connects two or more parts of a sentence that are equal.

Common Coordinating Conjunctions

and	but	or	nor
for	so	yet	as well as

A coordinating conjunction can connect two nouns, two verbs, or two adjectives.

Practice A

Write the conjunction in each sentence. Then write the words that the conjunction connects.

1. The games were fun but tiring.
2. Dario pedaled the bike, and Maurice cheered from the sidelines.
3. Dario won the high jump as well as the bike race.
4. His bike has hand brakes and ten speeds.
5. Selena did not enter the bike race, nor did she enter the high jump.

Coordinating conjunctions can connect words, phrases, or clauses in a **series**. A series is a list of three or more words, phrases, or clauses. Put a comma after each item in a series except the last one.

▶ **EXAMPLE 2**

Words in a Series
Dario, Maurice, and Joe entered the basketball game.

Phrases in a Series
They got in line, warmed up, and shot baskets.

Clauses in a Series
Maurice drew stars, Michelle cut them out, and Efran hung them in the gym.

Practice B

Write these sentences on your paper. Add the missing commas.

1. Have you seen Selena Megan or Neeru?

2. I am entering the bike race the basketball toss and the high jump.

3. I plan to win first second third or fourth prize.

4. They held the games in the gym the hall and the cafeteria.

5. I saw Dario eating popcorn peanuts and an orange.

They bike to school in September, October, April, and May.

Rule 1   Use *and* to connect two items when both are true.
Dario and Maurice entered the race.
(Both of them entered.)

Rule 1   Use *but* to point out a difference between two items.
Maurice entered the bike race, but Selena did not.
(Only Maurice entered.)

Rule 3   Use *or* to connect items that are choices or differences.
Dario or Maurice will enter the race.
(One of them will enter. You do not know which one.)

Rule 4   Use *nor* to show that neither of the subjects did the action.
Selena did not enter the contest, nor did Megan.
(Selena did not enter. Megan did not enter.)

Practice C

Write the conjunction that completes each sentence.

1. Selena dug through the sand, (and, but) she did not find anything.

2. Dario ate popcorn (and, but) an orange.

3. Ron is with Nathan (but, or) Steve.

4. Megan was not in the gym that day, (or, nor) was Jan.

5. I do not know who won, (and, but) Joe might know.

You can use a coordinating conjunction to join two or more sentences. Do not repeat the words that are the same in both sentences.

▶ **EXAMPLE 3**

Armando does not like tea. He does not like coffee.

Armando does not like tea or coffee.

Compound subject
Two or more subjects that share the same predicate

 NOTE

A *simple sentence* expresses one complete thought. It has one subject and one predicate. However, a simple sentence can have a compound subject. It can also have a compound predicate. Some simple sentences have both.

Reading Strategy:
Questioning

Ask yourself: Did I understand what I just read? If not, read it again.

Practice D

Use a coordinating conjunction to join each pair of sentences. Write the new sentence on your paper.

1. Emily saw Nathan. Emily saw Armando.

2. Angela ate popcorn. Emily ate grapes.

3. He is not at home. He is not at school.

4. Nathan likes to play baseball. Nathan does not like to play football.

5. I watched the bike race. I watched the high jump.

When you join two subjects, you may need to change the verb form. Before you join them, the subject and verb in each sentence might be singular. When the sentences are joined, the subject becomes plural. The verb must also be plural.

▶ **EXAMPLE 4**

| Singular Subjects | Mary plays tennis. Ana plays tennis. (singular form of verb) |
| Plural Subject | Both girls play tennis. (plural form of verb) |

A **compound subject** is two or more subjects that share the same predicate. Usually the subjects are connected by a coordinating conjunction. Compound subjects are plural and need the plural form of the verb.

▶ **EXAMPLE 5**

| Singular Subjects | Mary plays tennis. Ana plays tennis. (singular form of verb) |
| Compound Subject | Mary and Ana play tennis. (plural form of verb) |

Compound predicate

Two or more predicates that share the same subject

Practice E

Join each pair of sentences. Use a conjunction to make a compound subject. Check the verb form.

1. A steep hill was part of the race. A gentle slope was part of the race.

2. One contest was the high jump. Another contest was the treasure hunt.

3. Did Joe find a treasure in the sand? Did Neeru find a treasure in the sand?

4. They sold frozen yogurt. They sold popcorn.

5. Finally, Juan arrived. Finally, Angela arrived.

Sometimes, a sentence will have a **compound predicate**. A compound predicate is two or more predicates that share the same subject. Usually, the predicates are connected by a coordinating conjunction.

 Writing Tip

When you connect two predicates with a conjunction, do not use a comma between them. For example: *Angela played CDs and served pretzels.*

▶ **EXAMPLE 6**

Single Predicates   He plays drums. He leads the choir. (one subject, one predicate)

Compound Predicate   He plays drums and leads the choir. (one subject, two predicates)

Practice F

Join each pair of sentences. Use a conjunction to make a compound predicate.

1. Students jumped over the rope. They dug in the sand.

2. Dario won the bike race. He lost the high jump.

3. Martha plays soccer. Martha hopes her team will win.

4. The club made $300. The club used the money to buy costumes.

5. Megan helped clean up. Megan brought the extra popcorn home with her.

REVIEW

Write the coordinating conjunction in each sentence. Then write the words that the conjunction connects.

1. Dario rode the bike down the track and across the finish line.

2. Selena and Neeru arrived late to the party.

3. Megan entered the treasure hunt but not the bike race.

4. Some teachers entered the games, but others did not.

5. I will have lemonade or water.

Use a coordinating conjunction to make each set of sentences into one sentence. You may need to change the verb form or add commas.

6. Nathan likes oranges. Armando likes oranges. Joe likes oranges.

7. Armando entered the bike race. He did not enter the basketball toss.

8. Ana made paper snowflakes. She made paper cranes.

9. In the sand were polished stones. In the sand were coins.

10. One contest was the basketball toss. One contest was the bike race. One contest was the treasure hunt.

Correlative Conjunctions

Objectives

- To identify and use correlative conjunctions in sentences
- To use the correct verb form with a correlative conjunction

Correlative conjunction

Two words that act as a single conjunction connecting words or phrases in a sentence

Correlative conjunctions are pairs of words that act together as a conjunction. They show a relation between parts of a sentence.

Common Correlative Conjunctions

both…and	neither…nor	whether…or
either…or	not only…but also	

▶ **EXAMPLE 1**

Neither Yoko nor Nadia was on time.

Both Yoko and Nadia were late.

Either Miguel or Armando will win the next poster contest.

Not only are they talented, but they also work hard.

Whether they win or they lose, they enjoy painting posters.

Practice A

Write the correlative conjunction in each sentence.

1. Jackson plays neither soccer nor baseball.
2. Whether Emily performs or not, the concert will go on.
3. Not only will Neeru sing, but she will also give a speech.
4. Emily has either the flu or a bad cold.
5. Both Armando and Nathan received prizes.

Reading Strategy:
Questioning

Do you use correlative conjunctions when you speak or write?

Correlative conjunctions can be used with compound subjects. Sometimes a compound subject is made up of two singular subjects joined by *or, nor,* or *but also*. In those cases, use the singular verb form.

▶ **EXAMPLE 2**

Neither Carol nor Angela has signed up for that event.

Sometimes one of the subjects joined by *or, nor,* or *but also* is singular and one is plural. In those cases, the verb agrees with the subject nearest to the verb.

▶ **EXAMPLE 3**

Neither Carol nor her friends were on time.
(*Friends* is plural.)

Not only the students but also their teacher is lost.
(*Teacher* is singular.)

A compound subject connected with *and* uses the plural verb form. A compound subject with the correlative conjunction *both ... and* also uses the plural verb form.

▶ **EXAMPLE 4**

Megan and Selena are in the event.

Both Maurice and Dario are winners.

Practice B

Write the verb that completes each sentence.

1. Neither Neeru nor Angela (is, are) in the theater club.
2. Both Angela and Julie (is, are) looking forward to it.
3. Either the boys or their mother (walk, walks) the dog.
4. Either you or he (need, needs) a watch.
5. Not only Julie but also Nadia (was, were) late.

REVIEW

Write the correlative conjunction in each sentence.

1. Both Angela and Emily like flowers.

2. Not only do they like flowers, but they also like gardens.

3. She had to decide whether to go to a play or a movie.

4. Neither Emily nor Michelle has seen that movie.

5. I would like to see either a movie or a play.

Choose the correct verb for each sentence. Write the verb.

6. Both Emily and Julie (play, plays) the trumpet.

7. Either the coach or the players (have, has) to decide.

8. Neither Neeru nor Angela (are, is) at the party.

9. The race will begin whether you or she (are, is) ready.

10. Not only Maurice but also Dario (were, was) a winner.

SPELLING BUILDER

Spelling Words with *ie* or *ei*

How do you spell a word with the vowels *ie* or *ei*? This rhyme will help you:

> Put *i* before *e* (believe, thief)
> Except after *c* (ceiling, deceive)
> Or when sounded like *a*
> As in *neighbor* and *weigh*. (veil, sleigh)

There are a few exceptions to this rule, such as *either, height, reins, seize,* and *science.* If you are not sure if a word follows the rule, check a dictionary.

Add *ie* or *ei* to complete each word. Write the word.

1. *rec___ve*   2. *f___ld*   3. *___ght*   4. *p___ce*

Subordinating Conjunctions

Objectives

- To recognize and use subordinating conjunctions in sentences
- To tell the difference between a dependent clause and an independent clause

Independent clause

A clause that expresses a complete thought

Dependent clause

A clause that does not express a complete thought

Subordinating conjunction

A word that begins a dependent clause and connects it to an independent clause

Reading Strategy: Questioning

How do dependent clauses make writing more interesting?

An **independent clause** expresses a complete thought. An independent clause can stand alone as a sentence. A **dependent clause** does not express a complete thought. A dependent clause cannot stand alone as a sentence. A **subordinating conjunction** is a word that begins a dependent clause and connects it to an independent clause. The subordinating conjunction is part of the dependent clause.

Common Subordinating Conjunctions

after	as though	if	than	whenever
although	because	in order that	unless	where
as	before	since	until	wherever
as if	even though	so that	when	while

▶ **EXAMPLE 1**

We were in school   when it started to rain.
(independent clause) (dependent clause)

Practice A

Write each sentence on your paper. Draw a line between the independent and dependent clause. Underline the subordinating conjunction.

1. Ramon was very thirsty after he ate the popcorn.

2. The party was a success because everyone had fun.

3. The judges had to study the rules before they could pick a winner.

4. I could not leave the party unless Celia left also.

5. They drank water even though lemonade was offered.

Dependent clauses may be at the beginning or the end of a sentence. Use a comma after a dependent clause when it begins a sentence. Do not use a comma when a dependent clause ends a sentence.

▶ **EXAMPLE 2**

Comma	Because it rained, the game was canceled.
No Comma	The game was canceled because it rained.

Practice B

If a sentence has correct punctuation, write *correct*. If a sentence needs a comma, rewrite the sentence correctly.

1. Because she twisted her ankle Mrs. Choy could not go bowling.

2. Mrs. Choy will rest until her ankle is better.

3. If she feels up to it Mrs. Choy will go to the bowling alley.

4. Although she cannot bowl she can cheer on the team.

5. "I will keep score while you bowl," she said.

A dependent clause does not express a complete thought. It needs an independent clause to finish the thought.

▶ **EXAMPLE 3**

Dependent Clause	Since he was late
Complete Thought	Since he was late, he missed class.

Practice C

Write a sentence by adding an independent clause to each dependent clause. You may put the dependent clause at the beginning or end of the sentence. Use a comma if needed.

1. whenever he goes home

2. since March arrived

3. unless you finish your book

4. although Emily enjoys music

5. as time goes by

Some words can act as a subordinating conjunction or a preposition. The word is a conjunction when it begins a dependent clause. (A clause has a subject and a verb.) The word is a preposition when it begins a prepositional phrase. (A prepositional phrase has an object.)

▶ **EXAMPLE 4**

Conjunction	They halted the game until the rain stopped.
Preposition	They halted the game until the next day.
Conjunction	After the game ended, Jon went home.
Preposition	He went home after the game.

Practice D

Identify the word in bold as a *conjunction* or a *preposition*.

1. Neeru has art class **before** lunch.

2. Armando went to the gym for practice **before** he went home.

3. **Because** Dario pedaled so fast, he won the bike race.

4. In his opinion, the team won **because** of Maurice.

5. **Until** the rain stops, no one can play outside.

REVIEW

Write the dependent clause in each sentence. Underline the subordinating conjunction.

1. After the principal made a speech, the games began.

2. If you hurry, you will not miss the race.

3. They enjoyed the games even though it was cold.

Make a sentence by adding an independent clause to each dependent clause. Use a comma if needed.

4. before she left

5. unless he studies

6. after the games were over

Identify the word in bold. Write *conjunction* or *preposition*.

7. Armando left the gym **before** Nathan did.

8. **After** his last class, Joe went home.

9. They talked together **before** class.

10. **After** I called Neeru, we met at Tony's Cafe.

VOCABULARY BUILDER

Using Clipped Words

Sometimes you drop one or more syllables from a long word to make a shorter word. The result is called a clipped word. You probably use clipped words in conversation. In formal reports and business letters, use the complete words.

examination = exam   microphone = mike

Write the clipped word for each of these words: *hamburger, automobile, telephone, laboratory, gasoline.*

Interjections

Interjection

A word or group of words that expresses a feeling

Reading Strategy:
Questioning

Ask yourself: What feeling does each interjection express?

An **interjection** is a word or group of words that expresses a feeling. An interjection is not part of the subject or the predicate of the sentence.

Always separate an interjection from the rest of the sentence with a punctuation mark. The punctuation can be a period, a comma, a question mark, or an exclamation mark. It depends on the feeling that the interjection expresses.

▶ **EXAMPLE 1**

No kidding. I like cooked spinach.

So what? It is not important.

Say, could you help me?

Sometimes you use end punctuation after an interjection. When you do, capitalize the first word that follows the interjection. Sometimes you use a comma after an interjection. In this case, do not capitalize the next word unless it is a proper noun.

▶ **EXAMPLE 2**

Yes, indeed! That is really nice.

Hey, where did you get that?

Brrr! That snowball was cold! Yes, I know I deserved it.

Interjections usually appear at the beginning of a sentence. You can also use them at the end of a sentence. Use a comma or end punctuation to separate the interjection from the rest of the sentence. *We just made it. Whew!*

Reading Strategy:
Questioning

What interjections do you use most often?

Common Interjections

ah	hey	oh	really	thanks
alas	hurrah	oh no	so	well
fine	hurry	oops	sorry	what
gosh	hush	ouch	so what	whew
great	listen	please	stop	wow
ha	look out	quick	sure	yes
hello	my goodness	quiet	terrific	yum

Practice A

Write each sentence on your paper. Add punctuation at the end of each sentence. Add punctuation after each interjection. Use correct capitalization.

1. ouch that hurt my foot
2. wow do I have good news for you
3. yum that blueberry muffin tasted good
4. oh no I missed the bus again
5. no I do not need any help now

Practice B

Add an interjection to each sentence. Write the new sentence. Use correct capitalization and punctuation.

1. That is beautiful.
2. Would you like a break?
3. The test was difficult.
4. The party was fun.
5. I really needed that rest.

REVIEW

Write each sentence on your paper. Add the correct punctuation and capitalization.

1. my goodness you are right

2. what I did not hear that

3. ouch you stepped on my foot

4. whew it is hot today

5. ah that is just what I needed

Add an interjection to each sentence. Write the new sentence. Check the punctuation and capitalization.

6. Is that you?

7. I do not agree with you.

8. That is fantastic.

9. He finally arrived home.

10. The storm got worse.

PUTTING IT ALL TOGETHER

Write a paragraph that describes a recent event in the news. Use conjunctions to connect ideas. When you finish your paragraph, check your spelling and punctuation. Then circle the conjunctions you used.

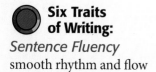

Six Traits of Writing:

Sentence Fluency
smooth rhythm and flow

ENGLISH IN YOUR LIFE

Telling What Happened

Ryan Stein fell while he was skateboarding. He hurt his ankle. His mother took him to the emergency room. Ryan told the doctor what happened. It was important for him to speak clearly when he told the story. It was also important for him to get the facts right. When you tell what happened, use details. Make sure that everything you tell is true and complete. Read what Ryan said to the doctor. Then follow the directions below.

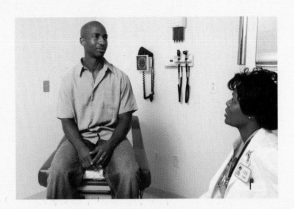

"I was skateboarding at the park. My friend showed me a trick. I tried it, but I fell and twisted my ankle. Ouch! It really hurt, and I could not move my foot. A woman who was watching gave me ice, and I put it on my ankle. Oh well, I guess I won't be skateboarding again for a while."

1. Write the four conjunctions in the report.

2. Write the two interjections in the report.

3. CRITICAL THINKING What effect do the interjections have in Ryan's story?

SPEAKING AND LISTENING

Work with a partner. Think about an event in your life. Tell the story to your partner. Then take notes while you listen to your partner's story. Now tell your partner's story to the rest of the class. Use as many conjunctions and interjections as you can.

Using an Almanac

An almanac is a book of facts. It may tell about weather, countries, businesses, people, or all of these things. Some almanacs include facts from the entire world. Others concentrate on one region or country. Some almanacs concentrate on only one subject, such as sports. Often, the information in an almanac appears in lists, tables, charts, and graphs. Almanacs usually come out with new information every year. Read this information from a 2005 almanac. Then follow the directions.

The **Taj Mahal** (1632–1650) at Agra, India, is thought to be the perfect example of **Mogul design**. Some people consider it the most beautiful building in the world. It was **built by Shah Jahan** as a tomb for his wife. Both the white dome and the slim white towers are considered unforgettable. It is **made completely of marble**.

1. Look at the first two sentences in the almanac entry. Use a conjunction to make these into one sentence. Write the new sentence.

2. Which sentence in the almanac entry contains a correlative conjunction? Write this sentence.

3. **CRITICAL THINKING** The almanac entry uses short sentences with few conjunctions. Explain why this is so.

TECHNOLOGY

There are hundreds of almanacs on the Internet. Type *almanac* into a search engine and hit *Go*. Some of the results of your search will be online almanacs. Some will be ads for almanacs you can buy. Now narrow your search. Type *sports almanac* into the search engine. The results will be almanacs related to sports. See if you can find an online almanac related to a subject that interests you. How is the information in this online almanac arranged? Suppose you are looking for a certain fact in this almanac. How would you find it?

CHAPTER 9

SUMMARY

- Use a conjunction to connect words, phrases, or clauses in a sentence.

- Use a coordinating conjunction to connect two or more equal parts of a sentence.

- Use a coordinating conjunction in a series. Use a comma after each item except the last one.

- Use a coordinating conjunction to join two or more sentences into one sentence.

- Some sentences have a compound subject that uses a conjunction. Make sure that the compound subject and the verb agree.

- Some sentences have a compound predicate that uses a conjunction.

- Use correlative conjunctions in pairs to connect related parts of a sentence.

- Use a subordinating conjunction to connect a dependent clause to an independent clause. The dependent clause can be before or after the independent clause.

- When *or, nor,* or *but also* are in a compound subject, the verb must agree with the nearest subject.

- When *and* is in a compound subject, the verb is plural.

- Use interjections to express feeling. They can appear at the beginning or the end of a sentence.

- If you use an end punctuation mark after an interjection, capitalize the word that follows it. If you use a comma after an interjection, do not capitalize the next word unless it is a proper noun.

GROUP ACTIVITY

Find a movie review on the Internet or in a newspaper. Have each person in the group choose one paragraph from the review. Read the paragraphs aloud. When you hear a conjunction, raise your hand.

Then write your own paragraph. Explain what you liked about a movie you saw recently. Underline each conjunction you use. Trade paragraphs with someone in your group. Check each other's work.

Word Bank

clause

compound subject

compound predicate

conjunction

coordinating conjunction

correlative conjunction

dependent clause

independent clause

interjection

series

subordinating conjunction

Part A Write the word or words from the Word Bank that complete each sentence.

1. A _____ is two or more predicates that share the same subject.

2. A _____ is a word that connects parts of a sentence.

3. An _____ expresses a feeling.

4. A _____ connects two or more equal parts of a sentence.

5. A list of three or more words, phrases, or clauses is a _____.

6. Any group of words with a subject and a predicate is a _____.

7. An _____ expresses a complete thought.

8. A _____ is two words that act as a single conjunction.

9. A _____ begins a dependent clause.

10. A _____ does not express a complete thought.

11. A _____ is two or more subjects that share the same predicate.

Part B Write the conjunction in each sentence.

12. Is the school dance on a Friday or Saturday?

13. Since Meg is working that weekend, she cannot go.

14. Neither Armando nor Nathan has asked anyone yet.

15. Let's decorate the gym with hearts and flowers.

16. Tonya is excited because this is her first dance.

17. Both Erica and Jameela bought new dresses.

Part C Use a conjunction to join each set of sentences into one sentence.

18. To make the decorations, Armando needs construction paper. He needs scissors. He needs tape.

29. Miguel will help him. Efran will help him.

20. Angela will serve fruit salad. She will serve cheese and crackers. She will serve mixed nuts.

Part D Write each sentence on your paper. Add correct punctuation and capital letters.

21. ah what a wonderful party this is

22. because the committee had planned so carefully the dance was a success

Part E Write the letter of your answer.

23. Which sentence uses correct punctuation and capitalization?
    A Wow that is a terrific idea.
    B Ouch! This paper cut really hurts!
    C Yuck! peanut butter on eggs tastes bad.
    D Hey have you met my cousin?

24. Which sentence uses a subordinating conjunction?
    A It has been years since I saw you.
    B Ellen or Marie will sing.
    C Beth went, but Amy stayed home.
    D Claire started early, yet she arrived late.

25. Which sentence uses a compound subject?
    A James brought apples and pears for the fruit salad.
    B Mindy could not go, so I went alone.
    C His mother and father own a restaurant.
    D My sister is in the play, but I am not.

Test Tip

You might not know what every word means in a test question. Read the question to yourself, leaving out the word. Try to figure out what the word means by how it is used in the sentence.

Recognizing Sentence Patterns

Look at the photo of a field. Do you see the lines running through the field? Do you see the neat stacks of hay on the horizon? When things are arranged in the same ways, they create patterns. Once you use a pattern to make something, you can use it again and again.

Languages have patterns, too. For example, English has six main sentence patterns. You hear these patterns as you listen to other people talk. You see these patterns as you read. You use these patterns to write and to speak.

In Chapter 10, you will learn the six basic sentence patterns in English. Then, you can use all six when you write.

GOALS FOR LEARNING

- To identify and use intransitive verbs in sentences
- To identify and use direct objects in sentences
- To identify and use indirect objects in sentences
- To identify and use object complements in sentences
- To identify and use predicate nouns in sentences
- To identify and use predicate adjectives in sentences

Reading Strategy: Predicting

 Previewing a text means to take a quick look at it before you read it. For example, skim through this chapter. Look at the lesson titles and vocabulary words. Think about what you already know about the topic. Previewing prepares you to read. It helps you look for new information. It helps you predict what will come next. To predict is to make a smart guess about what lies ahead. Keep these things in mind as you preview and predict:

- Make your best guess about what might follow.
- Use what you already know to predict meaning or order.
- Ask yourself why you think certain things will follow.
- Check your predictions. You may have to change them as you read.

Key Vocabulary Words

Intransitive verb An action verb that does not need a noun to receive its action

Compound verb Two or more verbs connected by a conjunction in a sentence

Direct object A noun or pronoun that receives the action of the verb

Indirect object A noun or pronoun that receives the direct object of an action verb

Object complement A noun or adjective that follows and tells about a direct object

Predicate noun A noun or pronoun that follows a state-of-being verb and renames the subject

Sentences with Intransitive Verbs

Intransitive verb

An action verb that
does not need a noun
to receive its action

NOTE

These abbreviations are
used in this lesson's
Examples:

S	subject
V	verb
Adv	adverb
Adj	adjective
HV	helping verb

Reading Strategy:
Predicting

Look for these kinds of
labels in the Examples
in this chapter.

Words are arranged in patterns to form sentences. The
simplest kind of sentences might be only two words long.
These sentences have verbs that stand by themselves.
These verbs do not need any help at all. They are called
intransitive verbs.

Subject + Intransitive Verb

▶ **EXAMPLE 1**

```
  S        V              S      V
Armando / froze.      The sun / shines.
```

Practice A

Write each sentence. Draw a line between the subject and
the predicate. Put an *S* over the subject and a *V* over the
intransitive verb.

1. The goose honked.
2. The candle flickers.
3. Both good and bad memories fade.
4. Everyone at the show laughed.
5. My little brother sneezed.

Intransitive verbs may have adverbs that answer questions
about them. An adverb can be at the beginning or end of
a sentence. It may also be between a helping verb and the
main verb.

▶ **EXAMPLE 2**

```
  Adv          S       V
Quickly, the hours / passed.

              S      V    Adv
Emily's friend / moved away.
```

Reading Strategy:
Predicting

You will learn about a new sentence pattern in each lesson in this chapter.

Practice B

Write each sentence with plenty of space between each one. Write *S* above each subject. Write *V* above each verb. Write *Adv* above each adverb.

1. The old mower still runs.

2. Javier runs fast.

3. The little girl giggled.

4. Megan practices often.

5. The stars shine brightly.

Sentences with intransitive verbs often contain prepositional phrases. They may be adjective phrases or adverb phrases.

▶ **EXAMPLE 3**

     S Adj phrase   V
The girl behind me / laughed. (Which girl?)

     S   V   Adv phrase
Amy / is jogging to the park. (Where is Amy jogging?)

Practice C

Write each sentence. Draw a line between the subject and the predicate. Underline each prepositional phrase.

1. No one in our family laughs at Uncle Mike's jokes.

2. My neighbor on the left has gone to the store.

3. My friend from California is visiting.

4. Everyone in our family sleeps late.

5. All of us are thinking about a vacation.

Compound verb

Two or more verbs connected by a conjunction in a sentence

You learned in Lesson 9-1 that a compound subject is two or more subjects that share one predicate. A **compound verb** is two or more verbs that share one subject. The verbs are connected by a conjunction.

▶ **EXAMPLE 4**

Armando and Dario left for school. (compound subject)

They walked to the corner and talked. (compound verb)

Practice D

Some of these sentences have a compound subject or verb. Write each sentence. Underline the compound part. Then write *S* above each subject and *V* above each verb.

1. Van and Ethan went to the concert.

2. Both students and teachers smiled.

3. We danced or talked all evening.

4. The band played English songs and Spanish songs.

5. Ann arrived with friends and danced with them.

A sentence that has an intransitive verb can be a command or request. This kind of sentence looks like it is just a predicate. The subject *you* is understood, even though it does not appear.

▶ **EXAMPLE 5**

   S   V
(You) Stop right now! (command)

   S   V
(You) Come with me to the mall. (request)

Practice E

In each sentence, the subject *you* is understood. Write the verb or verb phrase.

1. Stay at home today.

2. Please do not run.

3. Go to the store and shop for groceries.

4. Listen to the question.

5. Please leave for school now.

Sentences that have intransitive verbs can be questions. Part of the verb phrase may help form the question. It will come *before* the subject. At other times, a question may begin with an adverb or a pronoun.

▶ **EXAMPLE 6**

V   S   V
Are you going to the mall now?

HV   S   V
Does Maurice play on the team?

Adv   V   S
Where are my keys?

S   V   Adv phrase
Who is running in the park?

Practice F

Write each sentence. Write *S* above the subject. Underline the verb or verb phrase.

1. Where is Nathan going now?

2. Is there a sale at the mall?

3. Have you heard of Presidents' Day?

4. Do you know about the sales at the mall?

5. Why is Nathan leaving early?

REVIEW

Add an adverb, an adverb phrase, or an adjective phrase to each sentence. Write the new sentence on your paper.

1. Tanya and Angela were giggling.

2. Javier listens.

3. Some people arrived.

4. Her friend is visiting.

5. They are talking.

Write each sentence. Write *S* above the subject. Then underline the verb or verb phrase. In some sentences, the subject *you* is understood.

6. Who is coming for dinner?

7. Please wait at the door.

8. Why is Emily smiling?

9. Do not play with matches.

10. Has Joe arrived yet?

Sentences with Direct Objects

Sometimes an action verb "acts on" a person or thing. The person or thing that is acted on by the verb is the **direct object** (DO). A direct object receives the action of a verb. Verbs that have direct objects do not stand alone.

> **Subject + Action Verb + Direct Object**

To find the direct object, ask *what* or *whom* about the action in the sentence.

▶ **EXAMPLE 1**

    S   V   DO
Maurice hit the ball over the fence. (Hit *what*?)

    S   V DO
Javier found her in the store. (Found *whom*?)

Practice A

Write each sentence. Above each sentence, write *S*, *V*, and *DO* to identify the subject, verb, and direct object.

1. Armando plays baseball in the spring.
2. The coach chose Armando for the team.
3. Mr. Kwan drove his car.
4. Carmen dropped the glass on the floor.
5. Roberto mowed the lawn.

A verb may have a compound direct object. A conjunction connects the parts.

▶ **EXAMPLE 2**

Marta is bringing apples or pears to the party.

Pilar bought milk, bread, and fruit at the store.

Practice B

Write the compound direct object in each sentence.

1. Did Brittany order soup or salad at the restaurant?

2. Sasha has two dogs and a cat in her house.

3. Ben mailed a letter and a postcard to Sally.

4. Will you take a raincoat or an umbrella to school?

5. Mark visited New York, Boston, and Pittsburgh.

A command or a request can have a direct object. A question can also have a direct object.

▶ **EXAMPLE 3**

   S   V   DO
(You) Please get the pizza out of the oven. (request)

HV S   V   DO
Did you enjoy the party? (question)

Practice C

Write the direct object of each sentence.

1. Where did Mrs. Choy put her keys?

2. Eat an apple every day.

3. How did you climb such a giant tree?

4. Follow the directions to Diana's house.

5. Why did Regina close the door?

A direct object can be a pronoun. The pronoun can be singular or plural, but it must be in the object form.

▶ **EXAMPLE 4**

Nancy praised him. (singular pronoun)

A loud noise woke us last night. (plural pronoun)

Practice D

Write the direct object in each sentence.

1. Gerald helped us yesterday.
2. Mrs. Gravas gave this to my mother.
3. Lupe called me at home.
4. Nadia planted these last year.
5. You really surprised her.

Many verbs can take a direct object or not. Think about how you are using the verb in the sentence.

▶ **EXAMPLE 5**

| S | V | DO | | S | V | Adv |

Brad moved the book to his desk. Brad moved away.

| S | V | Adv phrase | S | V | DO | | DO |

We studied until dawn. We studied math and science.

Practice E

Write each sentence. If the sentence has a direct object, underline it. If the verb is intransitive, write *intransitive* after the sentence.

1. The old radio still works.
2. The choir sang holiday songs.
3. We must leave now.
4. Robins sing beautifully.
5. Marina brushes her hair every morning.

REVIEW

Write each sentence. Write *S* above each subject, *V* above each verb or verb phrase, and *DO* above each direct object.

1. He made sandwiches and put them in the picnic basket.

2. Patrice enjoys the beach in the summer.

3. Have you ever seen the Statue of Liberty?

4. Do you want this book or that one?

5. Take the flute out of the case.

Write the pronoun that completes each sentence.

6. Where did (she, her) go?

7. Armando saw (she, her) at the mall.

8. The young woman led (we, us) to our seats.

9. Please drive (I, me) to the store.

10. Dario returned (they, them) to the library.

Sentences with Indirect Objects

Objectives

■ To identify indirect objects

■ To write sentences with indirect objects

A sentence may have both a direct object (DO) and an **indirect object** (IO). An indirect object is a noun or a pronoun. It comes before the direct object. Indirect objects answer the question *to whom, to what, for whom,* or *for what.*

Subject + Verb + Indirect Object + Direct Object

Indirect object

A noun or pronoun that receives the direct object of an action verb

▶ **EXAMPLE 1**

   S   V   IO   DO

Miguel bought her some paint. (Bought paint *for whom*?)

   S   V   IO   DO

Gina gave the dog some food. (Gave food *to whom*?)

Reading Strategy:
Predicting

What do you predict this lesson will teach?

Practice A

Write the indirect object in each sentence. First, find the verb. Then, to find the indirect object, ask the question *to whom, to what, for whom,* or *for what.*

 NOTE

These abbreviations are used in this lesson's Examples:

S   subject
V   verb
IO indirect object
DO direct object
HV helping verb

1. Megan bought her dog a toy.

2. Michelle brought them a snack.

3. The camp gave the swimming students a picnic.

4. Angela brought them ribbons.

5. She handed the students their awards.

An indirect object can be a pronoun. The pronoun can be singular or plural, but it must be in the object form.

Practice B

Write the indirect object in each sentence.

1. The teacher gave us homework.

2. Darla gave me a pencil.

3. Julio mailed her an invitation.

4. She brought the group juice.

5. They awarded him the prize.

An indirect object can be compound. A conjunction connects the parts.

▶ **EXAMPLE 3**

S	V	IO	IO	DO

The man handed Max and me two sandwiches.

Practice C

Write the indirect object in each sentence.

1. Susan lent Pat and Emily a book.

2. Tell him and me the truth.

3. Are you giving Emily and me a straight answer?

4. Yes, I am telling you the whole truth.

5. Show me the pictures.

A command or a request can use an indirect object. A question can also use an indirect object.

▶ **EXAMPLE 4**

S	V	IO	DO

(You) Hand Maurice the hammer. (command)

HV	S	V	IO	DO

Would you give Megan this letter? (question)

Practice D

Write the indirect object in each sentence.

1. Will Ben tell Lisa the facts?

2. Does the school offer students different lunches?

3. Should David give Fred advice?

4. Bring me a book on motorcycles.

5. Mail the office the forms.

An indirect object is never part of a prepositional phrase. However, you can often change an indirect object into a prepositional phrase.

▶ **EXAMPLE 5**

I will buy *her* some paint. (*Her* is the indirect object.)

I will buy some paint *for her*. (*For her* is a prepositional phrase.)

Practice E

Write each sentence. Change the indirect object to a prepositional phrase using *to*.

1. The judges awarded Armando a prize.

2. Mr. Thomas gave every student a notebook.

3. Mrs. Choy taught Angela Chinese.

4. Patrice showed me her new soccer ball.

5. They offered the runners water.

REVIEW

Write each sentence. Write *S* above the subject and *V* above the verb or verb phrase. Then write *IO* above the indirect object and *DO* above the direct object. In a command, remember that the subject *you* is understood.

1. Emily offered Michelle her ideas.

2. Who gave Efraim the watch?

3. Allow yourself some time.

4. Will you tell me the time?

5. She gave me the answer.

Write the indirect object in each sentence.

6. My friends and I sent our teacher a get-well card.

7. Please pass me the bread.

8. Will you read Emma the story?

9. Nathan handed him the telephone.

10. She showed everyone the movie.

Sentences with Object Complements

A sentence with an *object complement* also has a direct object. An **object complement** (OC) tells about the direct object. It is always a noun or an adjective. In a sentence, an object complement follows the direct object.

Subject + Verb + Direct Object + Object Complement

Object complement

A noun or adjective that follows and tells about a direct object

▶ **EXAMPLE 1**

   S   V   DO   OC
The club made Hannah president.

(*President* renames *Hannah.*)

   S   V   DO OC
Carla colored her hair blue.

(*Blue* describes *hair.*)

NOTE

These abbreviations are used in this lesson's Examples:

S   subject

V   verb

DO   direct object

OC   object complement

HV   helping verb

Practice A

Write each sentence. Draw one line under the direct object. Draw two lines under the object complement.

1. They found the house deserted.

2. That made Jeremy angry.

3. They considered the noises strange.

4. The visitors made themselves comfortable.

5. The voters elected him mayor.

Reading Strategy:
Predicting

Use a lesson title to predict what a lesson will be about.

The words *complement* and *compliment* sound alike. A *complement* is something that completes something else. A *compliment* is praise.

An object complement can be compound. A conjunction connects the parts.

▶ **EXAMPLE 2**

          DO   OC   OC

They painted the house blue and white.

(compound object complement)

If the sentence has a compound direct object, each direct object can have an object complement.

▶ **EXAMPLE 3**

       DO   OC   DO   OC

We made Eli president and Tom treasurer.

(compound direct object)

If the sentence has a compound verb, each verb can have a direct object and an object complement.

▶ **EXAMPLE 4**

   V   DO OC   V DO OC

Lance made the soup spicy and served it cold.

(compound verb)

Practice B

Write each sentence. Write *DO* over each direct object. Write *OC* over each object complement.

1. The exercise made the players hot and tired.

2. Many students find their science class interesting and their computer class helpful.

3. The team named Armando the best player and voted him captain.

4. The fall weather turned the leaves gold and orange.

5. The delay made Jane sad and other people angry.

Reading Strategy:
Predicting

How are the lesson titles in this chapter alike? Does this help you predict what each lesson will be about?

A command, request, or question can have a direct object and an object complement.

▶ **EXAMPLE 5**

    V   DO   OC
Make Joe the leader. (command)

HV   S   V DO OC
Will that dark room make you sleepy? (question)

Practice C

Write the object complement in each sentence.

1. Will you make the cake chocolate?

2. Did the voters make him the winner?

3. Did Emily find the directions helpful?

4. Please make the sauce milder.

5. The heat in the oven turned the rolls brown.

She found the directions easy to follow.

REVIEW

Write each sentence. Write *S* above the subject and *V* above the verb or verb phrase. Then write *DO* above the direct object and *OC* above the object complement. Some sentences may not have an object complement.

1. Javier found the history class exciting.

2. Don't close the doors yet!

3. Does that loud noise bother you?

4. She painted the garage red and black.

5. The students voted Armando king and Emily queen.

Write the object complement in each sentence.

6. Selena thought *Titanic* the best film of all time.

7. Dean found that movie boring.

8. Armando named *Holes* the greatest.

9. That film made its actors famous.

10. "I judge them equal!" Nadia said.

VOCABULARY BUILDER

Choosing Names of Characters
Sometimes writers pick the names of characters based on sound and meaning. For example, in his book *A Christmas Carol*, Charles Dickens wrote about Tiny Tim. Tiny Tim was timid but kind. Look up the meaning of *timid*. Now look up the meaning *blaze* and *cane*. Write what a horse named Blaze might be like. Write what a character named Cane might be like.

Sentences with Predicate Nouns

Predicate noun

A noun or pronoun that follows a state-of-being verb and renames the subject

NOTE

These abbreviations are used in this lesson's Examples:

S subject

V verb

PN predicate noun

Reading Strategy: Summarizing

Review what a predicate is. How does this help you understand what a predicate noun is?

In some sentences, a state-of-being verb links the subject to a **predicate noun** (PN). The predicate noun renames the subject. It always follows the state-of-being verb. *Feel, look, become, remain,* and *be* are some state-of-being verbs.

> **Subject + State-of-Being Verb + Predicate Noun**

The predicate noun can be a noun or a pronoun. If it is a personal pronoun, it must be in the subject form: *I, you, he, she, it, we,* or *they.*

▶ **EXAMPLE 1**

    S   V   PN
Jane is the leader.

               S   V PN
The new leader is you!

Practice A

Write the predicate noun in each sentence.

1. Our new neighbors became friends.

2. Who is that?

3. Dario and Maurice remained members.

4. I am your father.

5. The teachers were once students.

A predicate noun can be compound. A conjunction connects the parts.

▶ **EXAMPLE 2**

        S   V   PN   PN
Mrs. Hernandez is a cook and a gardener.

A command, a request, or a question can have a predicate noun.

▶ **EXAMPLE 3**

    S   V   PN
(You) Be a good listener.

    V S   PN
Is that your house?

Practice B

Write each sentence. Draw one line under the state-of-being verb. Draw two lines under the predicate noun.

1. Did your brother become a pilot?

2. You have been a very good friend to me.

3. Ellen will be first or second in the race.

4. You are the champion of tennis in this town.

5. Was that your sister in the mask?

A sentence with a predicate noun can also have adverbs and prepositional phrases. These words answer questions about the verb. A predicate noun is never part of a prepositional phrase.

▶ **EXAMPLE 4**

    S   S   V   PN
Maurice and Dario have been friends for a long time.

(*For a long time* is a prepositional phrase that tells how long.)

Practice C

Number your paper from 1 to 5. Find the five prepositional phrases in the sentences in Practice B. Write each one.

REVIEW

Write each sentence. Write *S* above the subject, *V* above the state-of-being verb, and *PN* above the predicate noun.

1. Be a kind person!

2. Angela is a great swimmer.

3. Is Emily's father a musician?

4. Emily and her mother are the musicians in their family.

5. He and Jennifer are my classmates.

Write each sentence. Draw a line under the predicate noun.

6. Thomas Jefferson became the first secretary of state.

7. He was the second vice president and third president.

8. He was also the purchaser of the Louisiana Territory west of the Mississippi River.

9. Jefferson was a Virginian.

10. He was a very healthy man and always took a daily walk.

SPELLING BUILDER

Choosing the Right Homophone

Homophones are words that sound alike but have different spellings and meanings. You need to know the meanings of homophones to be sure you choose and spell the right ones. Each of the following words has a homophone. Write the homophone of each one.

1. here   2. sale   3. compliment   4. piece

Sentences with Predicate Adjectives

Objectives

- To identify and use predicate adjectives
- To write sentences with predicate adjectives

Reading Strategy:
Predicting

You learned about predicate nouns in the last lesson. How does this help you predict what predicate adjectives are?

 NOTE

These abbreviations are used in this lesson's Examples:

S   subject
V   verb
PA predicate adjective

As you learned in Chapter 4, a predicate adjective (PA) follows a state-of-being verb. It describes the subject of the sentence.

> **Subject + State-of-Being Verb + Predicate Adjective**

▶ **EXAMPLE 1**

　　　　S　　V　PA
This melon feels ripe.

(*Ripe* describes the subject, *melon.*)

　　　　S　V　PA
My dog is smart.

(*Smart* describes the subject, *dog.*)

Practice A

Write the predicate adjective in each sentence.

1. Yesterday the weather was warm.

2. The salad looks delicious.

3. The velvet jacket feels soft.

4. The new car is shiny.

5. Neeru seems cheerful today.

A predicate adjective can be compound.

▶ **EXAMPLE 2**

　S　V　PA　　　PA
He felt hot and thirsty after the game.

If the sentence has a compound state-of-being verb, each verb can have a predicate adjective.

▶ **EXAMPLE 3**

   S V PA   V PA

Efran was late for gym class and was early for health class.

Reading Strategy:
Summarizing

Do you think a predicate adjective can be part of a command, a request, or a question?

Practice B

Write the predicate adjectives in each sentence.

1. Everyone feels happy and cheerful today.
2. The spring weather is sunny and mild.
3. Yesterday everyone seemed gloomy and sad.
4. The weather was cold and rainy.
5. It was cold today but was warm yesterday.

A command or question can have a predicate adjective.

▶ **EXAMPLE 4**

    S   V PA

(You) Stay still.

 V   S   PA

Is that water cold?

Practice C

Write the predicate adjective(s) in each sentence.

1. Will the movie be good or bad?
2. The good weather report was welcome.
3. Remain calm, please.
4. Are you feeling silly today?
5. Is that meat too salty or spicy for you?

A predicate adjective is never part of a prepositional phrase.

▶ **EXAMPLE 5**

    S   V   PA
The air feels warm in early June.

(*Early* is an adjective in a prepositional phrase. It is not a predicate adjective.)

Practice D

Write each sentence. Underline each prepositional phrase. Label each subject *S*, each state-of-being verb *V*, and each predicate adjective *PA*.

1. Sam's Aunt Edna from Topeka, Kansas, has remained strong.

2. His aunt seems quite healthy in mind and body.

3. This 85-year-old woman feels great.

4. She is always cheerful.

5. Aunt Edna looks very young for her age.

My aunt is young at heart. She seems half her age!

REVIEW

Add a different predicate adjective to each sentence. Write the new sentence on your paper.

1. Was Angela's speech too _____?

2. No, her speech was just _____.

3. Her speech seemed _____.

4. Her listeners looked _____

5. Has she always been so _____ at speeches?

Write the predicate adjective in each sentence.

6. The surface of Mars appears hot and dry.

7. The soil looks red and sandy.

8. Small rocks are scattered around.

9. A couple of small holes were spotted on the surface.

10. They seem very deep.

PUTTING IT ALL TOGETHER

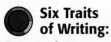

Six Traits of Writing:

Conventions correct grammar, spelling, and mechanics

Do you have a favorite relative? Write a paragraph that describes that person. Tell why you like him or her. Use sentences with direct and indirect objects. Use sentences with a predicate noun or a predicate adjective. Write one sentence with an object complement.

Video Store Clerk

Robert Vega just got a job in a new video store. He will greet customers, take money and give change, and keep the store tidy. He also will help people find the DVDs and videos they want. The store is getting ready for its grand opening. The store's owner asked Robert to make a poster to attract customers. Read Robert's poster. Then answer the questions.

Do you want the newest and most popular DVDs and videos?

Vince's Videos

is the place to get them!

We have the newest releases.

The store is open from 10:00 AM to 11:30 PM.

The owner, Vince Martelli, says, "Drop in and check us out!"

Vince's is awesome!

---

1. What predicate adjective appears in the poster?

2. What predicate noun appears in the poster?

3. **CRITICAL THINKING** Review superlative adjectives in Chapter 4. Find two of these adjectives in the poster. Why are they useful in a poster like this?

SPEAKING AND LISTENING

With a partner, make a poster for a store you like. Include a reason why customers should shop at the store. Also include the hours the store is open. Try to use predicate adjectives and predicate nouns. Use at least one direct object. Share your poster with the class.

Using Library Catalogs

Every library has a catalog. It is a list of everything the library contains.

In a card catalog, each book, magazine, or movie has its own card. The cards in the catalog are divided into three sections: title, author, and subject. You can find an item by looking in any of these sections.

Many libraries have their catalogs on a computer instead of on cards. An online catalog contains the same information as a card catalog. Look at the sample screen of an online catalog.

The *Keyword* box is where you type in a subject. You can also type in an author's name or a title. Then you choose the type of search from the *Search Type* menu.

Write the answer to each question.

1. What keyword has been entered on the sample screen? Is this a subject, a title, or an author's name?

2. If you wanted to find books by James Baldwin, what search type would you use?

3. **CRITICAL THINKING** Suppose you want to find a sports article. You decide to look in the most recent issue of a sports magazine. What search type would you use?

MEDIA AND TECHNOLOGY

You can read issues of many newspapers and magazines on the Internet. Most libraries have computers that allow you to use the Internet. Suppose you are in the library to do a report on the writer James Baldwin. How would you find information about him?

- Form simple sentences with one subject and one intransitive verb. An intransitive verb does not need an object to receive its action.

- Form compound verbs by connecting two or more verbs with a conjunction.

- Direct objects receive the action of verbs. To find them, ask *what* or *whom* about the action verb.

- Form a compound direct object by connecting two or more objects with a conjunction.

- Some verbs that take direct objects also take indirect objects. Indirect objects are also nouns or pronouns. They answer the question *to whom, to what, for whom,* or *for what.*

- Always use the object form of a pronoun when it is a direct or indirect object.

- Use nouns and adjectives as object complements. An object complement renames or tells more about a direct object.

- Use predicate nouns after state-of-being verbs to rename the subject.

- Use predicate adjectives after state-of-being verbs to describe the subject.

- Any of the sentence patterns can be in the form of a command, a request, or a question.

- Any of the sentence patterns can include prepositional phrases.

GROUP ACTIVITY

Think about a family party you remember. Find a partner. Tell about something that happened at the party while your partner listens and takes notes. Then switch roles. Listen carefully to your partner's story and takes notes.

Now tell your partner's story to the rest of the class. As the other students in class tell their stories, listen for direct and indirect objects. Also listen for predicate adjectives and predicate nouns.

Word Bank

compound verb

direct object

indirect object

intransitive verb

object complement

predicate adjective

predicate noun

Part A Write the words from the Word Bank that complete each sentence.

1. The noun or pronoun that receives the action of a verb is a _____.

2. The noun or pronoun that receives the direct object of an action verb is the _____.

3. A noun or adjective that follows and tells about a direct object is an _____.

4. A _____ follows a state-of-being verb and renames the subject.

5. A _____ is two or more verbs connected by a conjunction.

6. A _____ follows a state-of-being verb and describes the subject.

7. An _____ is an action verb that does not need an object to receive its action.

Part B Write a sentence using each sentence pattern.

8. Subject + Intransitive Verb

9. Subject + Verb + Direct Object

10. Subject + Verb + Indirect Object + Direct Object

11. Subject + Verb + Direct Object + Object Complement

12. Subject + State-of-Being Verb + Predicate Noun

13. Subject + State-of-Being Verb + Predicate Adjective

Part C Write each sentence. Write *DO* over a direct object. Write *IO* over an indirect object. Write *OC* over an object complement.

14. Mom made me the boss.

15. Grandmother made me a winter hat.

16. I served my brother a sandwich.

17. He poured me a glass of milk.

18. My family named our dog Champ.

19. We call her part of the family.

20. Champ has proven herself a great watchdog.

21. Cory bought his brother a cap.

22. I gave him a hug.

Part D How is the bold word used in each sentence? Write the letter of your answer.

23. Tamara seems **happy** about the visit with her grandmother.
A predicate noun   **C** indirect object
B predicate adjective   **D** object complement

24. Juan called Angela a great **swimmer**.
A predicate noun   **C** object complement
B predicate adjective   **D** indirect object

25. They have remained **friends** for years.
A predicate noun   **C** indirect object
B direct object   **D** object complement

Test Tip

Look over a test before you begin. See how many parts there are. Think about how much time you have to complete the test. Then plan how much time you can spend on each part.

Writing Compound and Complex Sentences

Wow! Look at the construction site on the opposite page. See how many floors there are! Look at all of the metal! There are so many points of connection. It looks very busy and complex, doesn't it?

Writing can be like a construction site. Words are arranged to form complete ideas. The more words you use, the more you need to find ways to connect them in your sentences.

You have already learned about independent and dependent clauses. In Chapter 11, you will learn more about these and other kinds of clauses and sentences. You will learn how to use them to make your writing better.

GOALS FOR LEARNING

- To use phrases and clauses to write simple sentences
- To write compound sentences using conjunctions
- To use adverb and adjective clauses in sentences
- To use noun clauses in sentences
- To write complex sentences
- To correct common sentence problems

Reading Strategy: Visualizing

To visualize means to imagine what something is like. Visualizing can help you understand what you are reading. It is like making a movie in your mind. Use these tips to visualize when you read:

- Look at the photographs and drawings.
- Pay attention to words that describe actions and objects. Imagine all five senses: sight, sound, smell, taste, and touch.
- Build pictures in your mind of what you are reading. Think about ideas from your own life to add to the pictures.
- Notice the order of events. Think about what might happen next.

Key Vocabulary Words

Phrase A group of words that work together; a phrase does not have a subject and a predicate

Simple sentence One independent clause

Compound sentence Two or more independent clauses that are connected with a conjunction

Adverb clause A dependent clause that works like an adverb in a sentence

Adjective clause A dependent clause that describes a noun or pronoun

Noun clause A dependent clause that works like a noun in a sentence

Appositive A noun, a noun phrase, or a noun clause that explains another noun in the same sentence

Complex sentence A sentence with one independent clause and one or more dependent clauses

Run-on sentence Two or more ideas written as one without proper punctuation or conjunctions

Phrases, Clauses, and Simple Sentences

A **phrase** is a group of words that work together. A phrase does not have both a subject and a predicate. Phrases are parts of a sentence. You have already learned about some kinds of phrases.

▶ **EXAMPLE 1**

Prepositional Phrase	near the road
Verb Phrase	has frozen

In Chapter 9, you learned that a clause is a group of words with both a subject and a predicate. Some clauses can stand alone as sentences. Others cannot.

▶ **EXAMPLE 2**

Phrase   about wind power

          S   V
Sentence   She wrote a report about wind power.

               S   V
Clause   after she came home

          S   V
Sentence   She wrote it after she came home.

Example 2 shows one phrase and three clauses. Each clause has a subject (*S*) and a predicate (*V* for verb). Two of the clauses are sentences. One is not.

Phrase

A group of words that work together; a phrase does not have a subject and a predicate

Reading Strategy:
Visualizing

Think of phrases and clauses as tools. People use them to write letters, poems, novels, and reports. People use them to create ads and movie scripts.

Practice A

Identify each group of words as a *phrase* or a *clause*. Write *phrase* or *clause* on your paper.

1. Toni went to Japan.

2. For three years.

3. She joined her family.

4. After they moved there.

5. Because her father had a job there.

Reading Strategy:
Visualizing

Picture words, phrases, and dependent clauses as building blocks. You use these "blocks" to build sentences.

A dependent clause has a subject and predicate, but it does not express a complete thought. A dependent clause usually starts with a conjunction or a pronoun. It needs to depend on an independent clause. An independent clause has a subject and a predicate. It is a complete thought.

▶ **EXAMPLE 3**

Grammar Tip

Do not write a dependent clause as if it were a sentence. This is a common writing mistake. A dependent clause that stands alone will confuse your readers.

	S V
Independent Clause (sentence)	Selena likes horses.

	S V
Dependent Clause (not a sentence)	who likes horses

Practice B

Identify the kind of clause. Write *independent* or *dependent* on your paper.

1. Because the sport is so popular.

2. Peru attracts many visitors in winter.

3. Since Terry got home in late January.

4. She has gone to school since March.

5. Whoever knew Tanya before the contest.

A **simple sentence** has one subject and one predicate. It expresses a complete thought. A simple sentence is one independent clause with no dependent clauses.

▶ **EXAMPLE 4**

> S   V
>
> Javier went to the mall.

A simple sentence can have a compound subject: two or more subjects that share the same predicate. It can have a compound predicate: two or more predicates that share the same subject. A simple sentence can have both a compound subject and a compound predicate. In each case, the simple sentence is still only one independent clause.

▶ **EXAMPLE 5**

> S V   V
>
> He called Maurice and met him at the music store.
> (compound predicate)
>
> S   S   V
>
> Javier and Maurice looked at CDs.
> (compound subject)
>
> S   S   V   V
>
> The boys and the other shoppers heard a noise and looked.
> (compound subject and compound predicate)

Practice C

Decide whether each sentence has a compound subject, a compound predicate, or both. On your paper, write *compound subject, compound predicate,* or *both.*

1. The wind and waves rocked the boat.
2. The sail and the flag hung in shreds.
3. The waves splashed against and pounded the dock.
4. The captain and passengers trembled and shouted.
5. A boat and a helicopter rescued the passengers.

REVIEW

Identify each group of words as a phrase or a clause. Write *phrase* or *clause* on your paper.

1. In the middle.

2. Because the poem has four verses.

3. Tanya saw the movie.

4. After the party.

5. She rented it and took it home.

Identify the kind of clause. Write *independent* or *dependent*.

6. Because she enjoyed rock climbing.

7. Tanya went home after the movie.

8. She had watched all three films in the series.

9. As soon as she saw the first one.

10. Tanya saw a movie about the FBI.

VOCABULARY BUILDER

Understanding Acronyms

FBI is an acronym. It stands for Federal Bureau of Investigation. An acronym is one kind of abbreviation. It is a short form of a phrase. An acronym is often formed from first letters. Most acronyms are written in all capital letters. The word *acronym* was first used in 1943.

Write these acronyms on your paper: *RBI, ASAP, NASA, www, UFO.* Guess what each one means. Use a dictionary to find out if your guesses are correct.

Compound Sentences

Objectives

- To recognize compound sentences
- To use conjunctions to form compound sentences
- To use correct punctuation in compound sentences

Compound sentence

Two or more independent clauses that are connected with a conjunction

Reading Strategy:
Visualizing

Picture a conjunction as a link between two parts.

When you form a compound, you put equal parts together. Any part of a sentence can be compound—subjects, predicates, objects, or phrases. We use conjunctions to join the equal parts together. Conjunctions are like links.

When you join two or more independent clauses with a conjunction, you form a **compound sentence**. Each clause has its own subject and predicate. Use a comma in front of the conjunction in a compound sentence.

▶ **EXAMPLE 1**

The wind grew cold, and we put on extra clothes.
(compound sentence made of two independent clauses)

Ty and Max studied hard and took the test.
(simple sentence, compound subject, compound predicate)

You learned about coordinating conjunctions in Chapter 9. These conjunctions join words, phrases, and clauses. They join things that are equal in importance.

Common Coordinating Conjunctions

and	but	for	or	so

Practice A

For each compound sentence, write *compound*. For each simple sentence, write *simple*. Remember that a simple sentence can have a compound predicate or subject.

1. Jim left his wallet in the car, and I found it.

2. Sam and I can make a salad or buy one at the store.

3. The students wrote papers and read them to the class.

4. Seth made lunch, but I cleaned up.

5. He fell quite a distance, yet he seems fine.

Reading Strategy:
Visualizing

Imagine the first clause of the compound sentence linked to the second clause.

A compound sentence can have three or more independent clauses in a series. Use commas to separate them. Use a conjunction before the last clause.

▶ **EXAMPLE 2**

Josh is on the debate team, Caren is in the science club, and Michelle is in the chess club.

Practice B

Change each set of simple sentences into one compound sentence. Use *and*, *so*, or *but*. Use commas correctly. Write the new sentences.

1. The wind howled. The lightning flashed. The sky finally poured down rain.

2. Amy does not have a test. She does have a project due.

3. The letter was lost in the mail. It was late.

4. We needed milk. We went to the grocery store.

5. Sandra called five people. Only one was home.

We have plenty of vegetables at home, but we need to buy some fruit.

Use a semicolon (;) to punctuate two independent clauses joined with one of the conjunctions below. Use a comma after the conjunction.

More Conjunctions

also	furthermore	nevertheless
besides	however	otherwise
consequently	instead	therefore

▶ **EXAMPLE 3**

Dario enjoys wrestling; however, he likes dancing more.

Yoko practiced for hours; nevertheless, she was nervous.

Practice C

Combine each pair of sentences into one compound sentence. Use one of the conjunctions in the table above. Separate the clauses with a semicolon. Use a comma after the conjunction.

1. Jesse went to the library to use a computer. They were all being used.

2. He needed some information. He wanted to use the Internet.

3. Jesse got a C on the test. He needed to write a report to raise his grade.

4. The report has to be typed. It has to include at least two charts.

5. Annie will help with the charts. Jesse will not finish in time.

REVIEW

Read each sentence. If it is a compound sentence, write *compound*. If it is a simple sentence, write *simple*.

1. The road had many curves, so I had to slow down.

2. Seth baked the muffins, Brita decorated the table, and I wrapped the gift.

3. The branches waved in the wind, but none broke.

4. The book was long but very interesting.

Join each pair of simple sentences into one compound sentence. Choose a conjunction that makes sense. Use the correct punctuation. Write the new sentences.

5. Francis Scott Key wrote a poem titled "The Star-Spangled Banner." Music was added to it later.

6. It was about a battle at sea with the British. The Americans won.

7. Katherine Bates visited Pikes Peak, Colorado. The beauty of the view led her to write "America the Beautiful."

8. "America the Beautiful" is a well-known song. People sing it on the Fourth of July.

Write each sentence. Add the missing punctuation.

9. Jane stretched her legs took a drink of water and waited at the starting line for the race.

10. Most of the runners were nervous however Jane felt prepared and calm.

Adverb and Adjective Clauses

Objectives

■ To use adverb
clauses in sentences
■ To use adjective
clauses in sentences

Adverb clause

A dependent clause
that works like an
adverb in a sentence

Reading Strategy:
Visualizing

Slow down as you read
these Examples. Think
about what an adverb
clause adds to
a sentence.

Some sentences have both independent and dependent
clauses. Remember that a dependent clause is not a
sentence by itself. It is always attached to an independent
clause. Dependent clauses are either adverb clauses or
adjective clauses.

An **adverb clause** is a dependent clause. It works exactly
like an adverb in a sentence. It tells something about the
verb, an adjective, or another adverb. Like all clauses, an
adverb clause has a subject and a predicate.

▶ **EXAMPLE 1**

Adverb	The snow started early.
Adverb Phrase	It began at three in the morning.
Adverb Clause	The snow started before the sun was up.

Like adverbs, adverb clauses tell where, when, why, how
much, how often, or how soon.

▶ **EXAMPLE 2**

He waited to use a computer until other students left.
(The adverb phrase tells *when.*)

He waited because all the computers were in use.
(The adverb phrase tells *why.*)

The computers are more popular than they were last year.
(The adverb phrase tells *how much.*)

Adjective clause

A dependent clause that describes a noun or pronoun

Dependent clauses often begin with subordinating conjunctions. An adverb clause always begins with a subordinating conjunction.

Common Subordinating Conjunctions

after	before	than	where
although	if	unless	wherever
as	in order that	until	whether
as though	since	when	while
because	so that	whenever	

If an adverb clause begins a sentence, use a comma after it.

▶ **EXAMPLE 3**

When the sun set, they sat around the campfire.

Practice A

Write the adverb clause in each sentence.

1. Tanya got a new computer when she returned from camp.

2. Her parents gave her the computer because she needed it for school.

3. Tanya plans to use her computer for homework whenever she can.

4. Because Tanya has a friend far away, she will send e-mails, too.

5. Her computer is much faster than older computers.

An adjective describes a noun or pronoun. An **adjective clause** is a dependent clause that describes a noun or pronoun. You can use an adjective clause in a sentence just like you would use an adjective.

▶ **EXAMPLE 4**

Adjective	Neeru is talented.
Adjective Phrase	She is a girl with many talents.
Adjective Clause	Neeru is a girl who is very talented.

Adjective clauses usually begin with relative pronouns. The relative pronoun is often the subject of the clause. The words *where* and *when* can also begin adjective clauses. An adjective clause usually follows the noun it describes.

Relative Pronouns

who	whom	that	whose	which	what

Practice B

Identify each bold word or group of words. Write *adjective, adjective phrase,* or *adjective clause.*

1. The **icy** river flowed under the bridge.

2. The river **of ice** flowed under the bridge.

3. The river, **which was full of ice,** flowed under the bridge.

4. The painting **that decorates the wall** shows a sailboat.

5. The painting **on the wall** is lovely.

Practice C

Write the adjective clause in each sentence.

1. Mandy had dinner with Carl, who is an old friend.

2. Josh went to the movie that he wanted to see.

3. The store where Emily works is open until nine.

4. Dario was the actor whom the audience liked best.

5. The book that Walter gave me has a surprise ending.

Reading Strategy:
Visualizing

Use the Examples and Practices in this lesson to help you see the difference between adverb clauses and adjective clauses.

REVIEW

Write the dependent clause in each sentence. Tell whether it is an *adverb clause* or an *adjective clause*.

1. Molly waved when she saw Jay.

2. I know the person who sent the letter.

3. Alex tried as hard as he could.

4. Did you see the movie that won three awards?

Add an adverb clause to each simple sentence. Write the new sentence.

5. He tried out for the play.

6. She improved her grades.

7. I shoveled the snow from our driveway.

Add an adjective clause to each simple sentence. Write the new sentence.

8. She bought a used car.

9. The policeman was helpful.

10. David works at the post office.

Noun Clauses

Objectives

■ To use noun clauses in sentences

■ To use appositives with correct punctuation

Noun clause

A dependent clause that works like a noun in a sentence

A noun names a person, place, event, or thing. You can use a **noun clause** in a sentence just like you use a noun. A noun clause can be a subject, a predicate noun, an object, or an object complement.

A noun clause often begins with a relative pronoun. The relative pronouns are *that, what, which, who, whom, whose, whatever, whichever, whoever,* and *whenever*. Other words that begin noun clauses are *if, whether*, and *why*.

▶ **EXAMPLE 1**

Subject	Whoever wins the race gets the prize.
Predicate Noun	She is who she seems to be.
Direct Object	Kate believed what I told her.
Indirect Object	Give whoever wants it my coat.
Object Complement	You can name the boat whatever you like.
Object of Preposition	Glen gave a ride to whoever needed one.

Practice A

Write the noun clause in each sentence. Tell how it is used in the sentence. Write one of these: *subject, predicate noun, direct object, indirect object,* or *object of preposition.*

  1. Order what you want.

  2. What you should do is ask for your money back.

  3. The salesperson handed whoever was in the store a free CD.

  4. Some hot soup is what I need right now.

  5. Nora sells peaches to whoever wants them.

Grammar Tip

Sometimes you name the person you are talking to in a sentence. The name is not an appositive. It is not part of the subject. It is a *noun of direct address*. For example:
I will be glad, Sara, to help.
That is a good idea, Sara.
Sara, are you ready?
Use commas to separate the name from the rest of the sentence.

Practice B

Use each clause in a sentence. Make sure that you use each clause as a noun.

1. that I am hungry

2. what the reason is

3. who saw the boat

4. that I got lost

5. which way I should go

An **appositive** explains another noun in the same sentence. An appositive can be a noun, a noun phrase, or a noun clause.

▶ **EXAMPLE 2**

My friend Tanya has a new computer.
(The appositive is a proper noun.)

Her computer, a small one, is easy to carry.
(The appositive is an adjective plus a pronoun.)

Tanya's computer, a present from her parents, is easy to use.
(The appositive is a noun plus an adjective phrase)

She showed me the computer, one that can do many tasks.
(The appositive is a pronoun plus a clause.)

Practice C

Write the appositive in each sentence.

1. Baseball, America's favorite sport, is popular in Japan.

2. Jeff, a friend of mine, will be in town tomorrow.

3. My neighbor, Mrs. Karr, asked me to mow her lawn.

4. We are going to Toronto, my hometown.

5. My cousin Michelle works for a law firm.

Writing Tip

To decide whether commas are needed with an appositive, ask yourself: Is there more than one possibility? If there is, then you do not need commas. For example, if you have two brothers, write *My brother Paul runs with me.* If you only have one brother, write *My brother, Paul, runs with me.*

If an appositive is a phrase or clause, you usually use a comma to separate it from the rest of the sentence. If an appositive is one word, you do not use commas.

▶ **EXAMPLE 3**

Armando's friend Josh plays soccer.

You can also use dashes to separate an appositive phrase or clause from the rest of the sentence.

▶ **EXAMPLE 4**

Judy Garland—a skillful actress—was in many movies.

An appositive can join two related sentences into one longer sentence. It is a way to avoid repeating words.

▶ **EXAMPLE 5**

Dr. Flores moved to a new office. Dr. Flores is my dentist.

Dr. Flores, my dentist, moved to a new office.

Practice D

Combine each pair of sentences by using an appositive. Write the new sentence.

1. Have you read *Alice In Wonderland*? It is a book by Lewis Carroll.

2. My lucky shirt is not in my closet. My lucky shirt is the one with the blue stripes.

3. Sharon is in *Romeo and Juliet*. She was the star of last year's play.

4. Nathan had a secret wish. Nathan wished he would become a scientist.

5. Ben Franklin was an important person in American history. He experimented with electricity.

Reading Strategy:
Visualizing

Use all five senses as you visualize what you read: *sight, sound, smell, touch,* and *taste.*

REVIEW

Write the noun clause in each sentence. Tell how it is used by writing one of these: *direct object, subject,* or *object of a preposition.*

1. We made dinner for whoever was hungry.

2. Tell the waiter what you want.

3. Whoever scores next will be the winner.

4. She said that my answer was right.

5. Give the job to whoever wants it.

Add an appositive to each sentence. Write the new sentence. Underline the appositive you added.

6. The horse ran across the field.

7. The store closed early on Friday.

8. Jason got a ride from Luke's dad.

9. The bicycle tour went through the mountains.

10. Elise caught a fish with her new rod.

SPELLING BUILDER

Pronouncing and Spelling Words

Are you meeting someone at the *libary* or the *library*? With some words, you may have trouble saying all the sounds in each syllable. To help you spell such words correctly, say the word aloud. Pronounce each syllable. If you are still not sure, look up the word in a dictionary.

Work with a partner. Write these words: *February, different, probably.* Say each word. Underline the part of the word that you might leave out when you say and spell it.

Complex Sentences

A **complex sentence** has one independent clause and one or more dependent clauses. The dependent clause may be an adverb clause, a noun clause, or an adjective clause.

▶ **EXAMPLE 1**

I will rent a movie tonight *if you will watch it with me.*
(independent clause)   (dependent clause)

Practice A

Write each sentence. Underline the independent clause once. Underline the dependent clause twice.

1. The friends who went to the party thought that Derek won the prize.

2. Andy's painting that hangs in the lobby is colorful.

3. The essay that Jamal wrote won a prize in the contest.

4. After he won the contest, he celebrated at Tony's Cafe.

5. Nathan could not go to Tony's because he was sick.

If Jamal's essay wins first prize, it will be printed in the newspaper.

You have now learned about three kinds of sentences: simple, compound, and complex.

- A simple sentence has one subject and one predicate.
- A compound sentence has two or more independent clauses connected with a conjunction.
- A complex sentence has one independent clause and one or more dependent clauses.

▶ **EXAMPLE 2**

Simple	The debate team won a trophy and a blue ribbon.
Compound	They wanted to celebrate, so they planned a party.
Complex	Because the team members enjoy using their debate skills, the party turned into a debate about where the trophy should be kept.

The complex sentence in Example 2 has one independent clause and two dependent clauses.

Practice B

Decide what kind of sentence each of these sentences is. Write *simple, compound,* or *complex* on your paper.

1. Janet's favorite singer is Roy Jeffers.
2. Jeffers, who is from Nashville, does not sing country music.
3. When Jeffers went to college, he entered a talent contest just for fun.
4. He won the contest and started to concentrate on his music.
5. He took guitar lessons, which made him a better performer.

REVIEW

Write the dependent clause in each sentence. Identify it as an *adverb clause*, an *adjective clause*, or a *noun clause*.

1. Because they are healthy and delicious, many people eat carrots.

2. The part of the carrot plant that people eat is the root.

3. Do you know what wild plant is related to carrots?

4. Queen Anne's lace, which is a small white flower, is a wild carrot.

5. The root of the wild carrot is not eaten since it is tough and dry.

Identify each sentence as a simple sentence, a complex sentence, or a compound sentence. Write *simple*, *complex*, or *compound* on your paper.

6. Parsley and carrots are in the same family of vegetables.

7. The top of the carrot, the part that is above ground, looks like parsley.

8. Many people eat the roots of carrots; however, they eat the leaves of parsley.

9. Some people say that the flavor is too strong.

10. Parsley looks attractive on a plate.

Common Sentence Problems

Reading Strategy:
Visualizing

When a dish breaks into pieces, the pieces are called fragments.

Sentence Fragments

A sentence has a subject and a predicate. It expresses a complete thought. Sometimes, a group of words may not express a complete thought. The words may start with a capital letter and have end punctuation, but they do not form a sentence. As you learned in Chapter 1, this group of words is a sentence fragment.

Some sentence fragments have a subject but no predicate. You know who or what is doing something, but you do not know what they are doing.

▶ **EXAMPLE 1**

Fragment   The cold winter weather.

Sentence   The cold winter weather made us grumpy.

Other sentence fragments have a predicate but no subject. You know what is happening, but you do not know who is doing the action.

▶ **EXAMPLE 2**

Fragment   Fell gently on the ground.

Sentence   The snow fell gently on the ground.

Practice A

Add either a subject or a predicate to each sentence fragment. Write the complete sentence.

1. The noise in the gym from the cheering students.

2. Found a coin on the street.

3. Wrote a report on frogs.

4. A cool fresh taste of milk.

5. The cold winter day.

Run-on sentence

Two or more ideas written as one without proper punctuation or conjunctions

A dependent clause has a subject and a predicate, but it does not express a complete idea. It is a sentence fragment. To correct this kind of sentence fragment, add an independent clause.

▶ **EXAMPLE 3**

Fragment   Because it was Saturday

Sentence   Because it was Saturday, we went shopping.

Practice B

Add an independent clause to each sentence fragment. Write the complete sentence.

1. Since they returned from the beach.

2. Because Emma wants to be a music teacher.

3. After they were done working.

4. Until spring arrived.

5. If you don't mind.

Run-on Sentences

Sometimes writers run two sentences together. They forget to use end punctuation or conjunctions between the sentences. This is called a **run-on sentence**.

▶ **EXAMPLE 4**

Run-on   I must catch the next bus I cannot be late.

The ideas in a run-on sentence must be separated or connected properly.

One way to fix a run-on sentence is to separate it into two or more simple sentences. Capitalize the first word in each simple sentence. End each sentence with the correct punctuation mark.

▶ **EXAMPLE 5**

Run-on   Just before spring came, there was a big storm school was closed for two days then the weekend came school opened again on Monday.

Fixed   Just before spring came, there was a big snowstorm. School was closed for two days. Then the weekend came. School opened again on Monday.

Practice C

Correct each run-on sentence by separating the ideas. Write the new sentences on your paper.

1. The storm lasted for two days the snow was more than one foot deep.

2. The horses needed to be fed we had to pour hot water in their pails to melt the ice.

3. The police closed our road no one could come or go for two days.

4. We had enough food and water we always have extra supplies.

5. The snowplow reached our farm two days after the storm ended we were happy to see it.

Another way to fix a run-on sentence is to use a conjunction to connect related ideas. However, do not string too many sentences together with conjunctions. The result can be a very long sentence that is hard to understand. Also, do not use *and* too many times. Use different conjunctions. Leave some sentences short if they express important ideas.

▶ **EXAMPLE 6**

Run-on Our dog is going to have puppies so we took her to the veterinarian and Dr. Cook said that she probably will have three puppies and they will arrive by March 26.

Fixed Our dog is going to have puppies! We took her to the veterinarian. Dr. Cook said that she probably will have three puppies, and they will arrive by March 26.

Practice D

The following groups of words are run-on sentences. Fix each one by using conjunctions or making separate sentences. You can add or change words. Write the new sentences. Use correct punctuation.

1. I took the bus to school and I missed the bus and I was late and my teacher was not happy.

2. Did you send me a letter if you did, I did not get it and I would like to hear from you.

3. I am so busy here in college and I have more homework than ever before and there are also all of my sports activities.

4. My friends and I want to go to a concert and I really need money and could you send me some?

5. Winter vacation is a month away and my friends are going camping and I want to go with them.

REVIEW

Rewrite each group of words. Fix each sentence fragment or run-on sentence.

1. The game was about to begin, the crowd cheered, the ball was tossed in the air.

2. Came in first in the road race.

3. Whenever I hear that song.

4. He said it was time to start and he began by going first and soon he was way ahead of everyone.

5. Given an award for his essay.

6. I wanted that computer it has better speakers.

7. Where the principal's office is.

8. Sara did not come back to camp, the sun went down.

9. Because the moon is closer to the earth than to the sun.

10. Lost my math book.

PUTTING IT ALL TOGETHER

What if you could trade places with someone for one day? Who would you be? Choose someone. You could choose a person from history, a book character, or someone you know. Write about how you would spend your day. Use a variety of sentences. Use at least one simple sentence. Use at least one compound sentence. Use at least one complex sentence.

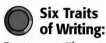

Six Traits of Writing:
Sentence Fluency
smooth rhythm and flow

Landscaper

Kurt Diaz works as a landscaper. A landscaper plants flowers and trims bushes and trees. He or she also mows lawns and waters gardens. Kurt reads about plants to help him do his job well. When he finishes a job, he writes a note to the owner of the yard. He tapes the note where the owner will see it. Before he leaves, he checks his writing. He makes sure that the words and sentences are correct. Read Kurt's note. Then answer the questions.

I finished several things today. I mowed the grass. I also trimmed the hedge by the street. I planted petunias last week, and I watered them well today. Although they are green now, they will bloom into many colors soon. I may cut a few tree branches next time. Your lawn is looking great!

I will be back next week. Thank you for your business.

Kurt Diaz

1. Identify one of the simple sentences in the note.

2. Identify the compound sentence and the complex sentence in the note.

3. CRITICAL THINKING Why is it a good idea for a landscaper to leave a note like this?

SPEAKING AND LISTENING

Think of a problem that a landscaper like Kurt might have while he is working. Think of a good way to solve the problem. Then work with a partner. Take turns speaking as if you were leaving a phone message for your boss. Describe the problem. Use conjunctions such as *after*, *while*, *when*, and *before*. Tell why the problem occurred. Use conjunctions such as *because* and *since*. Tell what you did to solve the problem. Use more conjunctions to explain your actions. After you have finished your phone message, listen to your partner's message. Pay attention to the dependent clauses he or she uses.

Searching the Internet

When you need information, a Web site on the Internet may have the facts you need. The World Wide Web can make finding information easy.

A search engine is a specific kind of Web site that leads you to other Web sites. Use a search engine to find the information you need. Enter one or two keywords that summarize your topic. A keyword can be a word or a phrase. The search engine will provide a list of Web sites that mention your keyword(s). Look at the list of sites. Visit several sites to decide which ones will help you.

Suppose you did a search using the keyword "shark attacks." Here are some results you might see:

Top 10 of about 135,190 found for: shark attacks

Nova Online/**Shark Attack!**
NOVA Online examines one of nature's most powerful predators, the shark,…
www.pbs.org/wgbh/nova/sharkattack/
[more from this site]

International Shark Attack File
Shark attack statistics including special sections for the great white shark and shark attacks…
www.flmnh.ufl.edu/fish/Sharks/ISAF/ISAF.htm
[more from this site]

Follow the directions below.

1. Suppose you want to find out how oil spills in oceans are cleaned up. Write three keywords that you could use in a search engine.

2. Think of a topic that interests you. Write two keywords related to the topic.

3. CRITICAL THINKING The search engine found more than 135,000 Web sites about shark attacks. How could you narrow this search?

 TECHNOLOGY

Choose a hobby or sport that you like. Use a search engine to find information about it. Enter two or three keywords. Scan the list of Web sites that appear on the screen. The sites with the most information about your topic are listed first. Choose three sites that sound interesting. Go to each site and look at the information found there. Which site do you think is best? Go to that site and write down its address. This address is in the address window near the top of the screen. It may start with http://www.

CHAPTER 11

SUMMARY

- Identify a group of words as a clause if it has a subject and a predicate.

- Identify a clause as an independent clause if it expresses a complete thought.

- Identify a clause as a dependent clause if it does not express a complete thought.

- Form a simple sentence with one subject and one predicate. A simple sentence can have a compound subject and a compound predicate.

- Form a compound sentence by connecting two or more independent clauses. Use a conjunction to join them. Use a comma after the conjunction.

- Use an adverb clause to answer a question about a verb, an adjective, or another adverb. Begin an adverb clause with a subordinating conjunction.

- Use an adjective clause to describe a noun or pronoun. Begin an adjective clause with a relative pronoun or the word *where* or *when*.

- Use a noun clause in a sentence exactly as you use a noun. A noun clause often begins with a relative pronoun.

- Use an appositive to explain another noun in the sentence.

- Form a complex sentence with one independent clause and one or more dependent clauses.

- Fix sentence fragments. Add what is missing: a subject, a predicate, or an independent clause.

- Fix run-on sentences. Either use conjunctions properly or break them into more than one sentence.

GROUP ACTIVITY

Work in a group. Choose a type of job. Write a note that someone with that job might leave at the end of the day. Tell what the worker did. Use at least one compound sentence and one complex sentence.

Make sure your note does not contain sentence fragments or run-on sentences. Also check the punctuation. Read your note to the other students in the class. See if they can guess the worker's job.

Word Bank

adjective clause

adverb clause

appositive

complex sentence

compound
 sentence

noun clause

phrase

run-on sentence

simple sentence

Part A Write the word or words from the Word Bank that complete each sentence.

1. A noun, a noun phrase, or a noun clause that explains another noun in the same sentence is an _____.

2. A _____ is two or more sentences written incorrectly as one sentence.

3. A _____ is a group of words that work together.

4. A _____ has one independent clause and one or more dependent clauses.

5. An _____ is a dependent clause that answers a question about a verb, adjective, or another adverb.

6. A dependent clause that describes a noun or pronoun is an _____.

7. A _____ is a dependent clause that works like a noun in a sentence.

8. A sentence with one subject and one predicate is a _____.

9. You form a _____ by connecting two or more independent clauses with a conjunction.

Part B Identify each sentence as *simple, compound,* or *complex.*

10. Before he rang the bell, he put the basket on the steps.

11. He put the basket on the steps and rang the bell.

12. He put the basket on the steps before he rang the bell.

13. He put the basket on the steps, and he rang the bell.

14. Before ringing the bell, he put the basket on the steps.

Part C Identify each group of words. Write one of these: *run-on*, *fragment*, or *correct*.

15. The apples that grew on the old tree were full of worms.

16. Because the apples that grew on the tree were full of worms.

17. The apples grew on the tree they were full of worms.

18. The juicy apples were full of worms.

Part D Identify each group of words in bold as a *noun clause*, an *adjective clause*, or an *adverb clause*.

19. Why you did it is not important.

20. Why do you want a car **that has so many miles on it?**

21. That you care so much is good to know.

22. When I laugh too hard, I get dizzy.

Part E Write the letter of the answer that completes the sentence.

23. An adjective clause usually begins with _____.
A an adjective
B a noun
C a subordinating conjunction
D a relative pronoun

24. *My truck, a red pickup, is for sale.* In this sentence, *a red pickup* is _____.
A an adjective clause
B an appositive
C a dependent clause
D a predicate

25. *After he climbed the mountain he could see for miles.* This sentence needs _____.
A a comma
B a conjunction
C a semicolon
D a predicate

Using Verbals and Verbal Phrases

Verbs can do many things. You have learned that they can express action. They can also show a state of being. There is more. Verbs can be used as other parts of speech. When you use verbs as other parts of speech, they are called verbals. Verbals can be nouns, adjectives, and adverbs in sentences.

Look at the photo. Then read the three sentences below. Each sentence uses a form of the verb *swim*.

Do you like to swim? (*To swim* acts as a noun.)

Swimming is good exercise. (*Swimming* acts as a noun.)

Swimming at full speed, he won the race. (*Swimming at full speed* acts as an adjective.)

In Chapter 12, you will learn about the three kinds of verbals: infinitives, gerunds, and participles.

GOALS FOR LEARNING

- To identify and use infinitives and infinitive phrases
- To identify and use gerunds and gerund phrases
- To identify and use participles and participle phrases

Reading Strategy: Text Structure

Information in a book or chapter comes in a certain order. Knowing that order can help you decide what information is most important. It can also help you see how the different parts fit together. This order and fit is called structure.

Before you begin reading this chapter, take a few minutes to look at the structure.

- Look at the chapter title, the lesson titles, and the headings.
- Notice that there are boldfaced words, highlighted words, and words in italic print.
- Ask yourself: What are the parts of each lesson? In what order do they come? How do important words and ideas appear?
- Summarize the text by thinking about its structure.

Key Vocabulary Words

Verbal A verb used as a noun, adjective, or adverb

Complement A word or phrase that completes the meaning of a verbal

Verbal phrase A verbal and its complements

Infinitive phrase An infinitive, its complements, and any other words that describe it

Gerund A verb ending in *-ing* that is used as a noun

Gerund phrase A gerund and its complements

Participle A verb form that can be used as an adjective

Participle phrase A participle plus any words that complement or describe it

Infinitives and Infinitive Phrases

Objectives

- To identify infinitives and infinitive phrases
- To use infinitives as nouns, adjectives, or adverbs in sentences

Verbal

A verb used as a noun, adjective, or adverb

Reading Strategy:
Text Structure

Read the Objectives for each lesson. They will help you identify the main ideas of the lesson.

A **verbal** is a verb that you use as another part of speech. There are three kinds of verbals: infinitives, gerunds, and participles. You will learn about infinitives in this lesson.

You learned in Chapter 5 that an infinitive is *to* plus a verb. An infinitive is a verbal. It can be used as a noun, an adverb, or an adjective. As a noun, an infinitive can be a subject, a predicate nound, or a direct object.

▶ **EXAMPLE 1**

Subject	To win is her goal.
Predicate Noun	Her goal is to win.
Direct Object	I like to swim.
Adverb	He practices to win. (*To win* tells why or how he practices.)
Adjective	We had lots of food to eat. (*To eat* describes *food*.)

Practice A

Write the infinitive in each sentence.

1. Julian needs to talk to you later.
2. I will need your help to move this table.
3. Kay learned to dive last Wednesday.
4. I want you to listen carefully.
5. My cousin wants to go home.

An infinitive is usually in the present tense. It can also be in the present perfect tense.

▶ **EXAMPLE 2**

Present   I am glad to meet you.

Present Perfect I am pleased to have caught six fish.

Practice B

Write the infinitive in each sentence. After it tell whether it is used as a *direct object* or an *adverb*.

1. A group met to plan the band's yearly picnic.

2. Emily agreed to be the leader.

3. What do you want me to bring?

4. Would you like to get the hot dogs?

5. Emily is happy to have served as the leader.

Sometimes *to* is missing from the infinitive. It is understood to be part of the sentence.

▶ **EXAMPLE 3**

Don't make me laugh. (to laugh)

Help me reel in the fish. (to reel)

Practice C

Write the infinitive in each sentence. The *to* is missing but understood.

1. We heard the audience cheer for the band.

2. Let me hear the sound of that music.

3. They watched Emily play her clarinet.

4. Their applause made Emily feel proud.

5. Will you let me thank everyone?

Complement
A word or phrase that completes the meaning of a verbal

Verbal phrase
A verbal and its complements

Infinitive phrase
An infinitive, its complements, and any other words that describe it

Reading Strategy:
Text Structure

How is bold type used in Practice D?

Do not mix up infinitives and prepositional phrases. An infinitive is *to* plus a verb. A prepositional phrase is *to* plus a noun or pronoun.

▶ **EXAMPLE 4**

| Infinitive | Armando likes to fish. |
| Prepositional Phrase | I gave the fish to Armando. |

Practice D

Write the bold words in each sentence. Then identify them as an *infinitive* or a *prepositional phrase*.

1. Will you walk with me **to school**?

2. I am going **to paint** now.

3. It is important **to get** there on time.

4. They planned **to begin** the picnic at 6:00.

5. Everyone went **to the park.**

Verbals often have **complements.** A complement is a word or phrase that completes the meaning of a verbal. A verbal with its complements is called a **verbal phrase.** There are three kinds of verbal phrases: infinitive phrases, gerund phrases, and participle phrases.

An **infinitive phrase** includes the infinitive, any complements, and any other words that describe it. Words that describe infinitives include adjectives, adverbs, adjective phrases, and adverb phrases. Infinitive phrases are often used as nouns. In Example 5, each infinitive phrase is in blue.

▶ **EXAMPLE 5**

Neeru wanted to earn money. (*Money* is a direct object.)

Their plan is to leave in the morning.
(*In the morning* is an adverb phrase that tells when.)

He wanted the meal to taste delicious.
(*Delicious* is an adjective.)

Write the infinitive phrase in each sentence. Remember that *to* is sometimes missing but understood.

1. They planned to get together after school.
2. Their wish was to have a picnic.
3. The cold rain made the students feel cold.
4. The rain caused them to cancel the picnic.
5. To gather their things took time.

An infinitive phrase can be a noun, an adverb, or an adjective.

▶ **EXAMPLE 6**

Noun	Neeru's hope is to find a job near home. (What is her hope?)
Adverb	Neeru will need new clothes to work in the store. (Why does she need new clothes?)
Adjective	She has plenty of clothes to wear today. (What kind of clothes does she have?)

Practice F

Write the infinitive phrase in each sentence. Identify each infinitive phrase as a *noun*, an *adverb*, or an *adjective*.

1. Neeru's goal is to get a job.
2. She has time to work on weekends.
3. She decided to look for a job at the mall.
4. A job will be fun to have.
5. She will work to earn money.

REVIEW

Write the infinitive or infinitive phrase in each sentence. Identify each as a *subject*, a *direct object*, a *predicate noun*, an *adjective*, or an *adverb*. There may be more than one infinitive in a sentence.

1. To describe an interesting person was the homework.

2. "I need to think about this," Emily said to herself.

3. She took the extra job to save money.

4. His goal was to be a performer.

5. He had the talent to sing, to dance, and to tell jokes.

Write the infinitive in each sentence. If the sentence does not have an infinitive, write *none*.

6. Can you help me find a ride?

7. I am going to the movies.

8. I want to see the newest film.

9. Jeff is sure to have seen it already.

10. I don't have the courage to watch scary movies.

VOCABULARY BUILDER

Using Internet Words

Because of the Internet, many new words have entered the English language. (*Internet* itself is a new word!) You cannot find these words in older dictionaries.

What do you think each word below means? Write a definition for each one. Then check your definitions in a newer dictionary.

1. online (adjective)
2. e-mail (noun and verb)
3. bookmark (verb)

4. Web site (noun)
5. download (verb)
6. key (verb)

Gerunds and Gerund Phrases

Gerund

A verb ending in *-ing* that is used as a noun

Gerund phrase

A gerund and its complements

Reading Strategy:
Text Structure

When a new vocabulary word is first used, it is in bold. Its definition appears in the left column.

A **gerund** is a verb that ends in *-ing*. In sentences, gerunds are used as nouns. Gerunds can be subjects, direct objects, objects of prepositions, and predicate nouns.

▶ **EXAMPLE 1**

Subject	Running is good exercise.
Direct Object	We enjoy cooking.
Object of Preposition	He is famous for his painting.
Predicate Noun	Angela's favorite sport is swimming.

Practice A

Write the gerunds in these sentences. Identify each gerund as a *subject*, a *direct object*, an *object of a preposition*, or a *predicate noun*.

1. Tanya's family returned to the United States after living in Switzerland.

2. Tanya enjoyed living in Switzerland.

3. While there, the family learned about skiing.

4. Tanya's favorite vacation was skiing in the Alps.

5. Cooking is one of Tanya's favorite things to do.

A **gerund phrase** is a gerund plus any adjectives, adverbs, prepositional phrases, or other complements. The progressive forms of a verb, like a gerund, end in *-ing*. Do not confuse progressive verb phrases and gerund phrases.

▶ **EXAMPLE 2**

Verb Phrase	Angela is swimming in the pool today.
Gerund Phrase	Angela likes swimming every day.

Is the bold word in each sentence part of a gerund phrase or part of a verb phrase? Write *gerund phrase* or *verb phrase*.

1. Angela was **enjoying** the TV program.

2. It was about deep-sea **diving**.

3. **Seeing** the unusual fish interested her.

4. Angela thought about **becoming** a deep-sea diver someday.

5. She is **planning** to learn more about the ocean.

A gerund phrase can have an adjective, an adverb, or a prepositional phrase. In each sentence in Example 3, the gerund is *singing*. The gerund phrase is in blue.

Reading Strategy:
Text Structure

In Example sentences, the words in blue are important.

▶ **EXAMPLE 3**

Adjective	Megan pleased the audience with beautiful singing.
Adverb	Megan enjoys singing loudly.
Prepositional Phrase	Megan enjoys singing in the choir.

If a gerund expresses action, it can have a direct object. The direct object is part of the gerund phrase. The gerund phrase below is in blue.

▶ **EXAMPLE 4**

Direct Object	Playing baseball is fun.

In Example 4, *baseball* is the direct object of the gerund *playing*.

Writing Tip

When you use a gerund as a subject, you can use an infinitive instead. For example:

To swim is fun. (infinitive)
Swimming is fun. (gerund)

NOTE

Not all words that end in *-ing* are gerunds. Some adjectives, nouns, and prepositions also end in *-ing*. To be a gerund, the word must be a verb used as a noun. These words are not gerunds: *during, interesting, king, morning, exciting, including, thing,* and *something.*

If the gerund is a state-of-being verb, it can have a predicate noun or adjective. The predicate noun or adjective is part of the gerund phrase. The gerund phrase in Example 5 is in blue.

▶ **EXAMPLE 5**

She liked being the oldest child.
(*Child* is the predicate noun of *being*.)

Practice C

Write each sentence. Underline each gerund phrase. In each phrase, identify a direct object, a predicate noun, or a predicate adjective. Above it, write *DO*, *PN*, or *PA*.

1. Henry enjoyed feeling prepared.

2. Knowing the answer is exciting.

3. Ping has thought about giving presents.

4. Sounding smart is easy if you read a lot.

5. Being a good friend means listening well.

Being a good listener is an important quality.

REVIEW

Write the gerund phrase in each sentence.

1. Saving money for college was Selena's goal.

2. She had thought about going to college long ago.

3. Selena thinks about studying music.

4. Teaching music in high school would be great.

5. Becoming a music teacher is her goal.

Write the gerund in each sentence. Decide whether it is used as a subject, a direct object, a predicate noun, or an object of a preposition. Write *S*, *DO*, *PN*, or *OP*.

6. When she was young, Emily began taking lessons.

7. Now one of her favorite activities is playing her flute.

8. She also enjoys writing short songs.

9. Learning new musical pieces is easy for her.

10. She learns about music by listening to it, too.

SPELLING BUILDER

Spelling the Sound /k/

Cat is one of the first words children learn to spell. In *cat*, the c is pronounced /k/. However, in English, the sound /k/ is not always spelled with a c. Read these examples:

a**cc**ount	s**ch**ool	sti**ck**	**k**eep	**qu**it

Now say the following words aloud: *dock, accuse, bank, cozy, chaos, occasion, quack, schooner*. (If you do not know how to pronounce a word, look it up in a dictionary.) How is the /k/ sound spelled in each one? Write a sentence using each of the eight words listed.

Participles and Participle Phrases

A **participle** is a verb form. You use participles to form the perfect tenses and the progressive tenses.

▶ **EXAMPLE 1**

| Present Perfect | Mrs. Young has baked bread. |
| Progressive | Mrs. Young is baking bread. |

You can also use a participle as an adjective.

▶ **EXAMPLE 2**

| Present Participle as an Adjective | We smelled the baking bread. (*Baking* describes bread.) |
| Past Participle as an Adjective | We ate the baked bread. (*Baked* describes bread.) |

Practice A

Write each participle and the noun that the participle describes. Look for verb forms that are used as adjectives.

1. Efran enjoys cooked carrots.
2. The howling wind kept us awake.
3. The movie was frightening.
4. The setting sun colored the sky orange.
5. We visited the Painted Desert in New Mexico.

A participle may be an adjective or part of a verb phrase.

▶ **EXAMPLE 3**

| Participle as an Adjective | Mr. Allen likes to wear a starched shirt. |
| Participle as Part of a Verb Phrase | Mr. Allen has starched his shirts for years. |

Participle phrase

A participle plus any words that complement or describe it

Reading Strategy:
Text Structure

As you work on a Practice activity, use the Example before it to guide you.

Practice B

Write whether each word in bold is used as an *adjective* or as a *verb*.

1. We **steamed** the vegetables.

2. She likes **steamed** vegetables.

3. Mark Twain wrote a story about a **jumping** frog.

4. The frog is **jumping** across the pond.

5. We **locked** the door as we left the car.

A **participle phrase** is a participle plus any words that complement or describe it. A participle phrase can be before or after the noun or pronoun that it describes.

▶ **EXAMPLE 4**

Jumping high, she cleared the fence.
(*Jumping high* describes *she.*)

Keys locked inside a car are useless.
(*Locked inside a car* describes *keys.*)

Practice C

Write each sentence. Underline the participle phrase. Draw two lines under the noun or pronoun that the participle phrase describes.

1. Emily mailed a letter addressed to the college.

2. Reading his book, he didn't hear his mother.

3. The granola made by Mrs. Cortez was a special treat.

4. The picture hanging on the wall was lovely.

5. Nadia made a phone call to a girl waiting at the store.

Writing Tip

Some verbs have irregular past participles. They do not end in -ed. For example, *taught* is the past participle of *teach*. *Broken* is the past participle of *break*. If you are unsure, look up the verb in a dictionary. If the verb has an irregular past participle, the dictionary entry will include it.

Reading Strategy:
Text Structure

Name two ways that the information in Example 5 is organized.

A participle can have a direct object, a predicate noun, a predicate adjective, an adverb, or a prepositional phrase. The participle phrase is always an adjective in the sentence.

▶ **EXAMPLE 5**

Direct Object	The boy jumping the fence tore his pants. (*Fence* is the direct object.)
Predicate Noun	Being a gifted singer, Allen started a band. (*Singer* is the predicate noun.)
Predicate Adjective	I saw the child being silly. (*Silly* is the predicate adjective.)
Adverb	Smiling brightly, he posed for the camera. (*Brightly* is the adverb.)
Prepositional Phrase	I saw a girl hiding behind a tree. (*Behind* is the preposition.)

Practice D

Write the participle phrase in each sentence. Then write the noun or pronoun it describes.

1. Reaching the high notes easily, Allen performed for the school.

2. The team, hoping for victory, ran out onto the field.

3. I wondered about the boy seeming so shy.

4. Looking bored, the tall girl won the race.

5. Did you see the dog standing by the side of the road?

Look at the participle phrase in bold. Decide whether it includes a *direct object*, *predicate noun*, *predicate adjective*, *adverb*, or *prepositional phrase*.

1. The robin, **sitting in a tree**, was a sign of spring.

2. **Appearing angry**, my father left the room.

3. **Painting the wall**, my aunt sneezed.

4. Greg said, **grinning broadly**, "Yes, I can!"

5. Alan, **becoming a chef**, loved food.

Mia's drawing ability is amazing!

REVIEW

Look at the participle or participle phrase in bold. Decide whether it acts as an *adjective* or is part of a *verb phrase*.

1. **Speaking quietly**, the girl introduced the song.

2. Sam typed his report **written about the Civil War**.

3. Willa has **played the piano** since she was three.

4. My brother's band is **playing Saturday night**.

5. **Sleeping soundly**, Brenna dreamed of world peace.

Write the participle or participle phrase in each sentence. Then write the noun that it describes.

6. Driving across the country, Julie and her cousin became good friends.

7. Seattle was their chosen goal.

8. They drove through mountains covered in snow.

9. They drove through Las Vegas, shining in the desert.

10. After two weeks, Seattle was welcoming!

PUTTING IT ALL TOGETHER

Think about one of your favorite things to do. It might be reading, writing, playing sports, or dancing. Write a letter to a friend or a relative. Tell him or her about the time you spend doing this activity. Use infinitive, gerund, and participle phrases in your sentences.

Six Traits of Writing:

Voice the writer's own language

Completing a Job Application

Jason Brock wanted a job at a movie theater. He applied for a job. The manager asked him to fill out an application form. On the form, he answered questions about his education. He answered questions about his past jobs. Other questions asked about what kind of worker Jason is.

Read part of the application form that Jason filled out. Then follow the directions below it.

Q: *What do you think you will like most about this job?*

A: I will like meeting other people and gaining work experience.

Q: *What are your best qualities?*

A: Being on time is important to me. I like to be busy. Completing a task feels good.

Q: *How do you keep track of details?*

A: I make organized lists to remember details.

1. List all of the verbals and verbal phrases in Jason's answers.

2. After each one you listed, write one of these: *infinitive phrase*, *gerund phrase*, or *participle*.

3. CRITICAL THINKING Read Jason's last answer. How can you change it so that all of the verbal phrases are the same type?

SPEAKING AND LISTENING

Work with a partner. Imagine that you are trying to get a job at a store. Your partner is the store owner and asks you questions. Answer the questions carefully and completely. Now switch roles. Listen for verbals and verbal phrases in your partner's answers.

Using a Biographical Dictionary

Suppose your teacher asks you to research a famous person. You need to find facts about the person's life. You might begin by looking in a biographical dictionary. A biography is a life story. A biographical dictionary contains short life stories of famous people. The entries in a biographical dictionary are arranged in alphabetical order by last name.

Here is the entry for César Chávez from a biographical dictionary. Read it and then follow the directions.

Chávez, César Estrada

César Chávez (SHAH vehz) was born in 1927 on a farm in Arizona. He was ten when his parents had to sell their farm to pay their bills. They became traveling farm workers. As Chávez grew up, he wanted to help farm workers have better lives. In 1962, he helped grape pickers in California get better working conditions. In the same year, he started the National Farm Workers Association. Until his death in 1993, Chávez spent his life improving the lives of others.

1. Find three infinitive phrases in the entry.

2. Write the part of speech of each phrase you found.

3. CRITICAL THINKING Think of a gerund phrase that would make a good title for a report on César Chávez.

MEDIA

When someone dies, the news often appears in a local newspaper. The article is called an obituary. It announces the person's death. It usually includes a short biography. It is often interesting to see what a newspaper writes about a person at this point. Find the obituary section in a newspaper at home. Cut out an obituary of an interesting person. Underline any verbals. Bring the article to class.

CHAPTER 12

SUMMARY

- Use verbals that act as other parts of speech in sentences.

- Form an infinitive with *to* and the present tense or present perfect tense of a verb.

- Form an infinitive phrase with an infinitive and words that complete its meaning.

- Use infinitives and infinitive phrases as nouns, adjectives, or adverbs.

- Use gerunds in your sentences. Gerunds are verb forms ending in *-ing* that are used as nouns.

- Use gerunds with words that complete their meaning to make gerund phases.

- Use gerunds as subjects and direct objects. Also, use them as objects of prepositions and as predicate nouns.

- Form a participle phrase with a participle and words that complete its meaning.

- Use participles and participle phrases as adjectives in your sentences.

GROUP ACTIVITY

Work in a small group. List four things that a teenager should think about before taking a part-time job. Use complete sentences. Use infinitives, gerunds, and participles.

Then trade lists with another group. Suggest ways that the other group can improve its list.

Word Bank

complement

gerund

gerund phrase

infinitive phrase

participle

participle phrase

verbal

verbal phrase

Part A Write the word or words from the Word Bank that complete each sentence.

1. A _____ is a verb used as a noun, adjective, or adverb.

2. A _____ is a verb ending in *-ing* that is used as a noun.

3. A participle and its complements are called a _____.

4. A _____ is a word or phrase that completes the meaning of a verbal.

5. An infinitive, its complements, and any other words that describe it are an _____.

6. A _____ is a verb that can be used as an adjective.

7. A _____ is a gerund and its complements.

8. A verbal and its complements form a _____.

Part B Write the infinitive phrase in each sentence.

9. Nathan has decided to buy a new CD.

10. His parents used to listen to records.

11. In 1979, CDs began to be popular.

12. Records began to disappear from music stores.

13. Some people now visit garage sales to look for old records.

14. Some search the Internet to find sellers of records.

15. Dario might start to collect record albums.

Part C Write the gerund phrase in each sentence.

16. People began traveling into space in 1957.

17. The United States played a big role in exploring space.

18. President Kennedy made traveling to the moon a national goal.

19. Reaching that goal happened in 1969.

20. In 1969, Americans celebrated Neil Armstrong's walking on the moon.

21. Space shuttles began making trips into space in 1981.

22. Landing humans on Mars is a major goal today.

Part D Write the letter of your answer.

23. Which sentence contains a participle phrase?
    A Maurice sings every day.
    B He loves to sing in the shower.
    C Singing loudly, he wakes his sister.
    D She yells, "Please stop singing!"

24. Which sentence contains a participle phrase?
    A The train is arriving at noon.
    B Arriving early is a good idea.
    C Selena is always early.
    D People arriving late have to stand.

25. Which sentence contains a participle phrase?
    A The dress, sewn with care, fit perfectly.
    B The dressmaker used a new pattern.
    C Have you ever sewn something?
    D Sewing is fun.

Test Tip

Read test questions carefully. Look for questions that have more than one part.

Writing Paragraphs

Sometimes you can express an idea in one sentence. Often, though, one sentence is not enough. You need a group of sentences to express an idea. A group of sentences on one topic is a paragraph.

Look at the photo of a large neighborhood. If each house is like a word, then each street is like a sentence. Many streets make a neighborhood or a town. Many sentences make a paragraph.

A paragraph is made of three parts. Every paragraph has a topic sentence, supporting sentences, and a conclusion. In Chapter 13, you will learn how to write a paragraph.

GOALS FOR LEARNING

- To write a paragraph with its three parts
- To write a topic sentence
- To write sentences that support the topic sentence
- To write a conclusion to end a paragraph

Reading Strategy: Inferencing

Sometimes the meaning of what you read is not directly stated in the words. You have to make an inference to figure out what the meaning is. An inference is a guess or conclusion about the meaning of what you read. It is based on what you already know and on what you read.

What You Know + What You Read = Inference

To make inferences, you have to think "outside" the words you read. Predicting what will happen can help you make inferences. Making connections between ideas as you read can also help.

Key Vocabulary Words

Paragraph A group of sentences about one idea

Indent To start a sentence a certain distance from the left margin

Topic sentence A sentence that states the main idea of a paragraph; usually the first sentence in a paragraph

Body The sentences in a paragraph that explain and support the main idea

Conclusion A statement that summarizes a paragraph, restates the main idea, or states an opinion that logically follows the paragraph's details

Prewriting Preparing to write; the planning step of the writing process

What Is a Paragraph?

A **paragraph** is a group of sentences about one idea. Every paragraph has one main idea. You use paragraphs to give order to your ideas. Paragraphs make ideas clear and easy to follow.

Indent the first line of each paragraph. To indent means to start the line a certain distance from the left margin. Margins are the edges of the writing on a page.

Parts of a Paragraph

A paragraph has three parts. A **topic sentence** states the main idea of the paragraph. The **body** of the paragraph explains and supports the main idea. The body is usually two or more sentences. The **conclusion** is a statement that summarizes the paragraph.

▶ **EXAMPLE 1**

People use computers for many purposes. People play games on their computers. People use computers to do homework. People use computers to send e-mail messages. A computer is a very useful tool.

The three parts of the paragraph in Example 1 are shown below.

▶ **EXAMPLE 2**

Topic Sentence — People use computers for many purposes.

Body — People play games on their computers. People use computers to do homework. People use computers to send e-mail messages.

Conclusion — A computer is a very useful tool.

The Main Idea of a Paragraph

Each sentence in a paragraph must relate to the main idea. Read Example 3. Each sentence is about one main idea.

▶ **EXAMPLE 3**

Poetry slams are becoming popular throughout the United States. A slam is a contest in which poets read their poetry. Volunteers judge the readings. They give each poem a score from 1 to 10. A poetry slam is like an Olympic event for poets.

The main idea of this paragraph might be stated like this: Poetry slams are popular contests for poets.

Practice A

Read each paragraph. Then write its main idea.

1.   Skiing is a popular sport. Many northern states have ski resorts. Thousands of people ski every day in the winter months. If there is not enough snow, the resorts use machines to make snow. Skiing is a big business.

2.   No one knows what happened to Amelia Earhart. She was a pilot. She flew alone across the Atlantic Ocean. In 1937, she took off to fly around the world. Her plane disappeared over the Pacific Ocean. She was never found.

3.   On the first warm day of spring, golfers drag out their clubs and find their golf shoes. They head to the nearest golf course. Now they take a practice swing and make their first drive of the season. They have been waiting all winter for this day.

4.   Did you hear about the mayor who put his city on a diet? He noticed that many people were overweight. He declared a citywide cutback on fattening foods. He asked citizens to exercise more and eat less. "We all need a healthier lifestyle," he said.

Practice B

Read each paragraph. Write the sentence that does *not* belong.

1. Camels can go without water for a long time. They can drink large amounts of water. Desert travelers also use horses. Camels do not lose water because they sweat very little. Camels are perfectly suited to dry regions.

2. There are many kinds of berries. Blueberries and strawberries are the most popular. A boysenberry is a cross between a blackberry, a raspberry, and a loganberry. Oddly, lemons and oranges also are berries. Orange juice is often served at breakfast. Which kind of berry is your favorite?

3. Many people today can work at home. Computers come in all shapes and sizes. Phone calls, faxes, and e-mails allow people to communicate. Conference calls let them have meetings without leaving home. Technology has helped many workers to do their jobs from home.

4. Many people are more afraid of sharks than of lightning. They should be more afraid of lightning. In the United States, the risk of death from lightning is 30 times greater than that from shark. There are 350 different kinds of sharks. Take the necessary precautions to be safe during lightning storms.

5. Many libraries have book clubs. Book club members choose a book to read. Each month they meet to talk about it. They share ideas and opinions. I really liked the book I finished last week. These discussions increase everyone's understanding and appreciation of the book. A book club can make your reading more meaningful and enjoyable.

NOTE

The topic of a paragraph must not be too broad. It must be something you can explain in several sentences. For example, it would take a whole book to write about *the history of music in America*. But you could write just one paragraph about *why you like a certain kind of music*.

Reading Strategy:
Inferencing

How does this lesson add to what you already know about paragraphs?

Prewriting

Before you can write a paragraph, you have some work to do. You need to choose a topic and a main idea. You need to gather the supporting details. All of this work is called **prewriting**. Prewriting is the planning step in the writing process. Follow these guidelines to plan a paragraph:

1. Read your writing directions carefully. Make sure you understand the assignment. The directions often tell you the purpose and length of your writing. They may provide the topic or main idea, too.

2. If you are not given a topic to write about, choose one that you are interested in. How do you think of a topic? Get ideas from your past experiences and from what you have read, seen, or discussed recently.

3. Choose the main idea of the paragraph. This is a statement about the topic. The main idea might express your opinion about the topic.

4. Finally, make a list of possible details to put in the body. For some topics, you may need to do research to find these details. Details can be facts, reasons, explanations, examples, experiences, or descriptions.

▶ **EXAMPLE 4**

Topic	Andrew Lloyd Webber
Main Idea	Andrew Lloyd Webber composed several popular musical plays.
Details	He composed *The Phantom of the Opera* and *Cats*. He also wrote *Evita*. One of his best-known songs is "Don't Cry for Me, Argentina."

Practice C

Imagine that you are going to write a paragraph about your favorite hobby or sport. Write the topic. Next, write the main idea. Then write at least three details to include in the paragraph.

REVIEW

Read the paragraph. Then answer each question.

   Tennis is harder to play than most people think. It takes both strength and speed. You must take the time to learn different shots. You must practice almost every day in order to improve. Clearly, tennis is a challenging sport.

1. What did the writer need to know in order to write the paragraph?

2. What is the main idea?

3. How many sentences make up the body of the paragraph?

4. What is the conclusion of the paragraph?

5. Two important words in the paragraph mean almost the same thing. One is in the topic sentence. The other is in the conclusion. What are the two words?

SPELLING BUILDER

Using Spelling Checkers

An electronic spelling checker is a great tool, but it can miss mistakes. For example, a spelling checker may not catch these mistakes in bold:

   They thought the dog was **there's**.
   He can come **two**.
   This **pear** of sentences can be combined.

Think of three other spelling mistakes that a spelling checker might not catch. Then test them on a computer.

Topic Sentences

Objectives

■ To identify the topic sentence of a paragraph

■ To write a topic sentence

Reading Strategy:
Inferencing

What do you already know about topic sentences?

In the last lesson, you learned that a topic sentence states the main idea of a paragraph. A topic sentence says what a paragraph is about. When your readers start to read a new paragraph, they expect to find a new idea. The topic sentence helps readers know what to expect. Usually, the topic sentence is the first sentence of a paragraph. The sentences in the body of the paragraph support the topic sentence.

▶ **EXAMPLE 1**

The first time my sister and I saw snow, we made snow angels. Fresh snow covered the ground. We lay down in the white stuff. Then we waved our arms and legs back and forth. Afterward, we stood up and admired our snow angels. We laughed at the tingling feeling of the cold snow and said, "Let's make some more!"

Practice A

Reread Example 1. Write a different topic sentence that expresses the same main idea?

A topic sentence is a general statement. It does not have details. Details appear in the body of the paragraph. Read Example 2. The first sentence is the topic sentence.

▶ **EXAMPLE 2**

Springfield is a pleasant place to live. The weather is beautiful most of the year. The town has many parks, stores, museums, and restaurants. The people are friendly and helpful. Springfield citizens are proud of their town.

Read each pair of sentences. One is the topic sentence of a paragraph. The other one is a supporting detail from the same paragraph. Write the letter of the topic sentence.

1. **A** Car owners must check their oil.
   B Car owners need to check their cars regularly.

2. **A** A topic sentence has two main jobs.
   B A topic sentence prepares readers for a new idea.

3. **A** Some go to college right after high school.
   B High school seniors have many decisions to make.

4. **A** Baseball has a long history.
   B The earliest games were played in the 1830s.

5. **A** Dogs are obedient and loyal.
   B Dogs make wonderful pets.

Read the three facts about a famous American painter. If they were used as supporting details in a paragraph, what might the topic sentence be? Write a possible topic sentence.

- Georgia O'Keeffe painted flowers and scenes from the American Southwest.
- New Mexico was the subject of many of her paintings.
- She died in 1986 at the age of 98.

Reading Strategy:
Inferencing

After reading a paragraph, look back at the topic sentence. What is the main idea of this paragraph?

Grammar Tip

Use *a* or *an* when naming a general person, place, or thing. Use *the* when naming a particular person, place, or thing. *An acorn fell in the birdbath.*

To write a topic sentence, think about the main idea you want to express about the topic. Notice how each topic in Example 3 is developed into a topic sentence.

▶ **EXAMPLE 3**

Topic	Topic Sentence
local police	Our police department helps the community in many ways.
hiking	Before you go hiking, you will need some equipment.
rap music	Rap music is a kind of poetry.

Practice E

Write a topic sentence about each topic.

1. sleep

2. a person you know

3. an easy food to make

4. your favorite place

5. a movie you like

Rob knows all about taking photos. For a writing assignment, he chose to write about digital camera features.

REVIEW

Each paragraph below is missing a topic sentence. Write a topic sentence that states the main idea of the paragraph.

1. It used to be unusual to live to be 90. Better foods and medicines have made 90 a more common age. Today, some people even live to be well over 100.

2. If you can sit down, you can go snow tubing. You need no special skills. Just grab the handles and hold on! Also, you do not need much equipment. All you need is a snow tube and warm clothes. Snow tubing is a fun winter activity for all ages.

3. Dogs need to be fed once or twice a day. They need clean water. They also need exercise, love, and attention. Most dogs need baths every few weeks. The love that dogs give back is worth all the work.

4. Libraries have books on different topics. They also have magazines and newspapers. Most libraries have computers that you can use. They also have videos, CDs, and DVDs that you can check out. Libraries are excellent resources of information.

5. You can see houses that were built in the 1700s. You can see the Old North Church. You can see where Paul Revere and Samuel Adams are buried. You can also see tall skyscrapers and new, modern hotels. The huge, new Boston Garden is home to basketball and hockey teams. If you want to see both the past and the present, visit Boston.

Imagine that you are going to write a paragraph about each topic below. Write a topic sentence for each one.

6. how to relax

7. school vacation

8. your favorite snack

9. air travel

10. your neighborhood

Supporting Details

Objectives

■ To develop the body of a paragraph

■ To write sentences that explain and support the main idea

What do you do after you have stated your main idea in a topic sentence? The next step is to support that main idea. The sentences that tell more about the main idea make up the body of a paragraph. The body is the place for details. In the body, you prove or show that your main idea is true.

▶ **EXAMPLE 1**

The speed of airplanes has changed greatly over the years. In North Carolina in 1903, the Wright brothers flew the first airplane. It flew for a few seconds at 30 miles per hour. By the 1920s, a small plane could fly about 135 miles per hour. The first jet reached 500 miles per hour in the 1950s. By the 1970s, supersonic jets were flying 1,200 miles per hour. Who knows how fast airplanes will fly in this century?

Reading Strategy:
Inferencing

Who, what, where, when, why, and *how* are called "reporters' words." Why do you think this is so?

Supporting details often answer the questions who, what, where, when, or why.

Who were the first people to fly an airplane? the Wright brothers

Where did the first plane fly? in North Carolina

When did the first jets fly? in the 1950s

How fast do jets fly today? about 1,200 miles per hour

Practice A

Copy the paragraph. Underline each supporting detail.

The new amusement park in town has many exciting rides. The roller coaster goes in a complete circle. The triple Ferris wheel is the tallest in the world. On a ride called the Drop, people feel like they are falling. The park is sure to thrill all who visit.

Supporting details can include facts, examples, reasons, descriptions, experiences, and quotations.

- A fact is something known to be true.
- An example is something that shows what the rest are like.
- A reason answers the question why.
- A description is a picture in words.
- An experience is someone's story.
- A quotation is someone else's words in quotation marks.

Reading Strategy:
Inferencing

The paragraph in Example 2 includes many facts. These details support the topic sentence by proving that the people who laughed were wrong.

▶ **EXAMPLE 2**

Many people laughed when the United States bought Alaska in 1867. Today, Alaska sends gas and oil to other parts of the United States. It offers some of the best fishing in the world. Alaska has more than 100 million acres of forested lands. There is gold in Alaska. Its rivers provide electric power. Alaska turned out to be a good buy.

Practice B

Write the topic sentence below. Then use the details about Springfield to write three supporting sentences.

Topic Sentence: Springfield is a great place to have fun.

Details:
- four city parks
- a sports arena
- a concert hall
- three basketball courts
- two swimming pools
- two golf courses
- nine tennis courts
- a museum
- an amusement park
- five movie theaters

Sometimes, writers make mistakes. They include details that do not support the topic sentence. When you write a paragraph, leave out unrelated details. If you find them in something you have written, take them out.

Practice C

Read the paragraph. Write the sentence that does not belong. Then write why it does not belong in the paragraph.

Our camping trip was awful! We froze all night and chased away bugs all day. No one caught a single fish! We enjoyed hiking through the woods. It took us an hour to start a fire. Then we burned the dinner. The strong winds blew down two tents. On top of it all, it rained. I am sure that is our last camping trip.

Many people like to camp because of the beautiful surroundings.

REVIEW

Read each paragraph. Write the topic sentence of each one. Then write the one sentence in each paragraph that does not support the main idea.

1. Bird watching is a popular outdoor activity. National parks are good places to do it. Trained guides teach visitors about different kinds of birds. Bird-watchers learn what birds look like and sound like. The Audubon Society is an organization that helps protect birds. Many people become hooked on bird watching after just one try.

2. Regular exercise keeps a person fit. People who exercise feel better and probably live longer. Exercise also helps people keep to a healthy weight. It makes the heart and lungs stronger. After people exercise, they will probably be sore and tired. Everyone should try to exercise every day.

3. Novels are popular for several reasons. A novel keeps people reading for a long time. It has many characters and events. Readers imagine all the events. They feel like they know the people. They can lose themselves in the story. They can't wait to see what happens. Poetry is also fun to read. Choose a novel to read tonight!

Write a short paragraph on each main idea. Use facts, examples, reasons, and descriptions to support the main idea. Each paragraph should have four or five sentences.

4. Music is important to teenagers.

5. Before you accept a job, consider these questions.

Conclusions

The last sentence in a paragraph is the conclusion. It announces the end. The conclusion wraps up the paragraph by doing one or more of these things:

- It may summarize the details in the paragraph.
- It may restate the main idea in slightly different words.
- It may give an opinion that logically follows the details in the paragraph.

A strong conclusion helps the reader remember what the paragraph was about.

▶ **EXAMPLE 1**

Since I started using a computer, writing is not such a chore. I can add and take out words. I can correct mistakes. I can even move sentences around. I can use the spelling checker. I do not need erasers. I do not have to recopy what I have written. A computer makes writing a lot easier.

Cal shows Erin how to use the spelling checker on his computer.

Write a conclusion for each paragraph.

1. For many people, drawing is a relaxing hobby. They enjoy using their imaginations. They like being creative. Each person can draw what he or she sees.

2. Camping is one way that people enjoy the outdoors. Campers have to take care of nature, though. They should always stay on paths when hiking. They should put out any fires they build. Campers should not dig up or pick plants. They should not feed animals. They should clean their campsites.

3. The Internet is a useful tool. It has information about current events. You can learn about many topics on the Internet. You can buy and sell products online. You can also communicate with people around the world.

4. It is important to protect yourself from the sun. To prevent sunburn, you should use sunscreen with an SPF of at least 15. SPF stands for sun protection factor. When you go to the beach, you should wear a hat. It is also a good idea to wear sunglasses.

5. Many people confuse alligators with crocodiles. An alligator has a wider, shorter mouth. The mouth of a crocodile is long and narrow. Both animals are reptiles. Both animals live in water.

VOCABULARY BUILDER

Understanding Blended Words

Have you ever been invited to *brunch*? The word brunch is a blend of breakfast and lunch. There are several blended words in English. More are being formed every day. Use a dictionary to find the two words that blend to make each of these words:

1. motel　　2. smog　　3. camcorder　　4. blog

REVIEW

Write a conclusion for each paragraph.

1. Angela thinks swimming is the best exercise. Very few swimmers become injured. Swimming tones many muscles at the same time. It is good for the heart. Many neighborhoods have swimming pools.

2. Most people recognize the Statue of Liberty. The statue was a gift from France. It has stood in New York Harbor for more than 100 years. It has a poem on it. The poem welcomes people to the United States.

3. Everyone should have emergency supplies. People can use them in case of a disaster. The supplies should include a flashlight and a first-aid kit. They should also include food and water.

Write a paragraph about each topic. Begin with a clear topic sentence. Include two or three supporting details. End with a good conclusion.

4. your favorite color

5. your favorite book

PUTTING IT ALL TOGETHER

At the end of the Lesson 13-2 Review on page 337, you wrote some topic sentences. Choose one of them to begin a short paragraph. Write the topic sentence. Write two or three sentences of details to support the topic sentence. End the paragraph with a strong conclusion.

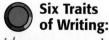

Six Traits of Writing:

Ideas message, details, and purpose

Writing a To-Do List

Tammy Garcia is leading the school talent show. She will also be the show's announcer. She has many things to do before the show. She is worried that she will not remember them all!

Tammy wrote a to-do list. It helps her remember her tasks. It also helps her put them in order. The most important tasks are first on the list. When she finishes a task, she checks it off her list.

Read Tammy's list. Then follow the directions below.

To-Do List

1. Make a list of the acts in the show.

2. Give the final list to the printer.

3. Write opening comments.

4. Write notes to introduce each act.

5. Write notes to close the show.

3. CRITICAL THINKING How might a to-do list help you in school?

SPEAKING AND LISTENING

People write to-do lists to remember the tasks they need to do. Make a to-do list for yourself. Write at least five tasks on it. Then get together with a partner. Read each other's lists. Ask each other questions about the tasks. Discuss which task on each list is most important. Which one should be done first?

1. Suppose the items on Tammy's list are used to write the body of a paragraph. Write a topic sentence for this paragraph.

2. Write a conclusion for this paragraph.

BUILDING RESEARCH SKILLS

Using Periodicals

Periodicals are magazines, newspapers, and journals. They are usually published daily, weekly, or monthly. They often have more up-to-date information than books. Some Web sites are online periodicals. They have new information and articles every day.

A magazine usually focuses on one subject, such as history, sports, health, travel, or a hobby. Magazines are written to inform and entertain their readers. A journal usually reports on scientific research or presents ideas related to a certain type of job.

Read this paragraph from a travel magazine. Then follow the directions.

FIESTA TIME!

"Fiesta San Antonio" is held each year in San Antonio, Texas. It is a citywide party that honors the heroes of Texas history. The fiesta lasts 10 days. It has more than 100 events. At the fiesta, you will learn about San Antonio's history.

San Antonio

1. Think of a better topic sentence for the paragraph. Write one that is interesting and will grab the reader's attention.

2. Write a conclusion for the paragraph.

3. CRITICAL THINKING This paragraph is from a travel magazine. What other kind of magazine might also include this information?

MEDIA

Advertisements, or ads, sell products and services. You find many ads in periodicals. You also find them on the Internet and on TV. Choose a product you would like to sell. Write a paragraph for an ad for the product.

SUMMARY

- Group sentences about the same idea into a paragraph.

- Prepare to write a paragraph by first choosing a topic that interests you. Then decide on the main idea and list the details you want to include.

- Indent the first line of every paragraph.

- Write a topic sentence that tells the main idea of the paragraph. It should be a general statement that does not include details.

- Develop the body of a paragraph by giving details that support the main idea.

- Write supporting sentences that answer *who, what, where, when, why,* and *how.*

- Use details such as facts, examples, reasons, experiences, quotations, and descriptions to support the topic sentence.

- Delete any sentence that does not support the topic sentence.

- End a paragraph with a conclusion. This sentence should summarize the details in the paragraph or restate the main idea. It may also leave the reader with an opinion.

GROUP ACTIVITY

With a group, create a travel brochure about the city or region where you live. Write a paragraph about the area's most interesting places. These might be historic sites, parks, or museums. Explain why someone should visit the area. Decorate your brochure with drawings or photos.

Word Bank

body

conclusion

indent

paragraph

prewriting

topic sentence

Part A Write the word or words from the Word Bank that complete each sentence.

1. A group of sentences about one idea is a _____.

2. The _____ tells the main idea of the paragraph.

3. The work you do before you write is called _____.

4. A _____ comes at the end of a paragraph.

5. To _____ a paragraph, start the first line a certain distance from the left margin.

6. The _____ of a paragraph explains and supports the main idea with details.

Part B Read the paragraph. Use it to answer items 7–10.

Ms. Lentz is always cheerful and friendly. She owns a gas station. I like to stop by her home to visit. She invites me in for a snack. We always have fascinating conversations. A visit with Ms. Lentz brightens my day.

7. What is the main idea of this paragraph?

8. Which sentence does not support the main idea?

9. How are the topic sentence and conclusion alike?

10. How are the topic sentence and conclusion different?

Part C Write a topic sentence and a conclusion for each paragraph.

11. Derek runs five miles every day. He has won three races already. He runs short races and long ones. Derek will continue to improve his time.

12. The air smells pleasant and clean. Flowers and trees are budding. Birds are nesting. The temperature rises. Insects fill the air.

Part D Read the paragraph. Use it to answer items 13–16.

Many games and sports that people play today came from other countries. For example, chess began in India. Pickup-sticks came from China. Football was invented in the United States. Football is more exciting than baseball. The Dutch invented bowling. The French were the first to play tennis. Games and sports come from all over the world!

13. What is the main idea of this paragraph?

14. What is the conclusion?

15. How many examples are given in the body?

16. Which sentence does not belong in the paragraph?

Part E Read the paragraph. Then answer items 17–20.

Habitat for Humanity is a group that builds houses for people in need. Costs are low because volunteers do the work. The homeowners also help with the project. There are many groups that feed the hungry. Many people give time and money to this worthy cause.

17. *Habitat for Humanity is a group that builds houses for people in need.* This sentence is _____.
A the topic sentence   C not related to the paragraph
B the conclusion   D part of the body

18. *There are many groups that feed the hungry.* This sentence is _____.
A the topic sentence   C not related to the paragraph
B the conclusion   D part of the body

19. *Costs are low because volunteers do the work.* This sentence is _____.
A the topic sentence   C not related to the paragraph
B the conclusion   D part of the body

20. Write a different conclusion for this paragraph.

Understanding Purposes for Writing

Honk! There are a lot of drivers in this photo. Each one is going to a certain place with a certain purpose. The driver of the school bus has a different purpose than the driver of a car. The driver of a minivan has a different purpose than the driver of a truck.

Every paragraph you write has a purpose. Sometimes you write to present facts. Sometimes you write to explain an idea or to tell what happened and why. Sometimes you write to tell readers how to do something. At other times, you write to express an opinion. For all of these purposes, you use paragraphs to organize your ideas.

In Chapter 14, you will learn about some common purposes for writing. You will also practice writing paragraphs for different purposes.

GOALS FOR LEARNING

- To write a paragraph that informs or explains
- To write a paragraph that persuades
- To write a paragraph that describes someone or something
- To write a paragraph that tells a story
- To write dialogue

Reading Strategy: Metacognition

Metacognition means "thinking about your thinking." Before you read something, scan the words and think about what you already know about the topic. As you read, pay attention to your thinking. Keep track of what you learn. Write down main ideas and details. If something does not make sense, stop and read it again.

Key Vocabulary Words

Inform To pass along information, especially facts

Cause and effect Something that happens (effect) because of something else (cause)

Compare To point out how two things are alike or different

Fact A piece of information that is known to be true

Opinion The way a person thinks about something; a belief or viewpoint

Persuade To convince someone to agree with an opinion, an idea, or a request; to change someone's opinion about something

Advertisement A message designed to attract the public's attention; also called an ad

Advertiser A person who uses an advertisement to sell a product or service

Fiction A piece of writing about imaginary people and events

Nonfiction A piece of writing about real people and actual events

Point of view The position of the storyteller in a story; either first-person or third-person point of view

Chronological order An arrangement of events according to time; usually from the earliest event to the most recent event

Dialogue The words that people or story characters say to one another; conversation

Direct quotation A quotation that reports someone's exact words; quotation marks are required

Quotation marks (" ") The marks placed at the beginning and end of a direct quotation

Indirect quotation A quotation that reports what someone said without using the speaker's exact words; quotation marks are not used

Writing to Inform or Explain

Objectives

- To write a paragraph that informs
- To write a paragraph that explains
- To write a paragraph that compares
- To write a paragraph that teaches

Inform

To pass along information, especially facts

Reading Strategy:
Metacognition

Look at the lesson titles in this chapter. How are they alike? How are they different?

Paragraphs That Inform

You learned that sentences have different purposes. Paragraphs have different purposes, too. The most common purpose of a paragraph is to **inform**, or to pass on information. When you write a paragraph that informs, you tell your readers about something you know. You support your topic sentence with details such as facts and examples.

▶ **EXAMPLE 1**

Kiribati is a small island country. It is made up of 33 islands in the Pacific Ocean. Kiribati covers just 266 square miles. It has about 105,000 people. It is about halfway between Hawaii and Australia. Kiribati has a hot, rainy climate. English is the official language of the country. Many coconut trees grow on Kiribati. This small island nation would be an interesting place to visit.

Practice A

Answer these questions about the paragraph in Example 1.

1. What is the topic of this paragraph?
2. Which sentence is the topic sentence?
3. What are three facts that support the topic sentence?
4. What is the conclusion?
5. Write a different conclusion.

Writing Tip

Good writers use details. For example, instead of just writing the sentence *Birds build nests,* you could give rich details about birds and nests. How do birds build nests? What do they build them out of? How long does it take? How big are the nests?

Reading Strategy:
Metacognition

You will not always understand something the first time you read it. Good readers will reread what they do not understand.

Paragraphs That Explain

A paragraph may explain something. Usually, this kind of paragraph answers the question *why* or *how*. Sometimes, the topic is something that happened (an effect). The paragraph explains why it happened (the cause). It explains a **cause and effect** relationship: something happened because of something else.

In the body of this kind of paragraph, you can use words like *because, so,* and *since.* These words help point to causes.

The paragraph in Example 2 answers this question: Why do so many people visit national parks? The paragraph answers *why* by giving facts and examples.

▶ **EXAMPLE 2**

National parks are very popular. These parks offer a change from people's usual lives. They provide a chance to get back to nature. Visitors see many birds and other wildlife. They see trees and wildflowers. National parks are often free or cost very little to enjoy. Everyone enjoys a break from day-to-day life, so they love to visit national parks.

Practice B

Choose one of the questions below. Write a paragraph to answer it. Start with a topic sentence. Include facts and examples. End with a conclusion.

- Why should you dress well when you are applying for a job?
- How did your family come to live in this town or city?
- Why do people visit amusement parks?

Compare

To point out how two things are alike or different

Paragraphs That Compare

When you **compare,** you show how two things are alike or different. Usually, the two subjects are alike in big ways. They are different in small ways. A paragraph that compares can show both.

▶ **EXAMPLE 3**

> Modern cars are much better than earlier cars. In the early days, drivers had to crank up a car just to get it going. Today, a turn of the key makes an engine roar. Modern cars can easily go 60 miles per hour. Early cars were racing at 30 miles per hour. Today's drivers expect to get where they are going. However, early drivers never knew for sure if their cars would make it. One thing has not changed: cars are definitely faster than walking!

Practice C

Write a paragraph about one of these topics.

- Compare two animals.
- Compare summer and winter.
- Compare two movies.
- Compare in-line skates and ice skates.

I think in-line skating is easier than ice skating.

Grammar Tip

Remember that adverbs and adverb phrases tell more about actions. Look at these sentences for example:

Press *evenly*.

Stir *for two minutes*.

Sew *using tiny stitches*.

Paragraphs That Teach

A how-to paragraph teaches the reader how to do or make something. The order of the details is usually important. In a how-to paragraph, use words such as *first*, *second*, *next*, *now*, *then*, and *finally*. They show the order of steps that the reader should follow. Also use adverbs and adverb phrases. They make your directions specific and clear.

▶ **EXAMPLE 4**

Bake a cake—it's easy! First, read the directions on the cake mix box. Gather everything you will need: water, oil, eggs, a baking pan, a mixing bowl, and a measuring cup. Next, turn on the oven to the desired temperature. Then measure the water and oil and combine them with the eggs. Add the cake mix. Beat the batter with an electric mixer or a hand beater. Finally, pour the batter into the cake pan and pop it in the oven. Set a timer. In less than an hour, the cake will be ready to enjoy.

Practice D

Read the how-to paragraph in Example 4. Then answer these questions.

1. What is the topic of this paragraph?

2. What does the writer do to encourage the reader?

3. What words help to show the order of the steps?

4. What is the final step in baking the cake?

5. What is another conclusion that could close the paragraph?

REVIEW

Read the paragraph. Write the answer to each question.

Sometimes you have to write about a famous person. You may want to get information from *Who's Who*. This commonly used book can be found at any library. *Who's Who* lists the names of famous living people in alphabetical order. You will find a short paragraph about each person. This paragraph gives a few facts about the person's life. *Who's Who* gives a little information about many people.

1. What is the main idea of this paragraph?

2. What are three facts you learned about *Who's Who*?

3. What is the purpose of this paragraph?

Follow each set of writing directions to write a paragraph. Introduce the main idea in your first sentence. Write three or four sentences that contain supporting details. End with a good conclusion.

4. Write a paragraph that explains one of the following:

   - how to study for a test
   - how to make a peanut butter and jelly sandwich
   - how to get from your home to school

5. Write a paragraph that answers one of these questions:

   - What happens when you do not get enough sleep?
   - Why would it be good to have a cell phone when you are driving alone?
   - How have computers changed the way our cars are repaired?

Writing to Persuade

Objectives

- To tell the difference between a fact and an opinion
- To write a paragraph that persuades
- To understand how advertising works

Fact

A piece of information that is known to be true

Opinion

The way a person thinks about something; a belief or viewpoint

Reading Strategy:
Metacognition

How are facts and opinions part of your daily life?

Fact or Opinion?

It is important in writing—and in life—to understand facts and opinions. A **fact** is a piece of information that is known to be true. Everyone agrees on facts. An **opinion** is the way a person thinks about something, It is a belief or viewpoint. Some people may believe an opinion is true, but others have different opinions.

▶ **EXAMPLE 1**

Fact	The Empire State Building is in New York City.
Opinion	It is fun to climb the steps of the Empire State Building.

You express an opinion when you use words that show what you like or dislike. These words include *better, best, good, bad, pleasant, unpleasant, poor,* and *great.* You express an opinion when you use words that show what you want or what should happen. These are words such as *should, ought to,* and *must.* You also express an opinion when you use words that predict what will happen. These are words such as *will, shall,* and *is going to.*

Practice A

Write *F* if the sentence is a fact. Write *O* if it is an opinion.

1. Mark Twain was a good writer.
2. Speeding is against the law.
3. Carrots taste better than celery.
4. Tomorrow, the robins will start to fly south.
5. Everyone should drink more milk.

Writing About an Opinion

Do you have a strong opinion? Do you have a good idea? Would you like others to agree with you? Then write to **persuade**. To persuade means to convince someone to agree with you. When you write a paragraph to persuade, keep these points in mind:

- In the topic sentence, clearly state your opinion or idea.
- Use facts, reasons, examples, and experiences to support your opinion.
- Write a conclusion that restates your opinion. The conclusion may also suggest that the reader take a certain action.

Suppose Derek wants to go to Western College. The college wants to know why Derek thinks he should be accepted. Here is Derek's response.

▶ **EXAMPLE 2**

    I deserve to be accepted at Western College. I take part in many high school events. I am on the track team. I want to continue running track in college. I was only a fair student when I began high school. Then I began to challenge myself at the end of my second year. My grades have improved. Now I work hard and take my studies seriously. More than anything, I want to continue my education. I hope you agree that I belong at Western College.

Practice B

Answer these questions about Derek's paragraph.

1. What main idea does Derek state in his topic sentence? Is this main idea a fact or an opinion?

2. What is one fact that supports Derek's main idea?

3. What is one opinion that supports Derek's main idea?

4. Why does Derek mention that his grades improved?

5. What is Derek trying to persuade his readers to do?

Advertisements

Advertisements, or ads, are messages designed to attract attention. They are everywhere. They appear on TV, in magazines, and on signs. The people who create them are **advertisers**. Advertisers combine words and pictures to try to sell a product or service. They try to make you want things you never knew you wanted before. For example, an advertiser might want you to believe that a certain cereal or car will make your life better.

Advertisers do not come out and say, "Buy this. It will make life better." Their message is less direct. For example, an ad might show a pair of athletic shoes with wings. This suggests that the shoes can make you run faster. Another ad might show a man cooking with a certain brand of oil. His children watch him and smile. This ad suggests that people who use that brand of oil have happy families.

Practice C

Cut an ad out of a newspaper or magazine. Study its words and pictures. What is the message of the ad? Summarize the message in one sentence. How convincing is the ad?

REVIEW

Add words to complete the sentence. Each sentence should state your opinion. Write the sentence.

1. I think that this city needs _____.

2. In my opinion, _____ is the best athlete.

3. I think that _____ is a waste of time.

4. I believe that people under age 25 are _____ drivers.

Follow the directions below to write a paragraph that persuades.

5. Choose one of your answers above. Use it as the topic sentence. Write at least three sentences to support your opinion. End your paragraph with a conclusion.

VOCABULARY BUILDER

Using Qualifying Words

When you write, make sure your opinions sound like opinions. Qualifying words can help you do this. They signal that a statement is not a fact. Notice the qualifying words in bold:

It will **probably** rain tomorrow.

Many dogs bark at cars.

Some teachers give too much homework.

Here are some other qualifying words: *sometimes, seems, may, in my opinion, most, I think, might, usually.*

Add qualifying words to the sentences below. Write the new sentences.

1. Police officers do not smile.

2. Teenagers love to dance.

3. Everyone loves Super Smoothies.

Writing to Describe

Objectives

- To write a paragraph that describes
- To write descriptions that appeal to the senses
- To write character descriptions

Reading Strategy:
Metacognition

When you read words that appeal to your senses, try to create a mental picture. Imagine the details.

Sometimes, you want your reader to imagine what you experience. When you write to describe, you paint a picture with words. Your purpose is to describe your topic as clearly as possible. When you write a paragraph that describes, you give details that create a vivid and clear picture in the reader's mind.

▶ **EXAMPLE 1**

The clock in my grandparents' house was old and valuable. When I was ten, the clock was as tall as an adult. It was made of smooth, dark wood. The clock had a white face painted with gold numbers. I called them "fancy numbers" because of their curly ends. Two heavy brass weights hung on chains down the front of the clock. It had loud, strong, even ticks that echoed through the house. Then, each hour, came the long, warm tones of the striking chimes. That old clock was an important part of my childhood.

Practice A

Write a paragraph that describes what you see from where you sit. Start with a topic sentence that lets readers know where you are. In the body of the paragraph, describe only what is right in front of you. End your paragraph with a conclusion.

Language that appeals to the five senses brings writing to life. The five senses are sight, hearing, smell, taste, and touch.

▶ **EXAMPLE 2**

The gently flowing stream seemed to be singing. (hearing)

He walked without shoes on the soft grass. (touch)

Practice B

Write a sentence that appeals to each one of the senses:
sight, *hearing*, *smell*, *taste*, and *touch*. After each sentence,
write the sense it appeals to.

Describing People and Characters

Sometimes, you need to describe a person. You may be
asked to describe a character from a book. You might want
to describe a real person you know. When you describe a
person, think about what he or she looks like. Think about
what he or she sounds like. Think about how he or she
acts.

▶ **EXAMPLE 3**

Connie entered the room with a jangle of bracelets
and a tinkling of bells. She had bright pink hair. She wore
matching pink, shiny eye shadow. She was in the room only
a moment. Then she was gone, leaving sweet perfume
hanging in the air.

Practice C

Think of a person you know well. Write a paragraph to
describe him or her. Use the list below to help you write
the details. You do not have to describe every item on the
list.

- hair
- eyes
- nose
- mouth
- skin
- height

- usual clothing
- what he or she likes to do
- what he or she does not like to do
- how he or she acts around others
- something unusual about him or her
- something he or she might say

REVIEW

Write each sentence on your paper. Underline the words that appeal to one of the senses. Write *sight, hearing, smell, taste,* or *touch.* Each sentence may appeal to more than one sense.

1. The clouds floated across the sky like huge balls of cotton.

2. The smell of the fresh bread made my mouth water.

3. From our camp, we could hear rocks crashing down the mountain.

4. The doctor placed ice packs around Lisa's aching knee.

5. The children laughed as several ducks quacked.

Write a sentence describing each item. Use words that appeal to the reader's hearing, smell, taste, or touch.

6. a barn

7. a busy street corner

8. a library

9. a park

10. a meal

Writing to Tell a Story

Objectives

- To identify fiction and nonfiction
- To write a paragraph that tells a story
- To identify a story's point of view
- To use chronological order

Fiction
A piece of writing about imaginary people and events

Nonfiction
A piece of writing about real people and actual events

Reading Strategy:
Metacognition

Why are some stories more interesting than others? What details make a story interesting to read?

A paragraph that tells a story answers the question *what happened*. **Fiction** is a story about imaginary people and events. **Nonfiction** writing is about real people and events. Stories are either fiction or nonfiction.

▶ **EXAMPLE 1**

The Day I Nearly Drowned
by Eliza Chevez

   When I was eight years old, I nearly drowned in the Gulf of Mexico. My cousin Julio and I were playing with a raft. Suddenly, he let go. The raft started to drift out to sea. As I swam toward the raft, the wind took it out farther and farther. People were yelling, but I could not hear them. A man on shore saw me and swam out to rescue me. When I got back to the beach, my mom and Julio were crying. We all thanked the man who had saved me from drowning. Almost drowning was an unforgettable experience!

Practice A

Read Example 1. Then write the answer to each question.

1. Does this story take place in the past, the present, or the future?

2. Who is the "I" in this story?

3. What event does this paragraph tell about?

4. Suppose Eliza is a real person. Is her story fiction or nonfiction?

5. Write a different sentence for the conclusion.

NOTE

A biography is a story of a real person's life. An autobiography is a biography that someone writes about himself or herself. A biography or autobiography might only tell about one part of someone's life. It can be as short as one paragraph or as long as a book.

Grammar Tip

Pronouns take the place of nouns in sentences. First-person pronouns can be singular (*I, me, my, mine*) or plural (*we, us our, ours*). Third-person pronouns can be singular (*he, she, it, him, her, his, its*) or plural (*they, them, their,* and *theirs*).

Point of View

Every story has a **point of view**. The point of view identifies the person telling the story. There are two main points of view.

When a story has a first-person point of view, the storyteller is a character in the story. The story is told from his or her point of view. The writer uses first-person pronouns such as *I, me, my,* and *we*.

When a story has a third-person point of view, the storyteller is an outside observer, not a character. The story is told using third-person pronouns such as *he, she* and *they*. Example 2 shows each point of view.

▶ **EXAMPLE 2**

| First Person | I entered the restaurant. I took a seat. I was hungry. |
| Third Person | The man entered the restaurant. He took a seat. He was hungry. |

Practice B

The story below is in first-person point of view. Rewrite it in third-person point of view. Use *he* or *she, his* or *her, they,* and *their*.

My family went crazy the day we lost my dog in the forest. My job was to walk Buddy on his leash. In the woods, I took his leash off, and Buddy ran. I called and called him. Then I went home and got my parents. We searched for an hour. Then we heard a dog bark. There was Buddy, begging for food at someone's picnic table. We all laughed.

Practice C

Look back at Example 1 on the previous page. What is this story's point of view?

Chronological Order

Stories are usually told in **chronological order**—according to time. When you use chronological order, you tell events in the order that they happened. You start with the earliest event and end with the most recent event.

▶ **EXAMPLE 3**

I had the most unusual morning yesterday. I was cooking eggs when the pipes burst. While I tried to stop the gushing water, the frying pan caught on fire. I ran toward it and tripped over the dog. I was sitting in an inch of water when my little brother came in. "Hey, what's for breakfast?" he asked. Just then, the phone rang. What a stressful way to start the day!

Practice D

The five sentences below tell a story, but they have been mixed up. Write the sentences so that they tell a story in chronological order.

- Finally, the meal was ready, and we sat down to eat.
- Early this morning, we put the turkey in the oven.
- Last evening, we baked bread and decorated the table.
- While the turkey baked, we cooked potatoes and beans.
- We finished our shopping yesterday morning.

We planned the meal, bought the groceries, and then spent the day in the kitchen.

REVIEW

1. Choose a topic from the list below. Write a paragraph that tells a story about this topic. Use first-person point of view. Your paragraph can be fiction or nonfiction.

   - a hurricane
   - learning something new
   - an electric guitar
   - a snake or insect
   - a bus or subway ride
   - a holiday event

2. Rewrite the paragraph you wrote above. This time, use third-person point of view. Make sure to use third-person pronouns.

SPELLING BUILDER

Spelling Words with Two Vowels in a Row
"When two vowels go walking, the first one does the talking." Have you ever heard this saying? It refers to words that have two vowels next to each other. In these words, the first vowel usually has a long sound. The second vowel is silent. That is why you write *team*, not *taem*; *coat*, not *caot*; and *wait*, not *wiat*. This rule will help you to put vowels in the right order. Think of three other words that have two vowels in a row. Write the words. Do they follow the rule?

Dialogue

Objectives

■ To use correct capitalization and punctuation in dialogue

■ To recognize direct quotations and indirect quotations

Dialogue is conversation. It is the words that real people or story characters say to one another. You can use dialogue in fiction and nonfiction stories. How people speak and what they say shows what they are like.

Written dialogue usually contains **direct quotations.** A direct quotation is someone's exact written or spoken words. Place **quotation marks** at the beginning and end of a direct quotation. Follow these rules of punctuation and capitalization when you write dialogue:

Rule 1   Put quotation marks around a speaker's exact words. Capitalize the first word.

▶ **EXAMPLE 1**

"Where are we going?" asked Amber.

"I thought you knew. We're going to see a rodeo," Eliza answered.

Rule 2   Use a period, question mark, or exclamation point at the end of a direct quotation. Put the end punctuation inside the closing quotation marks.

▶ **EXAMPLE 2**

"I want to see the horses," said Eliza.

Amber asked, "How long will we be there?"

Rule 3   You can name the speaker at the beginning of a direct quotation. Use a comma to separate the speaker from the quotation.

▶ **EXAMPLE 3**

Amber said, "I will see you later."

Dialogue

The words that people or story characters say to one another; conversation

Direct quotation

A quotation that reports someone's exact words; quotation marks are required

Quotation marks (" ")

The marks placed at the beginning and end of a direct quotation

Reading Strategy:
Metacognition

What do you already know about dialogue?

Writing Tip

Use different verbs to introduce dialogue. Do not always use the word *said*. Instead, try words like *exclaimed, shouted, whispered, responded,* or *suggested.*

Rule 4 You can name the speaker at the end of a direct quotation. Use a comma to separate the speaker from the quotation. Put the comma inside the closing quotation marks.

▶ **EXAMPLE 4**

"I will see you at the bus stop," said Eliza.

Rule 5 You can name the speaker in the middle of a sentence. Begin the second part of the sentence with a lowercase letter if it is in the middle of a sentence.

▶ **EXAMPLE 5**

"Maybe we will see the pie-throwing contest first," suggested Amber, "or the barrel-racing event."

"We want to see every event," she added. "We should stay longer."

Rule 6 Start a new paragraph with each new speaker.

▶ **EXAMPLE 6**

"Here we are at last!" said Eliza.

"I am glad we came to the rodeo," said Amber.

"Me, too!"

Reading Strategy:
Metacognition

Read the sentences in Practice A aloud. This may help you "hear" the direct quotations.

Practice A

Write each sentence. Add the correct punctuation.

1. Eliza said I am going to Centerville.

2. Why are you going there asked Amber.

3. I want to see a rodeo answered Eliza.

4. Amber said Take me with you.

5. Sure, come along replied Eliza.

Indirect quotation

A quotation that reports what someone said without using the speaker's exact words; quotation marks are not used

Practice B

Correct the punctuation and capitalization in each item. There may be more than one sentence in an item.

1. there are ten riders in this contest Amber said which one will win

2. the first rider will be Rudy Mendez said the announcer

3. Eliza called out come on, Rudy

4. that was a great ride Amber said

5. give Rudy a big cheer said the announcer

An **indirect quotation** reports what someone said but does not use the speaker's exact words. You do not need quotation marks when you write indirect quotations. The word *that* often introduces an indirect quotation.

▶ **EXAMPLE 7**

Direct Quotation	"I had fun," said Amber.
Indirect Quotation	Amber said that she had fun.

Practice C

Identify each sentence as either a direct quotation or an indirect quotation. On your paper, write *direct* or *indirect*.

1. "Do you come to the rodeo often?" Eliza asked the woman next to her.

2. "Yes, I enjoy rodeos," answered the woman.

3. The woman added that she lived nearby.

4. "Do you live in Centerville?" she asked Amber and Eliza.

5. Eliza explained that she and Amber lived in Springfield.

REVIEW

Rewrite the following dialogue. Begin a new paragraph wherever necessary. Add the correct punctuation and capitalization.

What do you want to do today asked Brandon. Derek said I think we should go to the mall. He continued I need a new pair of sneakers. Let's go to the movies said Amber. That's a wonderful idea Eliza replied. I want to see something funny Brandon told them. Will you come with us asked Eliza. Yes Derek said I can go to the mall tomorrow. Brandon said then it's decided. We will all go to the movies. I heard about one movie that is very funny.

PUTTING IT ALL TOGETHER

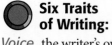

Six Traits of Writing:

Voice the writer's own language

Write a story about two people. One person is explaining how to do something to the other person. Use dialogue. Be sure that you use correct punctuation in your story.

Sports Commentator

Wanda Hanson works as a sports commentator for a TV station. She comments on sports events during the evening news show. Wanda writes her own reports. Her sentences must be clearly written. She wants her TV viewers to understand what she says.

Often, Wanda must write quickly. Sometimes, she makes mistakes. She corrects her report and reads it aloud before the show.

Read one of Wanda's reports. Then answer the questions.

There was a major upset in local basketball last night. The Dover Bears played well, but they just couldn't beat those Midland Tigers. Afterward, I asked Coach Miller if his team was surprised. Sure they were surprised, he said, but they were also thrilled. Beating the number one team in the league was awesome! When that last buzzer sounded, the Tigers won 63-57. Let's look at the tape.

1. Is the third sentence a direct quotation or an indirect quotation?

2. Add the correct punctuation to the fourth and fifth sentences.

3. **CRITICAL THINKING** The sixth sentence appeals to the sense of sound. What other detail could Wanda add to appeal to another sense?

 VIEWING

Watch a sports commentator on your local TV station. How does the commentator combine his or her own reporting with tapes of real sports events? How much of the report shows the commentator? How much of the report shows actual sports events?

Paraphrasing

When you write a report, you may use many sources of information. Your sources might include books, newspapers, and Web sites.

If you copy more than five words in a row from a source, use quotation marks and give credit to the author. Never use another person's words as your own.

However, do not use too many direct quotations in a report. Use your own words to retell, combine, and summarize the information you want to share. This is called paraphrasing.

Imagine that you are researching the writer Zora Neale Hurston. You have found a biography that provides the following information.

Hurston spent her early childhood listening to stories. The adults told these stories on the porch of a store in Eatonville.

In 1901, two visitors came to town. They were impressed with Zora's reading ability. The women gave Zora several books. These books included *Grimms' Fairy Tales*, Greek and Roman myths, and stories by Robert Louis Stevenson.

Follow the directions below using the information from the biography.

1. Paraphrase the first paragraph.

2. Paraphrase the second paragraph.

3. **CRITICAL THINKING** When is a quotation better than paraphrasing?

TECHNOLOGY

On a computer, it is easy to copy words directly from a Web site. This can make it easy to steal someone else's work. Using someone else's writing as your own is called plagiarism. It is a crime. Instead, use a quotation. Whether you use a direct quotation or an indirect one, give the author credit. Include his or her name with the quotation.

- When your write to inform, provide your reader with facts and examples.

- When your write to explain, answer the question *why* or *how*. In some cases you many be explaining a cause-and-effect relationship.

- When your write to compare two things, give details that show how they are alike and different.

- When your write to teach, explain how to do or make something.

- Know when you are writing facts and when you are writing opinions.

- When your write to persuade, try to convince your readers to accept your opinion or idea.

- When you see or hear an ad, think about the purpose of the message.

- When your write to describe, try to paint a picture with words. Use words that appeal to the senses: sight, sound, smell, taste, and touch.

- When your write to tell a fiction or nonfiction story, answer the question *what happened*.

- Be aware of a story's point of view. Determine if it has a first-person or third-person point of view.

- In most cases, place the events in a story in chronological order.

- Use dialogue to present what people or story characters say to one another.

- Check the capitalization and punctuation of direct quotations. Follow the rules in Lesson 14-5. Always use quotation marks with direct quotations.

- Use indirect quotations when you do not report the speaker's exact words.

- Make sure that all your paragraphs have the three parts: a topic sentence, a body, and a conclusion.

GROUP ACTIVITY

Work with a group to write a paragraph for a poster about your school cafeteria. Try to persuade students to buy the cafeteria food more often. Describe the food and the cafeteria. Use details that will appeal to the reader's senses.

Word Bank

advertisement

advertiser

cause and effect

chronological order

compare

dialogue

direct quotation

fact

fiction

indirect quotation

inform

nonfiction

opinion

persuade

point of view

quotation marks

Part A Write the word or words from the Word Bank that complete each sentence.

1. An _____ is the way a person thinks about something.

2. A _____ reports someone's exact words.

3. When you _____, you pass along information.

4. _____ are placed at the beginning and end of a direct quotation.

5. A _____ is a piece of information that is known to be true.

6. When you arrange events according to time, you are using _____.

7. When you show that something happens because of something else, you are showing _____.

8. A story about imaginary people and events is _____.

9. To _____ is to convince someone to agree with you.

10. An _____ reports what someone said without using the exact words.

11. To _____ means to tell how two things are alike or different.

12. An _____ is a message designed to get the public's attention.

13. The _____ is the position of the storyteller in a story.

14. _____ writing tells about real people and events.

15. The words that people or story characters say to one another is called _____.

16. A _____ uses an ad to try to sell something.

Part B Each sentence is the topic sentence of a paragraph. Decide on the purpose of the paragraph. Write the letter of your answer.

17. When I woke up yesterday morning, my furniture was gone!
    A to teach   **C** to persuade
    B to describe   **D** to tell a story

18. Why does Ali Lane deserve your vote for club president?
    A to teach   **C** to persuade
    B to describe   **D** to tell a story

19. You can learn the right way to wash a car.
    A to teach   **C** to persuade
    B to describe   **D** to tell a story

Part C

20. Choose one of the writing directions below. Write its letter. Then follow the directions to write a paragraph. Include a topic sentence, supporting details, and a conclusion.

    A Explain how to make or do something. Use words such as *first* and *finally* to make the order of the steps clear.

    B Persuade your reader to buy a product. Give reasons why the product will improve his or her life.

    C Describe your best friend. Introduce your friend in a topic sentence. Show what your friend looks like. Appeal to more than one sense.

    D Tell a fiction or nonfiction story. Put the events in chronological order.

Test Tip

If you do not know an answer, skip the question. Return to it if you have time. The answer may come to you later.

Writing Better Paragraphs

You know the basics of writing a paragraph. Now you will find out how to make your paragraphs better. Better paragraphs have lots of life. They use wonderful words. They have ups and downs. They have long sentences and short sentences.

Look at the photo on the opposite page. These people are enjoying quite a ride! Their ride is smooth and exciting. It appeals to all five senses. It is rich with detail. The motion of the ride certainly has every rider's attention.

You can write paragraphs that are lively and smooth. You can write paragraphs that grab your readers' attention. You can write paragraphs that thrill your readers like a roller coaster. In Chapter 15, you will learn how to write better paragraphs.

GOALS FOR LEARNING

- To revise your writing
- To improve topic sentences
- To include different kinds of sentences in your writing
- To use transitional words and phrases to connect ideas
- To choose more specific words
- To edit your writing

Reading Strategy: Summarizing

Before readers can summarize what they have read, they need to identify the topic and the main ideas. They need to look for details that show the main ideas. Then they can summarize the main ideas and details. They can create a shortened version of them. As you read this chapter, ask yourself questions like these:

- What is this chapter about?
- What is the main idea of each lesson?
- What details are important to each main idea?
- How can I summarize each lesson in one or two sentences?

Key Vocabulary Words

Draft An early version of writing; not the final version

Revise To change a piece of writing to make it better

Variety A collection of things that are different or vary in some way

Transition A change from one thing to another; often a change in time, place, situation, or thought

Active verb A verb form in which the subject is doing the action

Passive verb A verb form in which the action happens to the subject

Edit To correct mistakes in a piece of writing; to check spelling, grammar, punctuation, capitalization, and word choice

Proofread To mark editing changes on paper using proofreading marks

What Is Revising?

Objectives

- To revise a paragraph to match the purpose and audience
- To revise the organization of a paragraph
- To revise the content of a paragraph

Draft
An early version of writing; not the final version

Revise
To change a piece of writing to make it better

Reading Strategy:
Summarizing

The headings within a lesson can help you recognize the main ideas of the lesson.

When you write, your first try is called the first **draft**. At this step in the writing process, do not worry about writing a perfect paragraph. Just put your ideas down on paper. Make sure that your paragraph has a topic sentence, a body of details, and a conclusion. If you were given writing instructions, make sure you have followed them.

Practice A

Write a first draft of a paragraph about your favorite kind of movie. Include a topic sentence, supporting details, and a conclusion.

Once you have written a first draft, you are ready for the next step in the writing process. You are ready to **revise** your writing.

When you revise a piece of writing, you change it to make it better. To revise your first draft, read it over. It may help to read it aloud. Hear how your words and ideas sound. Listen for ways to improve them.

Many students like to write and revise on a computer.

Revising to Match the Purpose and Audience

Think about your purpose for writing when you revise.

- Does the paragraph match the purpose?

Also, think about your audience. These are the people who will read your paragraph.

- Will the paragraph be clear to the audience?
- How much do they know about the topic?

Perhaps you have used words that your readers may not know. If so, give the meaning of these words.

Look at the first draft in Example 1. Notice the details that support the topic sentence. The details show why rock music is the writer's favorite. The writer defined the word *lyrics* for the audience.

▶ **EXAMPLE 1**

Rock is my favorite kind of music. I like it more than country music. I like the messages in the songs. The lyrics, or words, tell about the way things are. The ideas in the songs make me think. It has a good beat. I can dance to it. Most of all, I like the sound of rock music. I listen to rock music whenever I can.

Practice B

Read your paragraph from Practice A to another student. Ask him or her these questions: Is there anything that is hard to understand? Are there words I should define? Then revise your paragraph based on the suggestions.

Revising the Organization

When you write a draft, your task is to put your ideas on paper. Sometimes, the details are not in the best order. When you revise, look at the organization of your writing.

- Does the order of the details make sense?

An organized paragraph will help your audience follow your ideas. Compare Examples 1 and 2. Notice how the order of details is improved in Example 2.

▶ **EXAMPLE 2**

Rock is my favorite kind of music. I like it more than country music. Most of all, I like the sound of it. It has a good beat. I can dance to it. I like the messages in the songs. The lyrics, or words, tell about the way things are. The ideas in the songs make me think about my own life. I listen to rock music whenever I can.

Practice C

Read your paragraph about your favorite kind of movie. Revise it if necessary by improving the order of the details.

Revising the Content

After you have revised the organization, you need to revise the content. The content is the information in the paragraph. Check your facts. Add missing or better details. Take out details that are not related or are unnecessary.

- What facts need to be checked?
- Are important details missing? Are there better details?
- Are there any details that do not support the main idea?

Read the revised paragraph in Example 3. The writer took out an unrelated sentence and combined two others. The writer also replaced weak words with more specific ones.

▶ **EXAMPLE 3**

Rock is my favorite kind of music. Most of all, I like its sound. It has a lively rhythm that I can dance to. The lyrics, or words, describe real-life situations. The messages in the songs make me think about my own life. I listen to rock music whenever I can.

Reading Strategy:
Summarizing

Write a one-sentence summary of what you learned in this lesson.

Practice D

Read your paragraph about your favorite kind of movie aloud. Revise it by improving the content.

In the next four lessons, you will learn more ways to revise your writing.

REVIEW

Write the answer to each question.

1. What does it mean to revise?

2. Why do you need to think about your audience when you revise?

3. Why is it important to organize your paragraph?

4. When you revise the content of a paragraph, what things might you do?

5. Read the paragraph below. Compare it to Example 3 on page 383. What has the writer done to revise the paragraph?

> Rock is my favorite kind of music. Most of all, I like its sound. It has a lively rhythm that my friends and I can dance to. In addition, the lyrics, or words, describe real-life situations. The messages in the songs make me think about my own life. I listen to rock music whenever I can.

SPELLING BUILDER

Using Words with the Prefixes *per-, pre-, and pro-*
It is easy to misspell words with the prefixes *per-, pre-,* and *pro-*. These prefixes often sound alike in words. It helps to say the words aloud and exaggerate the prefix. For example, say "PURR-fect" for *perfect*. Say "PREE-dict" for *predict*. This will help you remember where to write the *r*.

Write *per-, pre-,* or *pro-* to complete the words below. Look up each word in a dictionary to check the spelling.

1. ___duce

2. ___tend

3. ___form

4. ___vide

5. ___pare

6. ___mit

Interesting Topic Sentences

Objectives

- To write a better topic sentence
- To get the reader's attention
- To leave out unnecessary words

Reading Strategy:
Summarizing

One good way to summarize something you have read is to make a short list.

A good topic sentence does many things. It introduces the reader to the main idea of the paragraph. It gets the reader's attention. A lively topic sentence makes the reader want to find out more. A topic sentence may also express the writer's opinion about the topic.

To improve a topic sentence, get to the point. Take out unnecessary words. Add words that will grab the reader's attention. Compare the topic sentences in Example 1.

▶ **EXAMPLE 1**

Poor	Let me tell you about Toronto, which is a good place to visit.
Better	Toronto is a one-of-a-kind city that offers experiences you will never forget.

Practice A

Rewrite each topic sentence. Take out unnecessary words. Add words that will grab the reader's attention.

1. This paragraph is about a family vacation in Arizona.

2. I think I will begin by telling you that I just got a new CD player.

3. Let me tell you about what I want to be: a musician.

4. I am going to write about the trip my friends and I took last Saturday.

5. The topic I will tell about is Internet search engines.

One way to get your reader's attention is by asking a question.

► **EXAMPLE 2**

Have you ever wondered how Los Angeles got its name? Its name is a shortened form of "Reina de los Angeles." This Spanish phrase means "Queen of the Angels." Some people call Los Angeles "The City of Angels."

Practice B

Read each pair of questions. Decide whether *A* or *B* is the better topic sentence. Write the letter of your answer.

1. A Would you like me to tell you about our cat?
 B Have you met Harold, our family cat?

2. A Aren't some plants interesting?
 B Have you ever heard of a plant that eats meat?

3. A Would you like to live next door to a volcano?
 B What is a volcano?

4. A Are the foods you eat good for you?
 B Do you want me to tell you what foods are healthy?

5. A Why does poison ivy cause you to itch?
 B Have you ever had a bad case of poison ivy?

Practice C

Reading Strategy:
Summarizing

Write a one-sentence summary of this lesson.

Choose a topic listed below, or choose your own topic. Write a paragraph about it. Begin with a question that gets to the point and grabs the reader's attention.

- the perfect day
- learning to drive
- my favorite game to play

REVIEW

Read each pair of topic sentences. Which one is better? Write *A* or *B* on your paper.

1. **A** This paragraph is going to be about my cat.
   B Our cat Harold rules our home with an iron paw.

2. **A** Did you know there was an Earl of Sandwich?
   B Sandwiches are a popular lunch choice.

3. **A** Have you ever read a book with 1,037 pages?
   B *Gone with the Wind* is a story about the Civil War.

4. **A** Derek runs track at Springfield High School.
   B Meet Derek Anderson, a shining star of Springfield's track team.

Revise each topic sentence to make it better. Change at least one sentence into a question.

5. We saw a movie not long ago.

6. Let me tell you about a funny dream I had once.

7. The weather lately has been terrible.

8. Our science teacher makes us want to learn.

9. The book I read was about motorcycles.

10. Rock collecting is fun.

Sentence Variety

Spice up your paragraphs by giving your sentences **variety**.
Variety is a collection of things that are different. It is more
interesting to read a paragraph made of different kinds of
sentences.

You can add sentence variety in several ways. One way is
to begin some sentences with an adverb, an adverb phrase,
or an adverb clause. Remember to use a comma when you
begin a sentence with a dependent clause.

▶ **EXAMPLE 1**

I sent Lana an e-mail today. (Adverb is last.)

Today I sent Lana an e-mail. (Adverb is first.)

Lana was tired after she ran the race. (Adverb clause is last.)

After she ran the race, Lana was tired. (Adverb clause is first.)

Practice A

Revise each sentence. Move an adverb phrase or clause to
the beginning of the sentence. Write each new sentence.

1. Gardening is an art in my opinion.

2. Everyone applauded at the end of the concert.

3. The mystery was solved on the last page.

4. The team was behind until Kevin hit a home run.

5. They watched out of the window while the snow fell.

Grammar Tip

A simple sentence is one independent clause with a subject and a predicate. A compound sentence is two or more independent clauses connected with a conjunction. A complex sentence is an independent clause with at least one dependent clause.

Another way to add sentence variety is to use different types of sentences.

- Add a question or exclamatory sentence.
- Use simple, compound, and complex sentences.

By using a variety of sentence types, you will have sentences of different lengths. Read and compare the two paragraphs in Example 2. Which one uses a variety of sentence lengths?

▶ **EXAMPLE 2**

The mongoose is a small animal. It is very fierce. It lives in Africa and southern Asia. It eats all sorts of small creatures. It eats snakes. A mongoose will fight a deadly cobra. The mongoose moves very quickly. The cobra cannot strike it. Mongooses can be tamed. They are often kept around homes. They will drive away snakes.

The mongoose is a small, fierce animal that lives in Africa and southern Asia. It eats all sorts of small creatures, including snakes. A mongoose will even fight a deadly cobra! The mongoose moves very quickly, and the cobra cannot strike it. Since mongooses can be tamed, they are often kept around homes to drive away snakes.

In the first paragraph, all of the sentences are simple. The writing is choppy and flat. The second paragraph uses a variety of sentence types and lengths. It has two simple sentences, one compound sentence, and two complex sentences. It also has an exclamatory sentence. The paragraph is like a woven piece of cloth.

Practice B

Think of a problem you have at school. Then think of one way it could be solved. Write a paragraph to explain the problem and the solution. Write at least five sentences. Now study the sentences you wrote. Make two changes to add sentence variety.

REVIEW

Rewrite each sentence. Add an adverb, adverb phrase, or adverb clause at the beginning of each one. Write the new sentences on your paper.

1. The students arrived at school.

2. They had lunch in the cafeteria.

3. We bought bottles of juice.

4. Cold water is refreshing.

5. Our school building is 10 years old.

Follow the directions to write a paragraph with sentence variety.

6. Choose one of the topics below. Write a paragraph about the topic. Include at least one sentence that begins with an adverb, adverb phrase, or adverb clause. Use at least one short, simple sentence. Use different sentence types and lengths.

   - Tell about your favorite sport or hobby.
   - Explain why you prefer a particular kind of music.
   - Describe a pet or animal.

Transitions

Transition

A change from one thing to another; often a change in time, place, situation, or thought

A **transition** is a change from one thing to another. You can improve your paragraphs by making smooth, clear connections among your ideas. Transitional words and phrases make these connections and help the reader follow along. Transitional words and phrases link sentences together.

Here are some transitions that show a change in time:

Transitions That Show Time

at last	first	next	at this time
at the end	in the meantime	soon	during
before	later	then	now
finally	meanwhile	while	afterwards

▶ **EXAMPLE 1**

No snow fell for a month. Storm clouds appeared.

No snow fell for a month. At last, storm clouds appeared.

Practice A

Read the paragraph. Find four transitions, and write them on your paper. (Not every sentence has a transition.)

A computer has many uses. Sonia got hers a year ago. At first, she used her computer to play computer games. Then, Sonia began to write letters on her computer. Recently, she used her computer to print photos. Now, Sonia's computer is part of her daily life.

Reading Strategy:
Summarizing

Look at the two tables of words in this lesson. How do they help you understand the main idea of the lesson?

Transitional words and phrases can also show how two ideas are related or linked. For example, *also* points out how things are alike. *However* points out a difference. *Therefore* links a cause and effect.

Transitions That Link Ideas

also	for example	in addition
as a result	nevertheless	in conclusion
however	therefore	for that reason
such as	furthermore	as well as

▶ **EXAMPLE 2**

The Internet has many uses. Students use it to find information.

The Internet has many uses. For example, students use it to find information.

Practice B

Read the paragraph. Find five transitional words or phrases that link related ideas. Write them on your paper.

Planning a party for my friends was a big job. For example, my first task was making a guest list. In addition, I had to create a menu as well as a schedule of activities. Furthermore, I had to decide how to pay for the expenses. As a result of good planning, the party was a big success.

Practice C

Rewrite the paragraph. Add some transitions from the lists in this lesson. You may also use other transitions.

Would you like to improve the quality of your sleep? Give yourself a bedtime routine. Do something relaxing. Read a book. Listen to soothing music. Take a bath. Go to bed at the same time each night. Wake up at the same time each morning. You will feel more rested.

REVIEW

1. Read the paragraph. Find five transitional words or phrases that show connections in time. Write them on your paper.

    > Everyone I know wants to meet Selena. First, there is my mom. At least once a day, she asks me when she will meet Selena. Next, there are my friends Megan and Celia. All they talk about is Selena. Then, there is my best friend Kevin, who keeps asking, "When, Brad, when?" At last their lucky day is almost here! Finally, at the last track meet of the year, they will all meet Selena.

2. Write a paragraph about a recent event in your school or town. Include at least three transitional words or phrases. Underline each transitional word or phrase.

VOCABULARY BUILDER

Understanding Idioms

An idiom is a phrase that means something different from what the words actually say. It is hard for an English language learner to understand idioms. For example:

> The red bird *caught my eye.*

Caught my eye means "got my attention." It is an idiom.

Think about each idiom in bold below. Rewrite the sentence without using the idiom.

1. You could tell that the coach **meant business**.
2. She gave her answer **in a nutshell**.
3. It was raining **cats and dogs**.

Specific Words

Objectives

- To change passive verbs to active verbs
- To choose specific words

Active verb

A verb form in which the subject is doing the action

Passive verb

A verb form in which the action happens to the subject

Active and Passive Verbs

Action verbs can be **active verbs** or **passive verbs**. When the verb is active, the subject is doing the action. When the verb is passive, someone is doing the action to the subject.

▶ **EXAMPLE 1**

Active	Armando kicked the soccer ball.
Passive	The soccer ball was kicked by Armando.
Active	The coach chose Jacki.
Passive	Jacki was chosen by the coach.

Sentences with active verbs express energy. Sentences with passive verbs are wordy and slow down your writing.

Learn to spot sentences with passive verbs. Whenever you can, change them to active verbs. To do this,

- Use the object of the preposition *by* as the subject.
- Change the subject to the direct object.
- Remove the helping verb (*is*, *are*, *was*, or *were*).

Practice A

Change the verb in each sentence from passive to active. Write the new sentence.

1. The decision was reached by the committee.

2. The costumes for the play were designed by Tanya.

3. The winning goal was scored by Antoine.

4. All of the songs are being played by the band.

5. The best song was performed by Celia.

Sometimes the sentence does not have a prepositional phrase beginning with *by*. You have to figure out who did the action.

▶ **EXAMPLE 2**

The window was broken last night.

Someone broke the window last night.

The first sentence in Example 2 does not tell who broke the window. However, to make the verb active, you have to add a noun or pronoun as the subject. Because you do not know who broke the window, use the indefinite pronoun *someone*.

Practice B

Rewrite each sentence. Change the verb from passive to active. You may use an indefinite pronoun or a noun as the subject of the new sentence. You may add information to identify the person who did the action.

1. Celia was called on the telephone.

2. The e-mail that I received was sent by Michelle.

3. The party for Yoko was planned by her friends.

4. Deanna was hired by the manager of the store.

5. Tanya's lunch was packed by her mother.

Specific Words

You can improve your sentences by using specific nouns, verbs, adjectives, and adverbs. *Specific* means particular or exact. Specific words give a more detailed picture than general or vague words.

Reading Strategy:
Summarizing

As you read, ask yourself: What is the main idea of this lesson?

▶ **EXAMPLE 3**

| General | I took my pet to school. |
| Specific | I snuck my lizard into biology class. |

The second sentence gives the reader a clearer picture because it uses words that are more specific.

Practice C

Rewrite each sentence. Replace each word or phrase in bold with a more specific word or phrase.

1. I will not eat that **food**.

2. The **car rolled** down the street.

3. The **boat** sailed into the **spot**.

4. Mike **put all his things** into his locker.

5. **The girl** is from **another country**.

Some adjectives are more specific than others. Use specific adjectives and adjective phrases to make your writing clear and interesting.

Grammar Tip

An adjective describes a noun or pronoun. Adjectives usually tell what kind, which one, or how many.

▶ **EXAMPLE 4**

General   Nice flowers were in the pretty vase on the old table.

Specific   Fresh yellow flowers were in a crystal vase on the antique table.

Practice D

Add a specific adjective before each noun in the sentence. Write the new sentence.

1. The man approached the dog.

2. The computer sat on the desk.

3. Frozen yogurt is my sister's favorite treat.

4. The captain steered the ship toward the island.

5. The students entered the cafeteria.

Using specific adverbs and adverb phrases can also make your writing clearer and more interesting. Read the sentences in Example 5. Which one gives the clearest picture?

▶ **EXAMPLE 5**

Nina skated.

Nina skated well.

Nina skated gracefully.

The first sentence has no adverbs. It is hard to picture how Nina skated. The adverb *well* has been added to the second sentence. However, *well* does not tell much about her skating. It is not very specific. A more specific adverb in the last sentence gives the clearest picture.

Practice E

Add a specific adverb or adverb phrase to complete each sentence. Write the sentence.

1. That company treats its workers _____.

2. The flowers in the vase were arranged _____.

3. She sang _____.

4. She _____ rose out of bed to start her day.

5. The lion roared _____.

Reading Strategy:
Summarizing

How would you summarize this lesson for someone who has not read it? What two main ideas would you tell?

REVIEW

Rewrite each sentence. Change the verb from passive to active. You may use an indefinite pronoun as the subject of your new sentence. You may also add information to the sentence.

1. Nothing is better than being served dinner at home.

2. The dinner was prepared by Mrs. Choy.

3. The recipe had been handed down in the family for generations.

4. Mrs. Choy was given the recipe by her mother.

Add a specific adjective before each noun in each sentence. Write the new sentence.

5. The ship was docked near the city.

6. The wind blew the paper into the street.

7. The dog barked at the cat.

Add a specific adverb to complete each sentence. Write the sentence.

8. My elderly grandmother visits _____.

9. He spoke _____ about the issue.

10. The president wrote his speech _____.

What Is Editing?

Objectives

- To edit your writing
- To use proofreading marks

Edit

To correct mistakes in a piece of writing; to check spelling, grammar, punctuation, capitalization, and word choice

Reading Strategy:
Summarizing

Ask yourself: How are revising and editing different? How are they similar?

NOTE

Reading your writing from end to beginning will help you spot misspelled words.

Even the very best writers need to clean up their paragraphs before they publish them. To **edit** is to correct mistakes in spelling, punctuation, capitalization, and grammar. When you edit, you make sure that every word, every letter, and every mark is correct. Editing is like washing and waxing your car before you try to sell it. When you edit, you must pay attention to every detail.

Editing Checklist

- Add words that are missing. It may help to read your writing aloud slowly.
- Fix any run-on sentences and sentence fragments.
- Make sure each sentence begins with a capital letter.
- Make sure each proper noun is capitalized correctly.
- Check the use of punctuation: commas, periods, question marks, and exclamation marks.
- Check that apostrophes are used correctly. Possessive nouns and contractions need apostrophes.
- Replace weak words with more specific ones.
- Look for pronouns with no clear antecedents. Make sure each pronoun agrees with its antecedent.
- Fix all spelling mistakes. Use a dictionary to check words you are not sure of.
- Check the spelling and the form of irregular verbs.
- Make sure that each verb agrees with the subject.
- Read your paragraph for verb tense. For most paragraphs, the tense should be consistent.
- Indent each paragraph.

When you edit, you find mistakes. When you **proofread**, you mark the editing corrections on paper using proofreading marks. Here are the most common proofreading marks:

Proofreading Marks

Delete or take out	Insert an apostrophe
Spell out	Insert quotation marks
Insert	Change to lowercase
Insert space	Change to capital letter
Insert a period	Close up; take out space
Insert a comma	Begin a paragraph
Insert a semicolon	Transpose letters or words

▶ **EXAMPLE 1**

because Pine trees have *soft* wood, they bend and do do not break brake.

Practice A

Write each sentence. Use proofreading marks to edit it.

1. Dogs work as guard dog and patrol dogs

2. some dogs track birds and others track game like deer.

3. Dogs have show keen senses of sight, hearing, and smell.

4. Some dogs perform on Television.

5. Huskies pull sleds acrosssnow.

It is always a good idea to have someone else proofread your writing, too. He or she will catch mistakes that you might miss. Trading writing with another writer can help both of you practice your proofreading skills. Example 2 shows how one writer proofread a paragraph.

▶ EXAMPLE 2

Bob mitchell and the rockets was a ~~famus~~ *famous* rock band. ~~There~~ *Their* song "Rock and Roll Around the World" was recorded in 1964. it was ~~the~~ the bands first Worldwide hit. Young listeners, felt that the song said what they were thinking and feeling.

Practice B

Copy this paragraph as it appears here. Look for mistakes in punctuation, spelling, capitalization, and grammar. Use proofreading marks to correct the mistakes.

When I was a little girl. I had a poodle named Bear. This dog was not as fierce as a bare, he were the most sweetest dog I ever had Everyone loved him bear had a strange problem he liked to eat socks. No ones socks were safe. He also liked to eat bred along with the bag it was rapped in. "does he think he is a goat" asked my mother.

Good writers check for mistakes in all of their written work —even their test answers.

REVIEW

Correct mistakes in spelling, grammar, punctuation, and capitalization. Write the edited sentence or paragraph.

1. Do you work here.

2. That book belongs to emily.

3. Many short stories by that author has surprise endings.

4. Sharyls brother will pick us up after the game.

5. Josh said that he would bring him camera.

6. Its a cold day today, I think I'll wear my gloves.

7. The plane that has our suitcases leave tomorrow.

8. I am learning about adverbs in english class.

9. I stop at the store and then went to work.

10. Danny is a high school studant, he belongs to my writer's group. That meets every Tuesday. Danny is writing stories about his funy uncle Leo. Hes something else! The other peeple in the group. They think the story's are funny and they look forward to what Danny will write next about uncle leo?

PUTTING IT ALL TOGETHER

Write a paragraph about a day you will never forget. Write a topic sentence that will make the reader want to read more. Make sure each supporting detail adds to the main idea. Use transitional words and phrases to guide the reader. Use specific words and a variety of sentences. End with a strong conclusion. Then edit your paragraph.

Six Traits of Writing:

Organization order, ideas tied together

Giving Directions

Lauren Jackson is planning a birthday party for her friend. She will host the party at a local restaurant. She wants to include directions with the invitations. Her directions need to be clear so that guests can easily find their way to the party.

Lauren wrote a draft of the directions. Read her draft carefully. Then answer the questions below.

Take Route 19 north to Exit 5. Make a left onto Hamilton street. Go about 3 miles, you will see the Lakeview Shopping Center, witch will be on their right. Turn left onto Josey Lane. When the road splitts, stay to the right. Go straight until you see the Restaurant on the left or right. You may need to park acrost the street. Because the restaurant's Parking Lot often filled up quickly.

1. Edit Lauren's directions. Write the corrected directions on your paper.

2. Lauren plans to make a "test drive" to the restaurant to make sure her directions are right. Which sentence in her draft could she make more specific?

3. CRITICAL THINKING Why is it important to check for mistakes in the writing you plan to give to others?

SPEAKING AND LISTENING

Practice following spoken directions. Give directions from school to your house while a partner listens. Your partner should take notes or draw a map while listening. Your partner should ask questions about anything that is confusing. Check your partner's notes. Is anything missing or incorrect? Change roles and repeat the activity.

BUILDING RESEARCH SKILLS

Using a Table of Contents

Many nonfiction books have a table of contents. The table of contents is found in the front of the book. It shows you how the book is arranged. It lists the book's chapters and sections by title. It also gives the page numbers on which each chapter and section begins.

Scan the table of contents in the front of this textbook. Choose a lesson title. Then go to the page number shown to find that lesson.

Part of a table of contents is shown below. It is from a book that comes with a word-processing program. Scan the chapter and section titles. Then answer the questions.

1. How many sections are found in Chapter 10?

2. On what pages would you look for information about charts?

3. **CRITICAL THINKING** Should every book have a table of contents?

TECHNOLOGY

Many Web sites have menus. A Web site menu appears on the first page of the site. It is like a table of contents. It lists information that can be found on the site. It shows how the information is arranged. The items in a Web site menu are like chapter or section titles. Usually, clicking on an item in the menu will take you to that section of the Web site.

SUMMARY

- To begin writing, put your ideas on paper. Your first draft does not need to be perfect.

- Revise your draft to match the purpose and audience. Does your paragraph do what it is supposed to do? Will your paragraph be clear to readers?

- Revise the organization of your draft. Are your details in an order that makes sense?

- Revise the content of your draft. Are your facts correct? Do all of your sentences relate to the main idea? Are any details missing?

- Write topic sentences that get to the point and grab the reader's attention.

- Add variety to your paragraph by placing adverbs at the beginning of some sentences.

- Add variety to your paragraph by using different types of sentences.

- Use transitional words and phrases to make smooth, clear connections between sentences.

- Make your writing lively. Use specific nouns, verbs, adjectives, and adverbs. Choose active verbs instead of passive verbs.

- Edit your sentences to correct mistakes in spelling, grammar, punctuation, and capitalization. Check your choice of words.

GROUP ACTIVITY

Work with a group to create a travel brochure for the area where you live. Write a paragraph or two describing cities, parks, and other interesting places. Tell the best time of year to visit and why. As a group, edit and proofread the brochure.

CHAPTER 15
REVIEW

Word Bank

active verb

draft

edit

passive verb

proofread

revise

transition

variety

Part A Write the word or words from the Word Bank that complete each sentence.

1. A _____ helps the reader move from one idea to another.

2. When you _____, you check organization and content.

3. When you use an _____, the subject is doing the action.

4. A _____ is an early version of writing.

5. When you use a _____, the action happens to the subject.

6. When you _____, you fix mistakes in your writing.

7. A collection of things that are different shows _____.

8. When you _____, you use special marks.

Part B Write the letter of your answer.

9. When you edit, what do you do?
   A Write a draft.   **C** Add sentence variety.
   B Choose a topic.   **D** Correct mistakes.

10. How can you show links between sentences?
    A Add sentence variety. **C** Correct mistakes.
    B Use transition words.   **D** Fix sentence order.

11. Which topic sentence is the best?
    A I want to write about Dr. Ortiz.
    B Dr. Raymond Ortiz is my doctor.
    C Dr. Raymond Ortiz is wise and kind.
    D This paragraph is about Dr. Ortiz.

Part C Each sentence has a mistake. Edit the sentence. Write the corrected sentence.

12. This group of students have finished the test.

13. "Finding a summer job is hard" he said.

Part D Write a more specific word to replace the bold word.

14. I thought the team's performance was **good**.

15. The campers **walked** along the trail.

Part E Rewrite each sentence using the active form of the verb.

16. Have you read the lesson that was assigned by our teacher?

17. The puppy that was found by Nathan belongs to this family.

Part F Write the answer to each question.

18. How can you add sentence variety to a paragraph?

19. Describe a good topic sentence. What does it do?

Part G Revise and edit this paragraph. Write a better topic sentence. Add transitional words. Fix mistakes. Write the final paragraph.

20.   I want to tell you what I plan to do in the summer. It is the season for Part-Time Jobs. To me, working has two important purposes. I make money, I need cash to save and to spend. I use my spending money to pay for cloths, and fees for the water park, and gas for the car. A summer job give me work experience. I learn a lot when I work with other people. People who know more. A summer job gives me an idea about what the work world is like. So I hope I can find a good job this summer.

Test Tip

Read test directions carefully. If you do not understand them, ask a teacher for help.

CHAPTER 6

Writing Reports

The photo on the opposite page shows an assembly line. On it, cars are made, one step at a time. Each person or machine on the assembly line does one step. When you add all the steps together, you get a perfect automobile.

Before you can write a report, you need to follow a set of steps. First you choose a topic. You find information about it. Then you organize that information. If you follow these steps, you will have the three things you need to write a good report. You will have a topic, information about the topic, and a plan to follow as you write.

It takes time and planning to build a car. It also takes time and planning to write a report. In Chapter 16, you will learn the steps in preparing to write a report. Knowing these steps and following them will make the work easier.

GOALS FOR LEARNING

- To understand the steps in the writing process, and to identify the parts of a report
- To choose a topic
- To find information and take notes
- To organize information into an outline
- To write, revise, and edit a report
- To prepare a bibliography

Reading Strategy: Questioning

Asking questions can help you become a better reader. As you read, ask yourself:
- What do I already know about the topic?
- What can I learn by reading this?
- How might I use this new information?

When you write, remember that your readers will be asking questions, too. Your readers will be asking:
- What is the writing about?
- What are the most important ideas?
- When and how will I use this information?

Key Vocabulary Words

Publish To share your writing with others

Report An organized summary of information about a topic; usually involving research

Research To find information about a topic

Subtopic A division or part of a larger topic

Catalog A list of items arranged in a special way

Call number A number that tells where a book is located in the library

Keyword A word or phrase that you use to search for information about a topic

Bibliography A list of the sources used to write a report

Outline A writing plan that lists topics and subtopics in a certain order

What Is a Report?

Objectives

- To identify different types of reports
- To identify the parts of a report
- To identify the steps in writing a report

Publish

To share your writing with others

Report

An organized summary of information about a topic; usually involving research

Research

To find information about a topic

Reading Strategy:
Questioning

Some lesson titles in this book are questions. How is this helpful?

This chapter is different from the other chapters in this book. In this chapter, you will work through the writing process from beginning to end. You will do these steps:

1. **Prewriting**: choosing a topic, finding information, taking notes, and organizing the information

2. **Drafting**: writing the first draft of a report

3. **Revising**: changing a draft to make it better

4. **Editing**: correcting mistakes in spelling, punctuation, capitalization, and grammar; choosing better words

5. **Publishing:** sharing the final report with others

You have already practiced these steps. You have planned and wrote paragraphs. You have revised and edited them. You have also **published** them—you have shared them with your teacher or with other students.

Appendix A, which begins on page 456, is a Handbook on the Writing Process. It explains each of the five steps listed above. Use this appendix to help you plan and write paragraphs, essays, and reports.

In this chapter, you will write a **report**. A report is an organized summary of information about a topic. There are many kinds of reports. You might write a book report about a book you have read. You might write a report on a specific topic. Someday, you might write a business report for your job. For most reports, you will need to **research** your topic—you will need to find information about it. Research is part of the prewriting step.

You know that the building blocks of a paragraph are sentences. In the same way, the building blocks of a report are paragraphs. Some ideas are too big to be covered in one paragraph. These ideas can become topics for reports.

You learned that a good paragraph has three parts. A report also has three parts:

- the topic paragraph
- the body (paragraphs that give supporting details)
- the summary paragraph

The topic paragraph introduces the main idea of the report. The body of a report explains and supports the main idea. The body usually has at least two paragraphs. It includes details such as facts, examples, reasons, and experiences. It may include quotations from experts. The summary paragraph lets the reader know that the end has come. It summarizes the information in the report.

As you read the rest of this chapter, you will learn how to plan and write a report.

Practice A

Number your paper from 1 to 5. Write the names of the five steps in the writing process. After each one, write a few key words to help you remember that step.

Writing a report is like a building project. It takes planning and time.

REVIEW

Write the word or words that complete each sentence.

1. An organized summary of information about a topic is a _____.

2. When you _____ a topic, you look for information.

3. The _____ tells readers what a report will be about.

4. The _____of a report gives the supporting details.

5. A _____ goes at the end of a report.

6. In the _____ step of the writing process, you fix mistakes.

7. The _____ step includes choosing a topic.

8. In the _____ step, you write a first draft.

9. In the _____ step, you share your writing.

10. You change your first draft in the _____ step.

VOCABULARY BUILDER

The Prefix *Biblio-*

Read the words below. What do they have in common?

    bibliography   bibliology   bibliophile

They contain the prefix *biblio-*, which comes from a Greek word meaning "book." Use these words to answer the questions.

1. *Philo* means "love." Which word means a person who loves books?

2. The ending *-logy* means "study of." Which word means the study of books?

3. The ending *-graphy* means "a written or printed list." Which word means a list of books?

Choosing a Topic

Objectives

■ To choose a topic for a report
■ To narrow the topic

Subtopic
A division or part of a larger topic

The first step in writing a report is choosing a topic. Think of topics that interest you. You might start with a broad subject. Then list topics that fall within that subject. Look at the lists in Example 1.

▶ **EXAMPLE 1**

Science	History	Music
wind energy	World War II	popular dances
the atom	early explorers	the piano
weather	sports	African music

Practice A

Choose one subject listed below. List five topics that are in that subject area. Then underline the topics that interest you most.

- art
- jobs
- science
- travel

The best topic for a report is not too broad or too narrow. If your topic is too broad, you may find too much information. Make it easy on yourself. Narrow your topic to one that you can handle. Look for **subtopics,** or smaller parts within your topic. However, make sure that a subtopic is not too narrow. If it is, you may not be able to find enough information.

Reading Strategy:
Questioning

Ask questions to help you explore a topic. If your topic is the piano, you might ask: Who invented the piano? When was the first piano performance? What are different types of pianos? How are pianos tuned?

▶ **EXAMPLE 2**

Subject	music	Too Broad
Topic	the history of guitars	Too Broad
Subtopic	the lyrics of "Tears in Heaven"	Too Narrow
Subtopic	guitar music of the 1980s	Just Right

Catalog

A list of items arranged in a special way

 NOTE

In some libraries, the catalog may still be on cards in drawers. Most public libraries, however, have their catalogs on a computer.

Reading Strategy:
Questioning

What kinds of questions can help you narrow a topic that is too broad?

Practice B

Look at each pair of topics. Choose the topic that would be narrow enough for a three-page report. Write A or B on your paper.

1. **A** the history of automobiles
   B the Model T

2. **A** Native Americans
   B Navajo weaving

3. **A** the first telephone call
   B telephones around the world

4. **A** the use of fighter planes of World War I
   B airplanes throughout history

5. **A** fashion since the Middle Ages
   B skirt lengths in the 1900s

How can you find out if a topic is too broad or too narrow? Do a quick check at the library. Use the library **catalog** to look up your topic. A catalog is a list of items arranged in a special way. A library catalog lists every book and magazine in the library. If your topic is too broad, you will find a great number of books about it. If your topic is too narrow, you will find little or no information about it.

Practice C

Look over the report topics you underlined in Practice A. Use a library catalog to find out how much information is available on each topic. Choose the topic you think will be best for a report. Write the topic. To help you choose, ask yourself these questions:

- Am I interested in learning about this topic? (If not, choose another topic.)
- Is the topic too broad? (If so, narrow it.)
- Is the topic too narrow? (If so, make it broader.)

REVIEW

Write each subject. After each one, write a topic within that subject area that you could write a report about.

1. government

2. nature

3. history

4. inventions

5. art

Read each pair of report topics. Which one is more narrow? Write *A* or *B* on your paper.

6. A computer programs
   B using e-mail

7. A the human body
   B what your stomach does

8. A Robert Peary and the North Pole
   B world explorers

9. A working in theater
   B directing your senior class play

10. A the most popular breeds of dogs
   B bulldogs as pets

Finding Information

Objectives

- To find sources of information
- To use a library catalog
- To identify subtopics for a report
- To take notes and prepare bibliography cards

Call number

A number that tells where a book is located in the library

 NOTE

Also look for information in periodicals. Newspapers, magazines, and journals are periodicals. They often have more up-to-date information than books.

Reading Strategy: Questioning

Turn this lesson title into a question. Use it to guide your reading.

You have chosen a topic for your report. Now it is time to research your topic. Where can you find the information you need?

Reference Books

Reference books are good sources of general information. You do not read a reference book from cover to cover. You look up only the information you need. Here are some common reference books:

- Encyclopedias provide general information about many topics.
- Almanacs contain facts and records for a given year.
- Atlases are books of maps. They contain facts about cities, countries, and the world.

The Library Catalog

In your search for information, you will probably turn to books. A library is the best place to find the books you need. You can use the library catalog to search for information in three ways:

- Search by author: Authors' names are listed in alphabetical order by the last name.
- Search by title: Titles are listed in alphabetical order by the first important word.
- Search by subject: Subjects are listed in alphabetical order by the most important word. This kind of search is the most useful when you are researching a topic.

The catalog entry for a book will include the book's **call number**. This number tells you where the book is located in the library. The entry will also tell the year the book was published. If you want to find recent information, do not use books published long ago.

Practice A

Read each situation. Decide what you would look up in the library catalog. Write *author*, *title*, or *subject*.

1. You are writing a report about Albert Einstein.
2. You want to find books written by Patricia Lauber.
3. You are looking for facts about the North Pole.
4. You are looking for a book about bulldogs.
5. You are looking for a book called *The Long March*.

The Internet

Use a search engine to find Web sites with information about your topic. Enter one or more **keywords**. A keyword is a word or a phrase. It can be a topic, a name, or a title. The search engine will show you a list of Web sites that contain the keywords you entered.

Identifying Subtopics

After you have gathered various sources, look them over. Choose the ones that seem most helpful. Before you begin to read, make a list of subtopics that you will probably include in your report.

▶ **EXAMPLE 1**

Report Topic	growing vegetables
Subtopics	1. how to choose seeds
	2. how to prepare the soil
	3. when to plant
	4. when to harvest

Practice B

Use the report topic you chose in Practice C on page 415. List at least three subtopics to research. Then list at least three keywords you could use to search for information on the Internet or in a library catalog.

Bibliography

A list of the sources used to write a report

 Grammar Tip

Some of your notes may be quotations. Make sure that you use quotation marks around a writer's exact words.

Taking Notes

As you read, take notes on index cards. Use a separate card for each piece of information you collect. At the top of each card, write the subtopic that the information relates to. At the bottom of each card, write the author or title of the source. For a book or magazine, include the page number.

On a separate set of index cards, keep track of the sources you plan to use. Use one card for each source. Write these details:

- For a book, write the author's last name first. Underline the book title. Write the place the book was published, the publisher, and the year it was published.
- For a magazine article, write the author's last name first. Use quotation marks around the article title. Underline the magazine title. Include the volume number, date, and page numbers.
- For an article from a Web site, write the author's last name first (if the author is identified). Use quotation marks around the title of the article. Underline the name of the publication. Include the Web site address and the date that the site was last updated.

These cards are bibliography cards. You will use them to prepare your **bibliography**. A bibliography is a list of sources used to write a report. You will learn more about a bibliography in Lesson 16-6.

Practice C

Use the keywords you listed in Practice B to find three sources of information. If possible, use a library catalog as well as an Internet search engine. Write a bibliography card for each source.

REVIEW

Card 1

Chan, Maggie. <u>The Great Explorers</u>.
Toronto: Colby Publishing, 2000.

Card 3

Wilson, Kevin. "Admiral Byrd in the
Arctic," <u>Explorer</u> 5 (April 10, 2004)
34-38.

Card 2

"Arctic Exploration". April 9, 2001.
www.arctex.com (May 8, 2001)

Card 4

Admiral Richard Byrd
May 9, 1926, Byrd and Floyd Bennett
(the pilot) made "what may have been
the first airplane trip over the North
Pole." Flew from Norway to North
Pole and back. Flight took 15 1/2 hours.
Wilson, p. 36

Use the cards above to answer these questions.

1. Which card is a bibliography card for a magazine?

2. Which card is a bibliography card for a Web site?

3. Which card is a bibliography card for a book?

4. Who wrote the article "Admiral Byrd in the Arctic"?

5. Why do the words *Admiral Richard Byrd* appear at the top of card 4?

Creating an Outline

Objectives

■ To organize your notes

■ To create an outline for your report

When you are done taking notes, you will have many note cards. Sort the cards by the subtopic written at the top. See how much information you have about each subtopic. If you have very little information about one subtopic, you might combine it with a related subtopic or leave it out. If you have a large amount of information about one subtopic, you might divide that subtopic into parts.

Choosing an Order

Think about the subtopics you have listed for your report. How will you put them into an order that makes sense? There are many ways to organize information. Choose an order that best fits your report topic:

- Chronological order: From beginning to end according to time
- Order of importance: From most to least important, or from least to most important
- Order of size or cost: From largest to smallest, or from smallest to largest
- Other orders: From outside to inside, from easiest to hardest, from nearest to farthest, from most popular to least popular

Practice A

Decide on an order for the information in each report. Write the order that you think would work best.

1. Sarah is reporting on the five most popular breeds of dogs in the United States.

2. Derek researched four possible energy sources of the future.

3. Kara's report is about how tennis rackets have changed over the years.

Outline
A writing plan that lists topics and subtopics in a certain order

Practice B

Look over your list of subtopics for your report. Decide how you will order your information. Write what your order is and why you chose it.

Creating an Outline

An **outline** is a writing plan. It lists topics and subtopics in a certain order. A good outline makes writing a report easier.

The outline below is in chronological order. The main subtopics are listed after Roman numerals. The smaller subtopics are indented and listed after capital letters or numbers.

Reading Strategy:
Questioning

Study the sample outline. Does the order make sense to you?

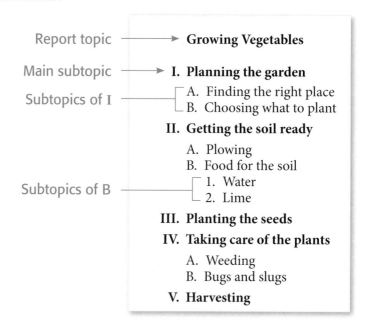

Report topic → **Growing Vegetables**

Main subtopic → **I. Planning the garden**

Subtopics of I →
   A. Finding the right place
   B. Choosing what to plant

II. Getting the soil ready
   A. Plowing
   B. Food for the soil

Subtopics of B →
     1. Water
     2. Lime

III. Planting the seeds
IV. Taking care of the plants
   A. Weeding
   B. Bugs and slugs

V. Harvesting

Practice C

Write an outline for your report.

REVIEW

Read the list of subtopics for a report on decorating your home. Put the subtopics into an order that makes sense. Write an outline. The outline will have two main subtopics (I and II). Use the outline on page 422 as a guide.

Report Topic: Decorating Your Home

Subtopics:
- Things you can use
- Wallpaper
- Posters
- Making pillows
- House plants
- Painting furniture
- Artwork
- Things you can do
- Making curtains

SPELLING BUILDER

Understanding Homographs

What is a round object that children play with? A ball. What is a fancy dance? A ball. How can that be? *Ball* (the toy) and *ball* (the dance) are homographs. Homographs have the same spelling but different meanings. To tell which meaning is used, look at the other words in the sentence.

Match each pair of meanings below with one of these homographs: *fleet, bear, light, school.*

1. large animal; carry or support
2. place for learning; group of fish
3. not heavy; not dark
4. quick; group of ships

Writing a Report

Objectives

- To write a topic paragraph
- To write a body of a report
- To write a summary paragraph

Reading Strategy:
Questioning

Which step of the writing process does this lesson cover? Which step of the writing process did the last three lessons cover?

You have decided on a topic for a report. You have done your research and made notes. You have organized your notes and written an outline. The prewriting is finished. You are ready to write the first draft.

The Topic Paragraph

You learned about the topic paragraph in Lesson 16-1. The topic paragraph introduces the topic of your report. It does not need to be long. Keep it simple and direct. State your topic. Let your reader know what to expect in the rest of the report.

Like any paragraph, your topic paragraph has three parts:

- a topic sentence that states the report topic
- a body that describes the main subtopics in the report
- a conclusion that leads your reader to the body of your report

The topic paragraph in Example 1 introduces the report topic: growing vegetables. Compare the sentences in this paragraph to the outline on page 422. Notice that the topic paragraph mentions only the main subtopics.

▶ **EXAMPLE 1**

Anyone can grow vegetables in his or her own backyard. To grow vegetables, you have to follow some important steps. Begin by planning the garden carefully. Next, prepare the soil well. Then plant your seeds. As the plants grow, take good care of them. This report will explain each of these steps. If you follow these steps at home, you will enjoy a harvest of ripe, tasty vegetables.

Practice A

Write a topic paragraph to introduce your report. Write one sentence about each main subtopic. Remember that this is a first draft—it does not have to be perfect.

The Body of the Report

The body of your report will have at least one paragraph for each subtopic. Remember that the paragraphs in the body of the report have a job to do. They must provide details that support the main idea. As you write, keep these points in mind:

- In each paragraph, follow your outline to guide your writing.
- Use the details on your note cards.
- Remember to begin each paragraph with a topic sentence and end it with a conclusion.
- Include only the details that relate to that paragraph.
- Use quotation marks around someone else's words.

Most of your report will be written in your own words. However, you may want to include some direct quotations. When you use a direct quotation, use quotation marks and name the author.

▶ **EXAMPLE 2**

Choosing high-quality seeds is important. Inexpensive seeds can be poor in quality. They may not grow. You will waste time and garden space if this happens. Gardener Bill White says, "It pays to buy seeds from garden stores that have been in business a long time." Mr. White also suggests that gardeners buy seeds well ahead of planting time.

Practice B

Write the paragraphs that will make up the body of your report. Use your outline as a guide. Write at least three paragraphs that support your main idea. Remember that this is a first draft. You will revise and edit it later.

The Summary Paragraph

End your report with a summary paragraph. This paragraph reminds your reader of your main idea. It leaves your reader with a strong, solid closing. It does not have to be long. Here is the summary paragraph from the report on growing vegetables.

Reading Strategy:
Questioning

As you write the summary paragraph, ask yourself: Will this paragraph leave my reader feeling satisfied?

▶ **EXAMPLE 3**

> Try growing vegetables at home—even if you do not have much garden space. Start by making a plan, preparing the soil, and planting good seeds. Take care of the plants as they grow. Harvest time will come sooner than you think!

Compare this paragraph to the topic paragraph in Example 1. How are they the same? How are they different?

When you have finished writing the first draft of a report, read it over. Take time to revise and edit it. Use the guidelines in Appendix A to help you.

Practice C

Write the summary paragraph for your report.

Growing vegetables requires some work, but the reward at the end is worth it!

REVIEW

Write the answer to each question.

1. What do you use as a guide when you write the body of your report?

2. Which part of a report is more than one paragraph?

3. Why should you put quotation marks around an author's exact words?

4. How do you end your report?

5. Revise and edit the first draft of your report. Use Appendix A and the questions below to guide you.

- Does your topic paragraph state the main idea and the main subtopics of your report?
- Do the sentences in each paragraph support the topic sentence of the paragraph?
- Do the paragraphs support the main idea of the report?
- Did you support your main idea with details such as facts, examples, reasons, and quotations?
- Did you end your report with a strong summary paragraph?
- Did you use transitions, sentence variety, and specific words?
- Is the report free from mistakes in spelling, grammar, capitalization, and punctuation?

Preparing a Bibliography

Objectives

- To prepare a bibliography

 NOTE

In a bibliography, the abbreviation *ed.* usually stands for "editor." Some books include articles by more than one author. It is the job of an editor to decide what articles are included.

Reading Strategy:
Questioning

Why might a reader want to look at a bibliography?

Most reports provide a bibliography on the last page. A bibliography is a list of the sources used to write a report. To make this list, start with the bibliography cards you wrote earlier. List the sources in alphabetical order by the author's last name. If an author is not identified, use the first important word in the title. Indent the second line of each entry. Also indent any lines after that.

Study the bibliography in Example 1.

▶ **EXAMPLE 1**

Allen, G., and M. K. Howard. *The History of Computers.* Chicago: Acme Books Co., 2005.

Brown, J. K., ed. *The Computer Encyclopedia.* New York: Computer Publications, Inc., 2003.

"Computer." *World Encyclopedia.* Vol. 3, 2002, 119-127.

"Computers of the Nineteenth Century." *Data World 8,* March 2006, 54-57.

Evan, Stacy. "Computers Yesterday and Today." *The Computer Journal* 2, August 2003. www.compjourn.com/evan.html (May 18, 2007).

Practice A

Use Example 1 to answer these questions.

1. Why is *The History of Computers* listed before *The Computer Encyclopedia*?

2. What information comes first in each entry?

3. Which entry is from a Web site?

4. Which entry is a magazine article?

5. What happens if the author is not identified?

Practice B

Rewrite each entry as it would appear in a bibliography. Use Example 1 as a guide.

1. Basic Car Care by Blakeley Richard. Automotive Publications published the book in Seattle in 2005.

2. "Fix It Yourself," an article by Jane Ramirez in The Car Magazine, Volume 7, March 2005, on pages 67-72.

3. "Automobiles," in Universal Encyclopedia, Volume 1, 2000, on pages 144-152. No author is given.

4. The History of Automobiles, K. L. Lee, editor. Cars and Company published the book in Boston in 2007.

5. The Auto Care Web site updated on December 13, 2002. www.autocare.org.

Practice C

Use your bibliography cards to make the bibliography for your report. Use Example 1 as your guide.

You are almost finished with the writing process! Before you make the final copy, do these things:

- Check the assignment directions, Does the report need a certain line spacing, margin size, or font size?
- Give your report a title. Choose a title that shows your topic. A good title will make your reader want to read your report.
- Make a title page like the one on the left.
- Put the pages in this order: title page, report, bibliography, blank page at the end.

Now you can publish your report! Hand it in on time. Share it with others who are interested in the topic.

Growing Vegetables Is a Snap!
Damon Holman
May 15, 2007

REVIEW

Read the five bibliography entries. Look for mistakes in order, capitalization, and punctuation. Fix the mistakes. Write the entries in the correct order.

1. Eating the right foods, A. L. Smith. <u>Good Food Journal</u>, May 2004, Volume 7, page 19.

2. Franklin, Sandra. <u>Food and You.</u> Nutrition Books, Inc., Chicago, 2006.

3. Gomez, Carlos "The Right Kind of Exercise." <u>Fast Fit.</u> June 7, 2004. (June 21, 2004). www.fastfit.com

4. W. L. Fisher. <u>Think Positive!</u> 2000, Boston: Good Thoughts Press, Inc.

5. Young, Jerry, ed. Carson City, NE: <u>A Good Night to All.</u> Carson City Press, 2001.

PUTTING IT ALL TOGETHER

Find an article in a science or history magazine. Read it carefully. How is the article like a report? Does it have the three parts of a report? What is the article's main idea? What are the subtopics in the body of the report? The author of this article probably created an outline before writing. What might it have looked like? Identify the main subtopics of the article. Then write a short outline that lists these subtopics.

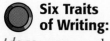

Six Traits of Writing:

Ideas message, details, and purpose

Computer Technician

Judy Woo is a computer technician in a big city. She takes care of and fixes computers for people and companies. Judy must use clear writing in her job. This helps her customers follow her directions.

Judy wrote an e-mail message to a customer. The customer had a problem with the hard drive of his computer. Read Judy's e-mail. Then answer the questions.

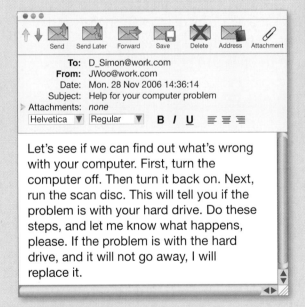

To: D_Simon@work.com
From: JWoo@work.com
Date: Mon. 28 Nov 2006 14:36:14
Subject: Help for your computer problem
▷ **Attachments:** *none*

Helvetica ▼ Regular ▼ **B** *I* U ☰ ☰ ☰

Let's see if we can find out what's wrong with your computer. First, turn the computer off. Then turn it back on. Next, run the scan disc. This will tell you if the problem is with your hard drive. Do these steps, and let me know what happens, please. If the problem is with the hard drive, and it will not go away, I will replace it.

1. What is the topic sentence of Judy's message?

2. What kind of words are used to begin the sentences in the body of the message?

3. **CRITICAL THINKING** Why did Judy include the last sentence in her e-mail?

VIEWING

Most e-mail programs allow you to view your messages in a list. You can choose to order your list of messages by date, by sender or receiver, or by subject. You can switch the order to search for a particular message.

Using Footnotes

Some reports include footnotes. A footnote is a short note for the reader. It is placed at the bottom of a page. Footnotes are numbered throughout a report. Each footnote is linked to a certain sentence in the report. A raised number appears after the sentence. The footnote with the same number appears at the bottom of the page.[1]

When do you use footnotes? Some writers use footnotes to identify their sources. Others use footnotes to add a piece of information that might be interesting to the reader.

According to the *Chicago Manual of Style*, writers must identify their sources, whether they are paraphrasing or quoting directly.[2] If a footnote identifies the same source as the previous footnote, writers use the abbreviation *ibid*.[3] *Ibid.* is short for the Latin word *ibidem*, which means "in the same place."

Look at the bottom of this page. The three footnotes you see go with the three numbers in the paragraphs above.

Answer these questions based on the footnotes at the bottom of this page.

1. Which footnotes identify a source?

2. What source does footnote 3 point to?

3. **CRITICAL THINKING** Why did the writer give the information in footnote 1 as a footnote?

TECHNOLOGY

Do not confuse footnotes with footers. A footer is a bit of text that appears at the bottom of every page. The page number is often part of a footer. Word processing programs can automatically insert footers at the bottom of pages. They can also add headers at the top of pages.

---

1. Sometimes, footnotes appear all together at the end of a report. Then they are called notes, endnotes, or backnotes.
2. *The Chicago Manual of Style*, Fifteenth Edition. Chicago: University of Chicago Press, 2003, p. 444.
3. *ibid.*, p. 466.

- Write a report to present facts and information about a topic.

- Choose a report topic that is not too broad and not too narrow.

- Use sources such as reference books, books, magazines, and Web sites.

- Use reference books to find specific kinds of information.

- Use the library catalog to search for information about a topic.

- Use keywords to search the Internet for information.

- Take notes on index cards. Organize them by subtopics.

- Keep track of your sources with bibliography cards.

- Order the subtopics in a way that makes sense. Write an outline as a guide for writing.

- Begin a report with a topic paragraph that introduces the topic and the main idea.

- In the body of a report, provide details that support the main idea. Write at least one paragraph for each subtopic on your outline.

- Summarize the main idea of a report in the summary paragraph.

- After writing the first draft of a report, revise and edit it.

- Complete a report with a bibliography. Use correct bibliography form.

GROUP ACTIVITY

With a small group, write a short report on the history of your school. As you plan, ask these questions: What sources might you use? What order will you use for your details? What direct quotation might you include? How would you divide the research among the members of your group? What might the outline for your report look like? If possible, give your report to the school newspaper or a local newspaper. If possible, find a good photo to include in your report.

Word Bank

bibliography

call number

catalog

keyword

outline

publish

report

research

subtopic

Part A Write the word or words from the Word Bank that complete each sentence.

1. A _____ is a division or part of a larger topic.

2. A list of items arranged in a special way is a _____.

3. When you _____, you find information about a topic.

4. A _____ is an organized summary of information about a topic.

5. A _____ shows where a book is located in the library.

6. When you _____ your writing, you share it with others.

7. A _____ is a word or phrase that you use to search for information about a topic.

8. A _____ is a list of the sources a writer used to write a report.

9. A writing plan that lists topics and subtopics in a certain order is an _____.

Part B Read each pair of topics. Which one is more narrow? Write *A* or *B*.

10. **A** where to find information for a report
    B using a search engine

11. **A** growing vegetables
    B growing carrots and potatoes

12. **A** computers from past to present
    B the first computers

13. **A** high schools in Canada
    B schools in Canada

14. **A** sun spots
    B the sun

15. A the history of Mexico
B the Mexican War

Part C Write your answer to each question.

16. What are the five steps in the writing process? List them in order.

17. What are the three parts of a report? List them in order.

18. Why is it important to narrow a report topic?

19. What are three ways to search for information in a library catalog?

20. Why does a writer make bibliography cards?

21. What do you write at the top of your cards to help you organize them later?

22. Write a bibliography entry for the article titled Smart Parenting in Parent Network magazine. Teri Kranz wrote it. It appears in Volume 7, Spring 2007, on pages 8–11.

Part D Write the letter of the answer to each question.

23. What do you use as a guide when you write a report?
A note cards   **C** an outline
B the title   **D** a library catalog

24. Which part of a report contains supporting details?
A the topic paragraph   **C** the summary paragraph
B the body   **D** the bibliography

25. Why do you use quotation marks?
A to show that you are using someone else's words
B to show that you are using your own words
C to show that you found a good source
D to show that the information is important

Test Tip

When you take a written test, show how well you can write. Pay attention to your sentences. Check punctuation, capitalization, spelling, and grammar.

Other Kinds of Writing

Look at the photo on the opposite page. Does this look like your school? Writing is a major activity inside school buildings. You write test answers. You work on many kinds of writing assignments. Writing happens outside of school, too. You need writing skills for most jobs. At home, you probably write messages, e-mails, letters—and homework.

Doing well on written assignments and tests will allow you to graduate. Good writing skills will help you get a good job or continue your education elsewhere. Whatever you do, you will need to give information to others. You will need to be able to write clearly.

In Chapter 17, you will learn how to write better school assignments and test answers. You will learn how to write business letters and memos. You will also learn how to write letters to stay in touch with friends.

GOALS FOR LEARNING

- To write answers to test questions, and to respond to writing prompts
- To write a business letter and a memo
- To write a personal letter and an invitation

Reading Strategy: Metacognition

Metacognition means "thinking about your thinking." When you think as you read, you understand and remember what you read. Here are some steps you can take:

- Before you read, scan the text. Make predictions about what you will learn.
- As you begin to read, ask yourself what you already know about the subject.
- Notice when you get distracted—when you stop thinking about the words you are reading.
- Keep track of what you have learned. Write down main ideas and details.
- If something does not make sense, read it again.

Key Vocabulary Words

Writing prompt The directions for a writing assignment

Essay A short piece of writing about one topic

Business letter A formal letter to a person or company

Block style The format of a letter in which all the parts begin at the left margin; paragraphs are not indented

Memorandum A formal business message with a special format; usually called a memo

E-mail An electronic message that you send from one computer to another

Personal letter An informal letter to a friend or relative

Assignment and Test Writing

You are asked to do many kinds of writing in school. You write short answers to questions. You write reports and other long assignments. You also take tests. Many tests ask for written answers. The answers may be a sentence, a paragraph, or several paragraphs. Whether you are writing for an assignment or a test, keep these things in mind:

- Read the directions carefully.
- Make sure that you understand the assignment or question. If you are not sure, ask for help.
- If an assignment or question has more than one part, make sure you answer each part.
- If you are asked to write one or more paragraphs, do prewriting tasks. Make a list of details, such as facts, definitions, reasons, and examples. Organize the details into a simple outline.
- As you write, remember the three parts of a paragraph.
- Revise your writing if you have time. Use specific words to show that you understand the topic.
- Edit your writing. Mistakes such as misspelled words can lower your grade.

Answering Questions

Some assignments and tests ask for short written answers. Whenever you can, write your answers in sentences. Remember that a sentence expresses a complete thought. It must include both a subject and a predicate.

A question may ask you to identify something or someone. Your answer should tell the most important details about that person, place, or thing. It should also describe any unique features.

Writing prompt

The directions for a writing assignment

Essay

A short piece of writing about one topic

NOTE

Make every word count when answering a test question. Use specific words. Use details such as names, dates, and numbers.

▶ **EXAMPLE 1**

Test Question	Who was Kate Chopin?
Poor Answer	She was an author.
Better Answer	Kate Chopin was the author of the book *The Awakening*.

Practice A

Write a sentence to answer each question. Use a reference book or the Internet to find the information you need.

1. Identify Sally Ride.

2. Why is Galileo famous?

3. Who was Jackie Robinson?

4. Identify Nelson Mandela.

5. What is a Nobel Prize?

Responding to Writing Prompts

Sometimes you will be asked to respond to a **writing prompt**. A writing prompt is the directions for a writing assignment. Your answer is often an **essay** of one or more paragraphs. An essay is a short piece of writing about one topic. Tests often include essay questions.

Plan your essay by doing these prewriting tasks:

- Read the prompt two or three times. It may identify the topic or ask you to choose one.
- Decide on the main idea of your essay. Make sure it matches the prompt.
- Think of details that support the main idea. Make a list of facts, definitions, reasons, and examples.
- Organize the details in an order that makes sense.

NOTE

Look for key verbs in writing prompts and essay questions. They will tell you what to do. For example, you may be asked to *describe*, *identify*, *explain*, *discuss*, or *give reasons*.

Reading Strategy:
Metacognition

Find a quiet place to read. This will help you focus on what the words mean.

When you have finished these tasks, you are ready to write:

- Begin your essay by stating the main idea in a topic sentence. (If you are writing several paragraphs, this will be a topic paragraph.)
- To write the body, look at the ordered list of details you wrote earlier.
- End with a conclusion (or summary paragraph).
- Revise and edit your essay.

▶ **EXAMPLE 2**

Prompt   Describe three uses of a helicopter.

Essay   Helicopters are very useful. For example, they can carry injured people from an accident to the hospital. Firefighters use helicopters to search for fires in the mountains. Military helicopters move troops and supplies. Helicopters do jobs no other vehicles can do.

Practice B

Read the essay in Example 2. Then write the answer to each question.

1. Why did the writer use the word *useful* in the first sentence?

2. How do the details in the body of the paragraph support the main idea?

3. What kind of order did the writer use to organize the details?

4. Does the essay match the writing prompt? Explain your answer.

5. Could the prompt have been answered with several paragraphs? Explain your answer.

REVIEW

Follow the directions to write an essay.

1. Write one paragraph about your favorite memory. Describe in detail what happened. Explain why this is your favorite memory.

Answer these questions about the essay you wrote.

2. What words in the directions helped you to know what to write?

3. What is the main idea of your essay?

4. What order did you use to organize your details?

5. What was the last step you took to complete your essay?

SPELLING BUILDER

Spelling Words with Silent Letters

Some letters in words are silent. You probably already know about the silent e in words such as *cane* and *fire*. Other letters can be silent, too. For some words, you just have to remember how to spell them. There are no rules to help you.

Say each word below. Write the silent letter in each one.

1. anchor
2. island
3. thumb

4. column
5. salmon
6. Wednesday

7. knee
8. sign
9. wrist

Business Writing

Objectives

- To identify the parts of a business letter
- To write a clear business message
- To explain the format of a memo

Business letter

A formal letter to a person or company

Block style

The format of a letter in which all the parts begin at the left margin; paragraphs are not indented

Reading Strategy:
Metacognition

How does this list compare to the sample letter on the next page?

At times, you will write for purposes other than school. You might write to a company about something you bought. You might write about getting a job. On the job, you might write to another company or to a customer.

Business Letters

Business letters are formal letters to a person or company. In formal writing, you use complete sentences. You do not use contractions or casual language. You stick to the topic.

Most business letters are typed on 8½- x 11-inch white paper. They follow a certain format called **block style**. All the parts of the letter begin at the left margin. The paragraphs are not indented. The parts appear as "blocks." A sample business letter is shown on the next page.

A business letter has eight parts. They appear in this order:

1. The *heading* is the address of the sender.

2. The *date* helps businesses keep track of letters.

3. The *inside address* is the address of the person who will receive the letter.

4. The *salutation* or *greeting* usually includes the name of the person being addressed. The salutation ends with a colon. Here are some salutations:
   Dear Dr. Ross: Dear Sir or Madam: Dear Editor:

5. The *body* is the message in one or more paragraphs.

6. The *closing* is where the sender signs off. Capitalize only the first letter of the first word. The closing ends with a comma. Here are some common closings:
   Sincerely,   Respectfully,   Best regards,

7. The sender signs his or her *signature*.

8. The sender's typed *name* (and sometimes the sender's *job title*) goes below the signature.

E-mail

An electronic message that you send from one computer to another

Reading Strategy:
Metacognition

As you study this letter, think about a business letter you have received.

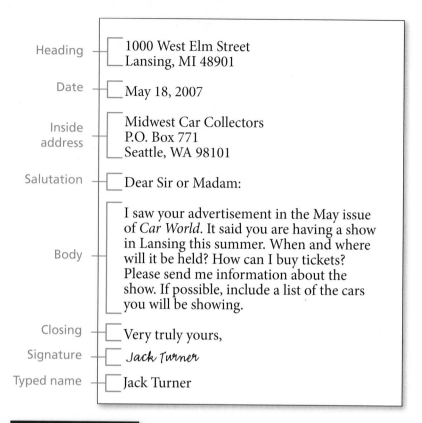

Heading
1000 West Elm Street
Lansing, MI 48901

Date
May 18, 2007

Inside address
Midwest Car Collectors
P.O. Box 771
Seattle, WA 98101

Salutation
Dear Sir or Madam:

Body
I saw your advertisement in the May issue of *Car World*. It said you are having a show in Lansing this summer. When and where will it be held? How can I buy tickets? Please send me information about the show. If possible, include a list of the cars you will be showing.

Closing
Very truly yours,

Signature
Jack Turner

Typed name
Jack Turner

Practice A

Draw the eight parts of a business letter. Use boxes of different sizes to show each part. Inside each box, write the name of the part.

Other Business Messages

In the world of work, you will not always write a business letter to share information. You may leave a phone message, write or type a message on paper, or send an **e-mail**. An e-mail is an electronic message that you send from one computer to another. In all of these messages, include:

- the time and date (automatically part of an e-mail)
- the name of the person to receive the message
- the message
- your name

Memorandum

A formal business message with a special format; usually called a memo

Grammar Tip

A colon is like an arrow. It points the reader to the information that follows it. Use a colon after each word in the heading of a memo.

A **memorandum** is a formal business message with a special format. A memorandum is also called a memo. Memos are usually not sent outside of a company. They are sent to other employees. A memo might be printed on paper or sent as an e-mail. The heading of a memo has four parts. The parts start with these words: *Date, To, From,* and *Subject.*

MEMO

Date: May 3, 2007
To: Ms. Hall, Principal
From: Mr. Garcia, Chairperson, Awards Committee
Subject: Awards Night

We will hold Awards Night on Monday, June 7, at 7:00 PM. Because the auditorium is small, we will invite only the seniors. The Awards Committee will meet again on May 12 at 3:30 PM in Room 216. We will choose a speaker and discuss how to set up the stage.
If you have questions about these plans, please let me know. Thank you for your support.

Practice B

Use the memo above to write the answer to each question.

1. What four pieces of information are always part of the heading of a memo?

2. There is no address on the memo. Why not?

3. Why did Mr. Garcia send the memo to Ms. Hall?

4. Does Ms. Hall need to write back to Mr. Garcia?

5. How does Mr. Garcia end his memo?

REVIEW

Follow the directions to write a business letter.

1. Imagine that you ordered a book from a catalog. After four weeks, the book has not arrived. Write a short business letter to the company. Explain the problem. Ask what the company will do to correct it. Here are some facts you will need:

Company:	Page Turner Books 999 Clark Street Chicago, IL 01943
Book title:	The Daily Life of Early American Indians by Curtis Lonewolf
Order date:	September 9, 2006
Today's date:	October 7, 2006

Read the memo below. Then answer the questions.

MEMO

Date: May 7, 2007
To: Ms. Hall
From: Mr. Garcia
Subject:

I have attached the bill for the flowers for Awards Night. You will notice that the bill is marked "Paid in Full." Mr. Bloom delivered the flowers himself. He told me that he was donating them, the flowers were gorgeous! The Awards Committee will write a thank-you note to him. In the meantime, here is the bill for your records.

---

2. What is missing from the heading of this memo?

3. Who sent this memo? Who received it?

4. What grammar mistake does the message contain?

5. What detail could have been left out of the message?

Personal Writing

You have probably written a letter to a friend or relative. Maybe you wrote to share some news or plans. Maybe you wrote just to stay in touch. In personal writing, you can use informal, or casual, language. However, you still need to follow the basic rules of grammar. You still need to express your ideas clearly so they can be understood.

Personal Letters

A **personal letter** can be written on paper of any size, color, or design. It is often written by hand. You can use both sides of the paper for a personal letter. It has five parts, as shown below.

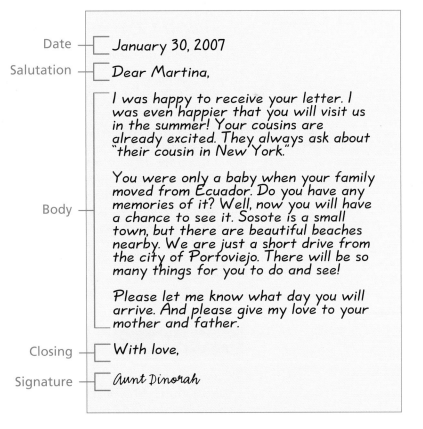

Date — January 30, 2007

Salutation — Dear Martina,

Body —
I was happy to receive your letter. I was even happier that you will visit us in the summer! Your cousins are already excited. They always ask about "their cousin in New York."

You were only a baby when your family moved from Ecuador. Do you have any memories of it? Well, now you will have a chance to see it. Sosote is a small town, but there are beautiful beaches nearby. We are just a short drive from the city of Portoviejo. There will be so many things for you to do and see!

Please let me know what day you will arrive. And please give my love to your mother and father.

Closing — With love,

Signature — Aunt Dinorah

NOTE

Personal messages can also be e-mails or short notes. With any message, remember to include the date and your name.

Reading Strategy:
Metacognition

After you write a personal letter, read it aloud. Think about how it sounds. Does it sound like you?

Practice A

Use the letter on page 447 to answer each question.

1. What punctuation mark follows the salutation?

2. What is the closing of this letter?

3. What punctuation mark follows the closing?

4. Which part of the letter contains the message?

5. What are three differences between a personal letter and a business letter?

Thank-You Letters

It is always polite to say thank you for a gift or favor. It is even more thoughtful to say it in a letter. A thank-you letter is a kind of personal letter. Read the letter below. Notice that the writer is specific about what she is saying thank you for. This shows that she appreciated the favor.

> August 9, 2007
>
> Dear Aunt Dinorah and Uncle Maceo,
>
> I can never thank you enough for the kindness you showed me this summer. Everything in Ecuador was new and strange to me—but you made me feel at home. The camping trip was the best! It was such a great way to see different parts of northern Ecuador. It was also a perfect way to get to know my cousins. Uncle Maceo, I want to thank you for taking time off work for that trip. I know it wasn't your usual vacation time. Now you must all come here to New York—please! Give my love to Adolfo and Eva.
>
> Love,
>
> Martina

Practice B

Write a thank-you letter to someone who has given you a gift or done a favor for you. Be specific. Make positive comments. Include the five parts of a personal letter.

NOTE

When you write by hand, take the time to write neatly and clearly.

Invitations

Suppose you are hosting an event. You want others to attend. You might write an invitation. An invitation can be written as a personal letter. Often, though, invitations only include the important details. In either case, make sure your invitation describes the event and tells when and where it will take place. Also include information such as how to get there, what to bring, and who to call if someone has a question.

> ### YOU'RE INVITED!
>
> **What:** A 20th birthday party for Reed Tinsley
> **When:** October 21, 2007
>   Supper at 6:00 PM and dancing at 8:00 PM
> **Where:** 260 Young Hill Road
>   Greenwood, Maine
>
> Bring your favorite dish and your dancing shoes!
> Call Sienna at 555-1122 if you need directions to the house.

I am so happy when I get a personal letter in the mail. That is why I like to send letters to others.

REVIEW

1. Write a short letter to a friend. When you are finished, label each of the five parts.

2. Write an invitation to a school event. The event can be real or imaginary. Include these headings: *What, When,* and *Where.* Add a sentence at the end telling what to bring or who to call.

VOCABULARY BUILDER

Using Formal and Informal Language

When you write a business letter, you use formal language. In a personal letter, you can use informal language. Informal language is more relaxed and casual. For example, in a business letter, you might choose this closing: *Sincerely yours,* In a personal letter, you might close with this: *Bye for now!*

In each pair, choose the one that is more formal. Write A or B.

1. **A** Yours truly,   **B** Love,
2. **A** Dear Mr. Smith: **B** Dear Jack,
3. **A** Call me later.   **B** Please call after 1 PM.
4. **A** Hi Mike,   **B** Dear Mike:

PUTTING IT ALL TOGETHER

Write a letter to the editor of a newspaper. Write about a problem that was in the news recently. Tell how you think the problem should be fixed. Offer positive suggestions. Put your ideas in order. Follow the business letter format shown on page 444. Then trade letters with a partner. Check your partner's letter for mistakes. Suggest ways to improve it. Check the format of the letter. Does it have all eight parts?

Six Traits of Writing:

Organization order, ideas tied together

Applying for a Job

If you need a job, look in the "Help Wanted" section of a local newspaper or magazine. To apply for a job, you may need to send a letter of application. This is a kind of business letter.

Begin a letter of application with a reference to the job and how you learned about it. Tell why you are the right person to hire. List past jobs you have had. Tell why you want the job. Show that you can organize your thoughts by writing clear, correct sentences. At the end of the letter, tell how you can be reached. Say that you look forward to meeting in person.

427 East Lincoln Drive
Denver, CO 80220

May 14, 2007

Oscar Chin
Snow Cap Cafe
602 Mountain Crest Road
Denver, CO 80220

Dear Mr. Chin:

I saw your ad for a waitress in the *Morning Advertiser*. I am very interested in the job.

I was a waitress at Martin's Restaurant in 2006. I also worked at Tom's Grocery last summer. I am a good student. I would like to learn more about the restaurant business. I dream of owning a restaurant someday.

I can start immediately. Call me at 555-6210 after 3:00 PM. I look forward to meeting you. Thank you.

Sincerely,

Marla Forman
Marla Forman

Answer these questions about the sample letter.

1. How did Marla learn about this job?

2. What job experience does Marla have?

3. **CRITICAL THINKING** Does the sentence about Marla's dream belong in this letter? Why or why not?

VIEWING

Go to an online posting of jobs. Search for jobs in your area. Scroll through the jobs that are listed. How many of the postings ask for a letter of application? What else do they ask for? What catches your eye as you read?

BUILDING RESEARCH SKILLS

Using a Grammar Reference Book

Even experienced writers have questions about grammar and punctuation. One place to find the answers is in a grammar reference book. A grammar reference book explains the rules about language. It shows how certain words are used. Your library has grammar reference books.

This book, *Basic English,* can also be used as a grammar reference. There are two easy ways to find information in this book. You can use the index, which begins on page 489. It lists topics in alphabetical order. Some of the topics have subtopics listed under them. You can also use the glossary, which begins on page 483. The glossary is a dictionary of vocabulary words used in this book. It provides a definition of each word. It also gives the page number where the word is first used.

Read the sentence below. Then answer the questions.

Writing well is not easy, it takes concentration, patience, and an understanding of basic grammar rules.

1. Identify the grammar mistake in the sentence.

2. On what pages in this book can you find information about this common mistake?

3. **CRITICAL THINKING** How is the English you write the same as the English you speak? How is it different?

MEDIA

Many Web sites provide useful information about grammar. Choose a grammar topic, such as proper nouns, conjunctions, or subject-verb agreement. Use this topic as a keyword for an Internet search. Look at three Web sites that discuss the topic. One Web site may explain the topic in a way that is easier for you to understand. Choose the site you think is best. Read some of the information on the site. Did you learn anything new?

- Make sure that you understand an assignment or a test question before you write the answer.

- Answer questions with complete sentences. For questions that ask you to identify something, answer by writing about the important details.

- Look for important words in writing prompts. They will tell you what to do.

- Plan the answer to a writing prompt by doing prewriting tasks.

- Support the main idea of an essay with details. Organize the details in a way that best fits the topic.

- Use complete sentences in business letters and messages. Do not use contractions or casual language.

- Include all eight parts in a business letter. Use block style.

- In any type of message, be sure to include the important details.

- Write a memo to share information within a company. Include all four parts in the heading.

- Write a personal letter to stay in touch with a friend or relative.

- Make sure that an invitation includes all of the important facts. Describe the event and tell where and when it will take place.

- Write a thank-you letter to show that you appreciate a gift or favor.

GROUP ACTIVITY

Work with a partner. Read the two roles described at the right. Decide which role you will take and which one your partner will take. Follow the directions in each. Make up any missing details. Then read your writing to the class.

- You are an office manager. Write a memo to employees about a new job opening. Explain that you have posted an ad for a truck driver.
- You want a job and see the ad for a truck driver. Write a business letter to apply for the job. Tell why you are the right person to hire.

Word Bank

block style

business letter

e-mail

essay

memorandum

personal letter

writing prompt

Part A Write the word or words from the Word Bank that complete each sentence.

1. A _____ is the directions for a writing assignment.

2. An _____ is a short piece of writing about one topic.

3. A _____ is a formal letter to a person or company.

4. An _____ is an electronic message.

5. A _____ is a business message with a special format.

6. In a letter with _____, all parts of the letter begin at the left margin.

7. A _____ is an informal letter to a friend or relative.

Part B Identify each item by writing one sentence about it. Use the information found on the pages in parentheses.

8. *Who's Who* (page 357)

9. Kiribati (page 353)

10. compound sentence (page 279)

Answer Bank

body

closing

date

heading

inside address

salutation

signature

typed name

Part C The eight parts of a business letter are described below. Match each description with a part from the Answer Bank. Write the name of the part.

11. the handwritten name of the sender

12. the greeting

13. the part that ends with a comma

14. the sender's address

15. the address of the person who will receive the letter

16. the month, day, and year

17. the message

18. the typed name of the sender

Part D Write the letter of the answer to each question.

19. Which is *not* included in prewriting?
- **A** taking notes
- **B** choosing a topic
- **C** revising and editing
- **D** writing an outline

20. Choose the best topic sentence for this prompt: Tell how apples and oranges are different.
- **A** Apples can grow in cold places.
- **B** How can two fruits look and taste so different?
- **C** Oranges are full of Vitamin C.
- **D** Both apples and oranges are healthy fruits.

21. Which statement is true?
- **A** Business messages use informal language.
- **B** Memos are usually sent only to other employees.
- **C** All business messages are memos.
- **D** Business messages do not need the date.

Part E Write the answer to each question.

22. A colon follows the salutation in a business letter. How is this different from a personal letter?

23. What four words are used in the heading of a memo?

Part F Follow each set of directions.

24. Draw the five parts of a personal letter. Use boxes of different sizes to represent each part. Inside each box, write the name of the part.

25. Choose one of the writing prompts below. Write a one-paragraph essay. Check spelling, punctuation, capitalization, sentence variety, and verb tense.
- Discuss a popular musician.
- Tell about a pet or an unusual animal.
- Explain why summer is a busy time of year.

▼ SIX TRAITS OF GOOD WRITING

Good writing is not a miracle. It is not an accident either. Good writing is part science and part art. It is the result of careful thinking and choices. To write well, you need to know about six important traits that determine the quality of writing.

Ideas

What message do you want to get across? What details are important to get your message across clearly? Ideas are the heart of any writing. So begin the writing process by developing strong, clear ideas. Set off your ideas with details that stand out and catch attention.

Organization

A piece of writing has a structure or pattern, just like a building. Organize your ideas into a structure that makes sense and fits the ideas well. For example, you may tell about events or steps in order. You may compare two things or explain a solution or an effect. Organization holds writing together and gives shape to ideas.

Voice

Your writing should "sound like you." It should capture your thoughts and your opinions. This is your "voice." In writing, your voice shows that you are interested in and understand the subject. Your voice also gives a personal tone to your writing that is yours alone.

Word Choice

Choose your words so that they are clear and interesting. Name things exactly. Use strong action verbs and specific adjectives. Good word choice helps you say exactly what you want to say. It helps your readers create a mental picture of what you want them to understand.

Six Traits of Writing:

Ideas message, details, and purpose

Six Traits of Writing:

Organization order, ideas tied together

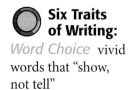

Six Traits of Writing:

Voice the writer's own language

Six Traits of Writing:

Word Choice vivid words that "show, not tell"

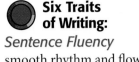

Six Traits of Writing:

Sentence Fluency smooth rhythm and flow

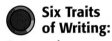

Six Traits of Writing:

Conventions correct grammar, spelling, and mechanics

Sentence Fluency

Well-made sentences make your writing easy to read. Aim for sentences that have the natural rhythms of speech. Vary sentence length and style. Then your sentences will flow. They will move your readers through your writing with ease.

Conventions

Once you have written something, ask yourself: Could this be published in a newspaper? Make sure your writing is free from mistakes in spelling, grammar, and mechanics. Mechanics includes things such as correct capitalization and punctuation.

The rest of Appendix A describes the writing process. As you follow this process, remember to include these six traits of good writing.

▼ STEPS IN THE WRITING PROCESS

When writers turn words into a paragraph or a report, they use a set of steps. These steps make up the writing process. The writing process helps you organize your ideas and form them into paragraphs. The five main steps in the writing process are prewriting, drafting, revising, editing, and publishing.

Prewriting

Prewriting is the planning stage. This is when you decide what to write about. You also think about your audience, your purpose for writing, and any assignment directions. You gather needed information, and then you organize your ideas about your topic.

Drafting

In the drafting step, you put your ideas into sentences. Then you build your sentences into paragraphs. You do not have to worry about mistakes in this step. You will find and fix them later.

Revising

When you revise, you improve your writing. You look for words and phrases that need to be changed. You may decide to add more information or take some information out. You may choose to arrange your ideas in a different way.

Editing and Proofreading

When you edit, you find and correct mistakes in spelling, grammar, punctuation, and capitalization. You also improve your word choice. The process of marking editing changes is called proofreading. After proofreading, you create the final draft.

Publishing and Presenting

There are several ways to publish, or share, your writing with others. One way is to read it to an audience. Other forms of publishing include giving someone a copy of your written work, or presenting it as a poster or in a slide show.

The five steps of the writing process are explained in more detail on the following pages.

▼ PREWRITING

Six Traits of Writing:

Ideas message, details, and purpose

Choosing Your Topic

Many writers find choosing a topic to be the hardest part of writing. Certainly, it is an important part. Without a good topic, you have nowhere to go with your writing. Here are some ways to look for a topic:

- Think about people you know, places you have seen, and activities you enjoy.
- Think about memories or experiences from your past.
- Read newspapers and magazines. Search the Internet. Listen to the radio. Think about what you have seen on TV recently. What is going on in the world around you?
- Write down anything that comes to mind. This is called *brainstorming*. When you brainstorm, you write down every idea as you think of it. You do not judge your ideas.
- Talk to other people. They may offer suggestions.

- Think of questions about a subject. A question can become a good topic.

Once you have a list of possible topics, check them against your writing assignment. Cross off topics that do not fit the assignment. Then cross off topics that do not interest you. Look at the remaining topics. Choose one that you feel strongly about. It may be something you like or dislike.

Six Traits of Writing:

Organization order, ideas tied together

Choosing Your Main Idea

Now think more about your topic. What is the main idea you want to talk about? To help you decide on your main idea, use a graphic organizer such as a diagram, word web, or chart. Write your topic as the title of the graphic organizer. Write down subtopics, or different parts of the topic. Then write details related to each subtopic. For example, suppose your topic is "teenagers and cell phones." You might create this graphic organizer as you prewrite:

Teenagers and Cell Phones

Problems	When Cell Phones Are Used	Popular Phone Features
cost of phone plan	to chat with a friend or family member	camera
use in school	to report an emergency	text messaging
losing your phone	to tell someone that your plans changed	games
remembering phone plan details	to ask a question	

A graphic organizer like this can help you organize your thoughts and see how ideas relate to each other. It can help you narrow your topic and choose your main idea. For example, after looking at the chart above, you might decide you want to write about why teenagers use cell phones. Your main idea might be: Besides talking with friends, teenagers use cell phones to make last-minute plans, to get information, to be entertained, and to call for help.

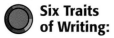
Developing Your Main Idea

Supporting details will make up the body of your writing. What details support or explain your main idea? Once you have chosen your main idea, you need to find information about it. There are several kinds of details:

- facts
- reasons
- examples
- sensory images
- stories or events
- experiences
- explanations

Where do you get these details? First, look back at anything you wrote when you were thinking about topics. Look at your brainstorm list, your notes, and any graphic organizers you made. To find more details to support your main idea, you might do the following:

- research
- interview
- observe
- remember
- imagine

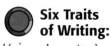

Six Traits of Writing:

Voice the writer's own language

Identifying Your Purpose and Audience

Before you begin to write your first draft, you also need to answer two questions:

- What is my reason for writing?
- Who is my audience?

Your reason for writing may be to entertain, to inform, to persuade, or a combination of these. Your audience may be your classmates, your friends, or another group of people. Knowing your reason for writing helps you focus. Knowing your audience helps you choose the information to include.

▼ Drafting

Now it is time to write your first draft. In a first draft, you put all your ideas on paper. Some writers make an outline or a plan first and follow it as they write. Other writers write their ideas in no particular order and then rearrange them later. Use the method that works best for you. Check your assignment directions before you begin writing.

Try to write the whole draft at once. Do not stop to rearrange or change anything. You can do that after you finish the draft. Remember, a first draft will be rough.

Writing the Introduction

How do you begin your writing? A good introduction can be a sentence or a whole paragraph. It should tell your reader what they will be reading about. The introduction usually states the main idea. It should also catch their attention. You might begin with:

- a story
- a fact
- a question
- a quotation

Writing the Body

The body of your writing contains details that explain or support your main idea. The body may be several sentences or several paragraphs. How can you arrange your details? Here are some suggestions:

- chronological order (from earliest event to latest event)
- order of importance (most important reason or detail first)
- comparison and contrast (different ways to compare two things)
- problem and solution (steps or different ways to solve a problem)

Six Traits of Writing:

Organization order, ideas tied together

Six Traits of Writing:

Sentence Fluency smooth rhythm and flow

If your draft is to be several paragraphs long, remember that most paragraphs begin with a topic sentence. The topic sentence tells the main point of the paragraph. All other sentences in the paragraph should relate to the topic sentence.

Writing the Conclusion

A good conclusion tells readers that the writing is coming to a close. It makes a closing statement about what you have written. Your conclusion should be logical—it should make sense with the details in the body. It should also leave a strong impression with your reader. You might end with:

■ a summary of what you wrote
■ a suggestion or opinion
■ the last event in a sequence

▼ REVISING

Now it is time to revise your draft. When you revise, you improve what you have written. You decide what you like and do not like. You decide what you want to change and how you will change it. You might add or take out words. You might rearrange sentences or paragraphs. Ask yourself these questions about your draft:

■ Does my draft fit the assignment directions?
■ Is my introduction interesting? Does it state the main idea?
■ Is the main idea supported and explained in the body?
■ Have I arranged the supporting details in a way that makes sense?
■ Is there any information that I should add?
■ Is there any information that I should leave out?
■ Do I use transitional words and phrases?
■ Do I use a variety of sentences?
■ Is my conclusion logical and strong?

Here are some tips to help you revise a draft:

- Set your draft aside for a while. Then read it. This will help you see your writing in a new way.
- Read your draft aloud. This will help you hear awkward sentences and notice places where information is missing.
- Ask someone else to read your draft. Encourage this person to tell you what you have done well and what needs work.

Adding Transitions and Sentence Variety

As you revise your writing, look for places that need a transition. A transition helps your reader move from one idea to the next. Here are some common transitional words and phrases:

also	finally	furthermore
next	in addition	therefore
first	for example	on the other hand

Also remember to use a variety of sentences in your writing. You can use declarative, imperative, interrogative, and exclamatory sentences. You can also use simple, compound, and complex sentences. Be sure to use a variety of sentence lengths. A mix of long and short sentences is more interesting. Do not begin every sentence the same way.

Creating a Final Draft

Rewrite your first draft, making the above changes in content and organization. Use a clean piece of paper or use a computer to type your draft. With a computer, you do not have to rewrite your entire draft every time you revise it. Using a computer also makes it easier for someone else to read your draft and make suggestions.

Then read your second draft and revise it. You may have to create several drafts before you have one that you like.

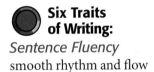

▼ EDITING AND PROOFREADING

Once you have a draft you like, edit it. When you edit, you find and correct mistakes in spelling, grammar, punctuation, and capitalization. These kinds of mistakes distract your reader. You want your reader to notice your ideas, not your mistakes. During the editing step, you also look at your choice of words. Replace any vague words with more specific ones. Ask yourself these questions as you edit:

- Did I spell each word correctly?
- Did I write complete sentences? Are there any fragments or run-on sentences?
- Did I use vivid and specific verbs, nouns, adjectives, and adverbs?
- Does the verb in each sentence agree with the subject?
- Did I use correct capitalization?
- Did I use correct punctuation?

Here are some other suggestions to help you edit:

- Use a computer spell checker, but remember that it cannot catch all spelling errors.
- Edit more than once. Look for a different kind of mistake each time.
- Read your work aloud. You may hear mistakes.
- Ask someone else to edit your work.
- Set your writing aside. Proofread it later. You may see mistakes more clearly.
- Keep a thesaurus nearby. It will help you find better words. It will help you replace words that you have used too often.
- Keep a dictionary and a grammar reference book nearby. You may have questions that they can help answer.

Proofreading Your Writing

The process of marking editing changes on paper is called proofreading. To make your proofreading faster and easier to follow, use proofreaders' marks. Draw the mark at the place where you want to make the correction. Here are some common proofreading marks:

Proofreading Marks

Delete or take out	ℐ	Insert an apostrophe	⌄
Spell out	ⓈⓅ	Insert quotation marks	⌄⌄
Insert	∧	Change to lowercase	/
Insert space	#	Change to capital letter	≡
Insert a period	⊙	Close up; take out space	◠
Insert a comma	∧	Begin a paragraph	¶
Insert a semicolon	⋏	Transpose letter or words	∿

▼ PUBLISHING AND PRESENTING

Think of publishing and presenting as sharing your writing with others. When you publish, you may decide to add photos, diagrams, or pictures. You may decide to add a cover. Many writers get their writing published in a newspaper or magazine or as a book. You publish a writing assignment by giving it to your teacher. However, there are other ways to publish your writing:

- Create a computer presentation such as a slide show.
- Create a poster, or post your work on the class bulletin board.
- Send your writing to a school or community newspaper or magazine.
- Give copies of your work to people who are interested in the topic. This could include family members and friends.
- Publish a class newspaper or magazine. Use it to present what you and your classmates have written.

- Get together with other writers. Take turns reading your work aloud and discussing it. Sharing aloud is one of the most common ways to publish writing.
- Present your writing as a speech. When you give a speech, you speak in front of an audience. To help you prepare and give a speech, read through Appendix C: Speaking Checklist.

Each time you write, think about the writing process you used. Ask yourself the following questions: What would I do the same next time? What would I do differently? What parts of the process do I need to work on? Use the answers to these questions to help you the next time you write.

▼ CAPITALIZATION RULES

Capitalization 1　**First word in a sentence**

Begin the first word of every sentence with a capital letter.

Who won the writing contest?

Capitalization 2　**Personal pronoun I**

Write the pronoun *I* with a capital letter.

At the last minute, I changed my mind.

Capitalization 3　**Names and initials of people**

Almost always begin each part of a person's name with a capital letter.

Hernando Jones　　Rosie Delancy　　Sue Ellen Macmillan

Some parts of names have more than one capital letter. Other parts are not capitalized. Check the correct way to write a person's name. Look in a reference book, or ask the person.

JoAnne Baxter　　Tony O'Hara　　Jeanmarie McIntyre

Use a capital letter to write an initial that is part of a person's name.

B. J. Gallardo　　J. Kelly Hunt　　John F. Kennedy

Capitalization 4　**Titles of people**

Begin the title before a person's name with a capital letter.

Dr. Watson　　Governor Maxine Stewart　　Ms. Costa

Use a lowercase letter if the word is not used before a person's name.

Did you call the doctor?

Who will be the next governor?

Capitalization 5	Names of relatives

A word like *grandma* may be used as a person's name or as part of a person's name. Begin this kind of word with a capital letter.

Only Dad, Grandma, and Aunt Ellie understand it.

A word like *grandma* is usually not capitalized when a possessive pronoun comes before it.

Only my dad, my grandma, and my aunt understand it.

Capitalization 6	Names of days

Begin the name of a day with a capital letter.

She does not go to work on Saturday or Sunday.

Capitalization 7	Names of months

Begin the name of a month with a capital letter.

My favorite months are March and September.

Capitalization 8	Names of holidays

Begin each important word in the name of a holiday with a capital letter. Words like *the* and *of* do not begin with a capital letter.

They meet on the Fourth of July and on Thanksgiving.

Capitalization 9	Names of streets and highways

Begin each word in the name of a street or highway with a capital letter.

Why is Lombard Street the most crooked road in the world?

Capitalization 10	Names of cities and towns

Begin each word in the name of a city or town with a capital letter.

In 1997, they moved from Sparta to New Brighton.

Capitalization 11	**Names of states, countries, and continents**

Begin each word in the name of a state, country, or continent with a capital letter.

> The movie was set in Peru, but it was filmed in Mexico.

Capitalization 12	**Names of mountains and bodies of water**

Begin each word in the name of a mountain or river with a capital letter. Also use a capital letter for lakes and oceans.

> Amelia Earhart's plane was lost over the Pacific Ocean.

Capitalization 13	**Abbreviations**

If a word would begin with a capital letter, begin its abbreviation with a capital letter.

> He wrote "Tues.—Dr. Lau" on a piece of paper.

Capitalization 14	**Titles of works**

Use a capital letter to begin the first word in the title of a work. Also capitalize the last word and every main word in a title. Only capitalize *the*, *a*, or *an* if it is the first word. Coordinating conjunctions and prepositions do not begin with a capital letter.

> Joe and Jen are characters in the TV series *Friends for Life*.

Capitalization 15	**Other proper nouns**

Begin each major word in a proper noun with a capital letter. A proper noun is the name of a particular person, place, idea, or thing.

> Matt went to Mario's Restaurant and ate Spaghetti Romano.

Capitalization 16	**Proper adjectives**

Begin a proper adjective with a capital letter. A proper adjective is an adjective that is formed from a proper noun. If the proper adjective is made with two or more nouns, capitalize each of them.

> That American author writes about English detectives.

> She loves Alfred Hitchcock movies.

▼ PUNCTUATION RULES

Punctuation 1

Punctuation at the end of a sentence

Use a period, question mark, or exclamation point at the end of every sentence. Do not use more than one of these marks at the end of a sentence. For example, do not use both a question mark and an exclamation point. Do not use two exclamation points.

Use a period at the end of a sentence that makes a statement.

> A hockey player can skate backward at top speed.

Use a period at the end of a sentence that gives a command.

> Keep your eye on the puck.

Use a question mark at the end of a sentence that asks a question.

> Who is the goalie for their team?

Use an exclamation point at the end of a sentence that expresses excitement.

> That was a terrific block!

Punctuation 2

Periods with abbreviations

Use a period at the end of each part of an abbreviation.

Most titles used before people's names are abbreviations. These abbreviations may be used in formal writing. (*Miss* is not an abbreviation and does not end with a period.)

> Dr. Ramas   Mr. Bill Tilden   Ms. Mia Connolly

Most other abbreviations may be used in addresses, notes, and informal writing. They should not be used in formal writing.

> Lake View Blvd.   Thurs.   Fifth Ave.   Dec. 24

Do not use periods in the abbreviations of names of government agencies and certain other organizations.

> Station MLT will broadcast a special program about the FBI.

Do not use periods after two-letter state abbreviations in addresses. This kind of abbreviation has two capital letters and no period. Use these abbreviations in addresses.

> His address is 187 Third Street, Los Angeles, CA 90048.

Punctuation 3   Periods after initials

Use a period after an initial that is part of a person's name.

> Chester A. Arthur   C. C. Pyle   Susan B. Anthony

Punctuation 4   Commas in dates

Use a comma between the number of the day and the year in a date.

> Hank Aaron hit a record-breaking home run on April 8, 1974.

Use a comma after the year if it comes in the middle of the sentence.

> April 8, 1974, was an exciting day for Hank Aaron's fans.

Do not use a comma with only the name of the month and the year.

> Aaron hit his final home run in July 1976.

Do not use a comma with only the month and the number of a day.

> April 8 is the anniversary of his record-breaking home run.

Punctuation 5   Commas in place names

Use a comma between a city or town and the state or country.

> The chocolate factory is in Hershey, Pennsylvania.

Sometimes the two names do not come at the end of a sentence. Use another comma after the state or country if this is the case.

> Hershey, Pennsylvania, is the home of a chocolate factory.

Punctuation 6	**Commas in compound sentences**

Use a comma before the conjunction *and*, *but*, or *or* in a compound sentence.

> Many people tried, but no one succeeded.

Punctuation 7	**Commas in series**

Three or more words or groups of words used in a sentence form a series. Use commas to separate the words or groups of words in a series.

> Jamie, Mitch, Kim, Lou, and Pablo entered the contest.

> They swam one mile, biked two miles, and ran five miles.

Punctuation 8	**Commas after introductory phrases and clauses**

Use a comma after a phrase placed before the subject of the sentence. The phrase should give additional information about the main thought of a sentence.

> In the old dresser, Juan found the diamonds.

Do not use a comma if the predicate comes before the subject of the sentence.

> In the old dresser lay the diamonds.

Use a comma after an adverb clause at the beginning of a sentence.

> When he was named MVP, Wayne Gretzky was 18 years old.

Punctuation 9	**Commas with nouns of address**

Use a comma after a noun of direct address at the beginning of a sentence.

> Fernando, that was a terrific pitch!

Use a comma before a noun of direct address at the end of a sentence.

> That was a terrific pitch, Fernando!

Use a comma before and after a noun of direct address in the middle of the sentence.

That, Fernando, was a terrific pitch!

Punctuation 10 **Commas with appositives**

Use a comma before an appositive at the end of a sentence.

The speech was given by Shelley, our class president.

Use a comma before and after an appositive in the middle of the sentence.

Shelley, our class president, gave the speech.

Punctuation 11 **Commas or exclamation points with interjections**

Almost always use a comma after an interjection.

Well, we should probably think about it.

Use an exclamation point after an interjection that expresses excitement.

Wow! That is a terrific idea!

Punctuation 12 **Commas after greetings in personal letters**

Use a comma after the greeting in a personal letter. Begin the first word in the greeting of a letter with a capital letter.

Dear Karla,   Dear Uncle Theodore,

Punctuation 13 **Commas after closings in letters**

Use a comma after the closing in a letter. Begin the first word in the closing of a letter with a capital letter.

Love,   Yours sincerely,

Punctuation 14 **Quotation marks with direct quotations**

A direct quotation is the exact words a person said. Use quotation marks at the beginning and end of a direct quotation. Begin the first word in a direct quotation with a capital letter.

"Look!" cried Tina. "That cat is smiling!"

"Of course," Tom joked, "it's a Cheshire cat."

Punctuation 15   Commas with direct quotations

Usually, use a comma to separate the words of a direct quotation from the speaker.

Jay asked, "Who won the game last night?"

"The Tigers won it," said Linda, "in 14 innings."

Punctuation 16   Quotation marks with titles of works

Use quotation marks around the title of a story, poem, song, essay, or chapter.

"Have a Happy Day" is a fun song to sing.

Sometimes a period or a comma comes after the title. Put the period or comma inside the closing quotation mark.

A fun song to sing is "Have a Happy Day."

Punctuation 17   Underlines with titles of works

Underline the title of a book or play when you write it by hand. Also underline the title of a magazine, movie, TV series, or newspaper.

One of the best movies about baseball is <u>The Champion</u>.

Put the title of a book or play in italic type in a word-processing program. Also put the title of a magazine, movie, TV series, or newspaper in italic type.

One of the best movies about baseball is *The Champion*.

Punctuation 18   Apostrophes in contractions

Use an apostrophe in place of the missing letter or letters in a contraction.

is not—isn't   Mel is—Mel's   I will—I'll

| Punctuation 19 | Apostrophes in possessive nouns |

Use an apostrophe and -*s* to write the possessive form of a singular noun.

> This cage belongs to one bird. It is the bird's cage.

Use an apostrophe for the possessive form of a plural noun that ends in -*s*.

> This is a club for boys. It is a boys' club.

Use an apostrophe and -*s* for a plural noun that does not end in -*s*.

> This is a club for men. It is a men's club.

| Punctuation 20 | Colons after greetings in business letters |

Use a colon after the greeting in a business letter. Capitalize the first word in a greeting.

> Dear Ms. Huan: Dear Sir or Madam:
>
> Dear Senator Rayburn: To Whom It May Concern:

| Punctuation 21 | Colons in expressions of time |

When you write time in numerals, use a colon between the hour and the minutes.

> 5:45 PM   9:00 AM   12:17 PM

| Punctuation 22 | Hyphens in numbers and fractions |

Use a hyphen in a compound number from twenty-one to ninety-nine.

> thirty-seven   fifty-eight   seventy-three

Use a hyphen in a fraction.

> one-quarter   two-thirds   seven-eighths

Appendix C: Speaking Checklist

Speaking in front of an audience is one way to communicate. Common types of public speaking include speeches, presentations, debates, group discussions, interviews, storytelling, and role-playing. Use this checklist to help you plan a speech or presentation.

Define Your Purpose and Audience

✔ If the speech is an assignment, read the instructions carefully. What will you be graded on? Will the speech be formal or informal? Will you stand in front of a podium? Can you interact with the audience?

✔ Decide on your purpose. Do you want to inform, entertain, persuade, explain, or describe something? Do you want to get the audience to act on an issue? Do you want to involve them in a discussion or debate?

✔ Identify your audience. Who are they?

✔ Think about what your audience already knows about the topic. Predict their questions, concerns, and opinions. What words are familiar to your audience? What may need explanation?

✔ Think about how your audience prefers to get information. Do they like visuals, audience participation, or lecture?

Decide on Your Topic

✔ Choose a topic that is right for the purpose and assignment. Choose one that you know and enjoy, or choose one that you want to learn more about.

✔ Make sure the topic is important or interesting to the audience.

✔ Determine how long your speech should be. Is your topic narrow enough? Do you have enough time to share the details?

✔ Think about the kinds of details that will help you get across the main idea.

Draft Your Speech

✔ Include an introduction, a body, and a conclusion.

✔ In the introduction, state your topic and purpose. Give your position.

✔ Establish yourself as an expert. Tell why you are the right person to give the speech based on your experiences.

✔ Get the attention of your audience so they want to listen. You might start your speech by asking a question, telling a story, describing something, giving a surprising fact, sharing a meaningful quotation, or making a memorable entrance.

- ✔ In the body of your speech, tell more about your main idea.

- ✔ Try to prevent listener confusion.

- ✔ Include supporting details such as facts, explanations, reasons, examples, stories or experiences, and quotes from experts.

- ✔ Check the order of your supporting details. Do they build on each other? Is the order logical?

- ✔ If you are describing something, use figurative devices, specific words, and words that appeal to the senses.

- ✔ If you are telling a story, make sure it has a beginning, middle, and end.

- ✔ Repeat key phrases or words to help people remember your point. If something is important, say it twice.

- ✔ Use transitions such as, "This is so important it is worth repeating," or "As I said before, we must act now."

- ✔ In the conclusion, tie your speech together.

- ✔ If you asked a question in your introduction, answer it in the conclusion.

- ✔ If you outlined a problem in your introduction, offer a solution.

- ✔ If you told a story in your introduction, refer to that story again.

- ✔ You may want to ask your audience to get involved, to take action, or to find out more about your topic.

- ✔ Revise your speech. Add missing details. Make sure the details support the main idea. Make sure the body is organized in a logical way.

- ✔ Edit and proofread your script. Choose more specific words. Check your grammar.

Select Audio/Visual Aids

- ✔ Decide if a visual aid would help your audience understand the main idea. Visual aids include posters, displays, objects, models, pictures or words on a screen or blackboard, and slide shows.

- ✔ Decide if handing out printed material, such as a list or diagram, would help the audience follow along.

- ✔ Decide if an audio recording or video clip would be helpful or interesting.

- ✔ Think about how the room is set up. Can the room be darkened for a slide show or video presentation? If the room is large, do you need a microphone or projector?

- ✔ Make sure the right technology and props are available. Do you need a projector, video or tape player, computer, overhead screen, display table, or easel? Do you need someone to hold or adjust something?

- ✔ Make sure the audience will be able to clearly hear or see your audio and visual aids.

Know Your Speech

Every speaker is afraid of forgetting his or her speech. Choose one of the following ways to remember your speech.

✔ Hold a copy of the script. Highlight key phrases to keep you on track.

✔ Write a sentence outline of your main points and supporting details. Write down anything that you want to say in a certain way.

✔ Write an outline of key words. Choose words that will remind you what to say.

✔ Write key words, an outline, or your entire speech on note cards. They are less obvious than paper. Number the cards to keep them in order.

✔ Memorize your speech.

Practice Your Speech

✔ Practice your speech several times so you are familiar with the words.

✔ If you plan to use a script, practice with it. Do not just read your script. Practice looking out at the audience.

✔ If you plan to use note cards or an outline, practice with them. Revise them as you practice.

✔ If you plan to use visual aids, practice with them. Decide when in the speech you will introduce them.

✔ If you plan to use technology, be familiar with how it works.

✔ Practice sounding natural and confident. Giving a speech is more than talking. Your voice and appearance are powerful parts of your speech.

✔ Decide what you will wear when you give your speech.

✔ Practice how you will move. Will you stand in one place or move around? What gestures will reinforce your message?

Give Your Speech

✔ Body language: Stand tall. Keep your feet shoulder-width apart. Do not cross your arms or bury your hands in your pockets. Use gestures to make a point. Try to relax; that way, you will be in better control of your body.

✔ Eye contact: Look at your audience. Spend a minute or two looking at each side of the audience. The audience will feel as if you are talking to them. Do not just look at your teacher, the front row, or one side.

✔ Voice strategies: Clearly pronounce your words. Speak at a comfortable rate that is not too fast. Speak loud enough for everyone to hear you. Vary your volume, rate, and pitch. For example, you could say, "I have a secret. . . ." Then, you could lean toward the audience and speak in a loud, clear whisper as if you are telling them a secret. This adds dramatic effect and gets attention.

Appendix D: Listening Checklist

Listening is an important skill. You hear messages all the time—from other people and from the media. You are a listener at school, at home, at social events, at work, even in the car. You are a listener whenever you are part of a conversation or a discussion. It is important to understand and analyze the messages you hear. Use this checklist to become a better listener.

Listen Actively

✔ Be prepared to listen. Complete any reading assignments that are due before a speech or presentation.

✔ Sit near the person speaking and face the speaker directly.

✔ Sit up straight to show you are alert.

✔ Look at the speaker and nod to show you are listening.

✔ Focus on what the speaker is saying. Do not be distracted by other people.

✔ Take short notes during the speech or presentation.

✔ After the speech, ask the speaker to explain unfamiliar words or confusing ideas.

Be Appreciative and Thoughtful

✔ Relax and enjoy the listening experience.

✔ Think of the listening experience as an opportunity to learn.

✔ Respect the speaker and his or her opinions and ideas.

✔ Do not talk or make distracting gestures.

✔ Do not cross your arms. Open your arms to show you are open to receiving information.

✔ Try to understand the speaker's background, experiences, and feelings.

Analyze the Message

✔ Predict what the speaker is going to say based on what you already know.

✔ Identify the main idea of the message.

✔ Determine the purpose of the message.

✔ Note details such as facts, examples, and personal experiences. Does each detail support the main idea?

✔ Determine if a supporting detail is a fact or an opinion. Watch for opinions that are not supported. Watch for unfair attacks on a person's character, lifestyle, or beliefs.

- ✔ Identify any details intended to trick or persuade. Watch for exaggerations of truth. Watch for cause-effect relationships that do not make sense.

- ✔ If there are audio/visual aids, do they contribute to the message? What effect do they have?

- ✔ After the speech, ask about any words or ideas you did not understand.

- ✔ Form your own conclusions about the message.

Analyze the Speaker

- ✔ Analyze the speaker's experience and knowledge. Is he or she qualified to speak on the topic?

- ✔ Does the speaker seem prepared? Does the speaker appear confident?

- ✔ Analyze the speaker's body language. Is it appropriate?

- ✔ Consider the speaker's tone, volume, and word choices. What do they show?

Take Notes

- ✔ Write down key ideas and phrases, not everything that is said. Abbreviate words.

- ✔ Summarize the main points of the message in your own words.

- ✔ Copy important visual aids, such as graphs, charts, and diagrams. Do not copy every detail.

- ✔ Use stars or underlining to highlight important information or main points.

- ✔ Use arrows to connect related information.

- ✔ Use lists, charts, bullets, or dividing lines to organize information.

- ✔ Circle anything that is confusing or needs to be explained. Ask about these items later.

- ✔ Use the note-taking guidelines described on page xv of this textbook.

Appendix E: Viewing Checklist

Visual messages are messages that you see. They may or may not contain words. Visual messages include artwork, posters, diagrams, videos, photos, slide shows, and ads. Use this checklist to help you analyze a visual message.

Analyze Photos and Videos
✔ Identify the parts and features of the photo or video. What does it show?

✔ For videos, think about how movement is used to create the message. Is it fast or slow?

✔ Are written or spoken words part of the message? If so, how do the words affect what you see?

✔ Think about how the photo or video makes you feel. What mood is created? What are you reminded of?

Analyze Artwork
✔ Notice how colors, shapes, lines, and textures are used. Do certain features seem important?

✔ Think about the artist's purpose. What message does the art express? Does it represent something? Does it show an opinion or a mood?

Analyze Graphs, Charts, and Diagrams
✔ Graphs and charts are used to organize information. What information is shown? Is it clear?

✔ Graphs and charts often compare facts or numbers. What is being compared?

✔ Diagrams use shapes, lines, and arrows to show a main idea. What does the diagram show?

Analyze the Overall Message
✔ Think about the main idea. What is the author/artist trying to say? Is he or she successful?

✔ Think about the purpose of the message. Is the author/artist trying to inform, persuade, or entertain?

✔ Look for facts and opinions. Is information presented fairly? Does the message express an opinion? Is exaggeration used?

✔ Think about how the parts of the message work together. Does each part support the main idea? Do any parts take away from the main idea?

✔ Sometimes a visual message is part of a presentation, display, or speech. How does the visual message tie into the whole presentation? Does it help the presenter make a point?

✔ What conclusion can you make after viewing this message?

✔ What will you remember most about this message?

Appendix F: Reading Checklist

Good readers do not just read with their eyes. They read with their brains turned on. In other words, they are active readers. Good readers use strategies as they read to keep them on their toes. The following strategies will help you to check your understanding of what you read.

✔ **Summarizing** To summarize a text, stop often as you read. Notice these things: the topic, the main thing being said about the topic, and important details that support the main idea. Try to sum up the author's message using your own words.

✔ **Questioning** Ask yourself questions about the text and read to answer them. Here are some useful questions to ask: Why did the author include this information? Is this like anything I have experienced? Am I learning what I thought I would learn?

✔ **Predicting** As you read, think about what might come next. Add what you already know about the topic. Predict what the text will say. Then, as you read, notice whether your prediction is right. If not, change your prediction.

✔ **Text Structure** Pay attention to how a text is organized. Find parts that stand out. They are probably the most important ideas or facts. Think about why the author organized the ideas this way. Is the author showing a sequence of events? Is the author explaining a solution to a problem? Is the author showing cause and effect?

✔ **Visualizing** Picture what is happening in a text or what is being described. Make a movie out of it in your mind. If you can picture it clearly, then you know you understand it. Visualizing what you read will help you remember it later.

✔ **Inferencing** The meaning of a text may not be stated. Instead, the author may give clues and hints. It is up to you to put them together with what you already know about the topic. Then you make an inference—you conclude what the author means.

✔ **Metacognition** Think about your thinking patterns as you read. Before reading a text, preview it. Think about what you can do to get the most out of it. Think about what you already know about the topic. Write down any questions you have. After you read, ask yourself: Did that make sense? If the answer is no, read it again.

Glossary

A

Abbreviation (ə brē vē ā′ shən) A short form of a word (p. 29)

Abstract noun (ab′ strakt noun) A word that names something you cannot see or touch (p. 32)

Action verb (ak′ shən vėrb) A word that tells what someone or something did, does, or will do (p. 115)

Active verb (ak′ tiv vėrb) A verb form in which the subject is doing the action (p. 394)

Adjective (aj′ ik tiv) A word that describes or tells about a noun or pronoun (p. 85)

Adjective clause (aj′ ik tiv klȯz) A dependent clause that describes a noun or pronoun (p. 284)

Adverb (ad′ vėrb) A word that tells more about a verb, a verb phrase, an adjective, or another adverb in a sentence (p. 169)

Adverb clause (ad′ vėrb klȯz′) A dependent clause that works like an adverb in a sentence (p. 283)

Adverb of degree (ad′vėrb ov di grē) An adverb that tells how much, how little, or how often something happens or is present (p. 172)

Adverb of negation (ad′ vėrb ov ni gā′ shən) The adverb *never* or *not* (p. 175)

Advertisement (ad′ vər tīz′ mənt) A message designed to attract the public's attention; also called an ad (p. 360)

Advertiser (ad′ vər tīz′ er) A person who uses an advertisement to sell a product or service (p. 360)

Antecedent (an′ tə sēd′ nt) The noun or nouns that a pronoun replaces (p. 55)

Apostrophe (’) (ə pos′ trə fē) A punctuation mark that you use to show that a noun is possessive (p. 43)

Appositive (ə poz′ ə tiv) A noun, a noun phrase, or a noun clause that explains another noun in the same sentence (p. 288)

B

Bibliography (bib′ lē og′ rə fē) A list of the sources used to write a report (p. 419)

Block style (blōk stīl) The format of a letter in which all the parts begin at the left margin; paragraphs are not indented (p. 443)

Body (bod′ ē) The sentences in a paragraph that explain and support the main idea (p. 329)

Business letter (biz′ nis let′ ər) A formal letter to a person or company (p. 443)

C

Call number (kôl num′ bər) A number that tells where a book is located in the library (p. 417)

Capital letter (kap′ ə təl let′ ər) The uppercase form of a letter such as *A* (p. 4)

Catalog (kat′ l ôg) A list of items arranged in a special way (p. 415)

Cause and effect (kôz and ə fekt′) Something that happens (effect) because of something else (cause) (p. 354)

a	hat	e	let	ī	ice	ȯ	order	u̇	put	sh	she	ə	a in about
ā	age	ē	equal	o	hot	oi	oil	ü	rule	th	thin		e in taken
ä	far	ėr	term	ō	open	ou	out	ch	child	ŦH	then		i in pencil
â	care	i	it	ȯ	saw	u	cup	ng	long	zh	measure		o in lemon
													u in circus

Chronological order (kron´ ə loj´ ə kəl ôr´dər) An arrangement of events according to time; usually from the earliest event to the most recent event (p. 367)

Clause (klôz) A group of words with a subject and a predicate (p. 219)

Collective noun (kə lek´ tiv noun) The name of a group of people, places, or things (p. 24)

Common noun (kom´ ən noun) The name of any person, place, thing, event, or idea (p. 27)

Comparative form (kəm par´ ə tiv fôrm) The form of an adjective used to compare two people or things (p. 103)

Compare (kəm per´) To point out how two things are alike or different (p. 355)

Complement (kom´ plə mənt) A word or phrase that completes the meaning of a verbal (p. 309)

Complex sentence (kəm pleks´ sen´ təns) A sentence with one independent clause and one or more dependent clauses (p. 291)

Compound (kom´ pound) Two or more sentences or sentence parts that are connected with a conjunction (p. 132)

Compound noun (kom´ pound noun) Two or more words that work together to name one thing (p. 24)

Compound predicate (kom´ pound pred´ ə kit) Two or more predicates that share the same subject (p. 223)

Compound relative pronoun (kom´ pound rel´ ə tiv prō´ noun) One of these pronouns: *whoever, whomever, whichever,* or *whatever* (p. 64)

Compound sentence (kom´ pound sen´ təns) Two or more independent clauses that are connected with a conjunction (p. 279)

Compound subject (kom´ pound sub´ jikt) Two or more subjects that share the same predicate (p. 222)

Compound verb (kom´ pound vėrb) Two or more verbs connected by a conjunction in a sentence (p. 245)

Conclusion (kən klü´ zhən) A statement that summarizes a paragraph, restates the main idea, or states an opinion that logically follows the paragraph's details (p. 329)

Concrete noun (kon´ krēt noun) A word that names something you can see or touch (p. 32)

Conditional verb (kən dish´ ə nəl vėrb) A verb that shows that the action is possible or necessary (p. 138)

Conjunction (kən jungk´ shən) A word that connects parts of a sentence (p. 219)

Contraction (kən trak´ shən) Two words made into one by replacing one or more letters with an apostrophe (p. 75)

Coordinating conjunction (kō ôrd´ n āt ing kən jungk´ shən) A word that connects two or more equal parts of a sentence (p. 219)

Correlative conjunction (kə rel´ ə tiv kən jungk´ shən) Two words that act as a single conjunction connecting words or phrases in a sentence (p. 225)

D

Declarative sentence (di klar´ə tiv sen´ təns) A sentence that gives information (p. 11)

Definite article (def´ ə nit är´ tə kəl) The word *the*; it means a particular person or thing (p. 88)

Demonstrative adjective (di mon´ strə tiv aj´ ik tiv) The word *this, that, these,* or *those* used as an adjective (p. 101)

Demonstrative pronoun (di mon´ strə tiv prō´ noun) A pronoun that points out a particular person or thing (p. 69)

Dependent clause (di pen´ dənt klôz) A clause that does not express a complete thought (p. 228)

Dialogue (dī´ ə lôg) The words that people or story characters say to one another; conversation (p. 369)

Direct object (də rekt´ ob´ jikt) A noun or pronoun that receives the action of the verb (p. 248)

Direct quotation (də rekt´ kwō tā´ shən) A quotation that reports someone's exact words; quotation marks are required (p. 369)

Double negative (dub´ əl neg´ ə tiv) A sentence with two negatives (p. 175)

Draft (draft) An early version of writing; not the final version (p. 381)

E

Edit (ed´ it) To correct mistakes in a piece of writing; to check spelling, punctuation, capitalization, and word choice (p. 399)

E-mail (ē´ māl´) An electronic message that you send from one computer to another (p. 444)

End punctuation (end pungk´ chü ā´ shən) A mark at the end of a sentence that tells the reader where a sentence ends; there are three end punctuation marks: a period (.), a question mark (?), and an exclamation mark (!) (p. 4)

Essay (es´ ā) A short piece of writing about one topic (p. 441)

Exclamatory sentence (ek sklam´ ə tôr´ ē sen´ təns) A sentence that expresses strong feelings (p. 11)

F

Fact (fakt) A piece of information that is known to be true (p. 358)

Fiction (fik´ shən) A piece of writing about imaginary people and events (p. 365)

First-person pronoun (fėrst pėr sən prō´ noun) A pronoun that refers to the speaker (p. 58)

G

Gerund (jer´ ənd) A verb ending in -ing that is used as a noun (p. 312)

Gerund phrase (jer´ ənd frāz´) A gerund and its complements (p. 312)

H

Helping verb (hel´ ping vėrb) A verb that combines with a main verb to form a verb phrase (p. 119)

I

Imperative sentence (im per´ ə tiv sen´ təns) A sentence that gives a command or makes a request (p. 11)

Indefinite article (in def´ ə nit är´ tə kəl) The word a or an; it means any one of a group of people or things (p. 88)

Indefinite pronoun (in def´ ə nit prō´ noun) A pronoun that does not refer to a specific person or thing (p. 72)

Indent (in dent´) To start a sentence a certain distance from the left margin (p. 329)

Independent clause (in di pen´ dənt klòz) A clause that expresses a complete thought (p. 228)

Indirect object (in də rekt´ ob´ jikt) A noun or pronoun that receives the direct object of an action verb (p. 252)

Indirect quotation (in´ də rekt´ kwō tā´ shən) A quotation that reports what someone said without using the speaker's exact words; quotation marks are not used (p. 371)

Infinitive (in fin´ ə tiv) The word to plus the present tense of a verb (p. 122)

a	hat	e	let	ī	ice	ȯ	order	u̇	put	sh	she	ə	a	in about
ā	age	ē	equal	o	hot	oi	oil	ü	rule	th	thin		e	in taken
ä	far	ėr	term	ō	open	ou	out	ch	child	ᵗħ	then		i	in pencil
â	care	i	it	ȯ	saw	u	cup	ng	long	zh	measure		o	in lemon
													u	in circus

Infinitive phrase (in fin´ ə tiv frāz´) An infinitive, its complements, and any other words that describe it (p. 309)

Inform (in fôrm´) To pass along information, especially facts (p. 353)

Interjection (in´ tər jek´ shən) A word or group of words that expresses a feeling (p. 232)

Interrogative pronoun (in´ tə rog´ ə tiv prō´ noun) A pronoun that asks a question (p. 66)

Interrogative sentence (in´ tə rog´ ə tiv sen´ təns) A sentence that asks a question (p. 11)

Intransitive verb (in tran´ sə tiv vėrb) An action verb that does not need a noun to receive its action (p. 243)

Irregular plural noun (i reg´ yə lər plür´ əl noun) A plural that does not follow the normal rules (p. 39)

Irregular verb (i reg´ yə lər vėrb) A verb whose past tense and past participle are formed in different ways (p. 122)

K

Keyword (kē´ wėrd) A word or phrase that you use to search for information about a topic (p. 418)

M

Memorandum (mem´ ə ran´ dem) A formal business message with a special format; usually called a memo (p. 445)

N

Negative (neg´ ə tiv) A word or phrase that means "no" (p. 175)

Nonfiction (non´ fik´ shən) A piece of writing about real people and actual events (p. 365)

Noun (noun) A word that names a person, place, thing, event, or idea (p. 23)

Noun clause (noun klôz´) A dependent clause that works like a noun in a sentence (p. 287)

O

Object complement (ob´ jikt kom´ plə mənt) A noun or adjective that follows and tells about a direct object (p. 256)

Object of the preposition (ob´ jikt ov thə prep ə zish´ ən) A noun or pronoun at the end of a prepositional phrase (p. 193)

Opinion (ə pin´ yən) The way a person thinks about something; a belief or viewpoint (p. 358)

Outline (out´ līn´) A writing plan that lists topics and subtopics in a certain order (p. 422)

P

Paragraph (par´ ə graf) A group of sentences about one idea (p. 329)

Participle (pär´ tə sip əl) A verb form that can be used as an adjective (p. 316)

Participle phrase (pär´ tə sip əl frāz) A participle plus any words that complement or describe it (p. 317)

Passive verb (pas´ iv vėrb) A verb form in which the action happens to the subject (p. 394)

Past participle (past pär´ tə sip´ əl) The verb form used to form the perfect tenses (p. 122)

Perfect tense (pėr´ fikt tens) The present perfect, past perfect, or future perfect form of a verb (p. 119)

Personal letter (pėr´ sə nəl let´ ər) An informal letter to a friend or relative (p. 447)

Personal pronoun (pėr´ sə nəl prō´ noun) A pronoun that refers to a person or a thing (p. 58)

Persuade (pər swād´) To convince someone to agree with an opinion, an idea, or a request; to change someone's opinion about something (p. 359)

Phrase (frāz) A group of words that work together; a phrase does not have a subject and a predicate (p. 275)

Plural noun (plùr´ əl noun) The name of more than one person, place, thing, event, or idea (p. 34)

Point of view (point ov vyü) The position of the storyteller in a story; either first-person or third- person point of view (p. 366)

Positive form (poz´ ə tiv fôrm) The form of an adjective used to describe people or things (p. 103)

Possessive noun (pə zes´ iv noun) A word that shows ownership or a relationship between two things (p. 43)

Possessive pronoun (pə zes´ iv prō´ noun) A pronoun that shows that something belongs to someone or something (p. 60)

Predicate (pred´ ə kit) The word or words in a sentence that tell something about the subject; it always contains a verb (p. 8)

Predicate adjective (pred´ ə kit aj´ ik tiv) An adjective that follows a verb and describes the subject of the sentence (p. 86)

Predicate noun (pred´ ə kit noun) A noun or pronoun that follows a state-of-being verb and renames the subject (p. 260)

Preposition (prep ə zish´ ən) A word that shows how a noun or pronoun relates to another word or phrase in a sentence (p. 193)

Prepositional phrase (prep ə zish´ ən nəl frāz) A group of words that begins with a preposition and ends with a noun or pronoun (p. 193)

Present participle (prez´ nt pär´ tə sip əl) The form of a verb that ends in -*ing* (p. 127)

Prewriting (prē rī´ting) Preparing to write; the planning step of the writing process (p. 332)

Progressive verb phrase (prə gres´ iv vèrb frāz) A form of *be* plus the present participle of a verb (p. 127)

Pronoun (prō´ noun) A word that takes the place of one or more nouns (p. 55)

Proofread (prüf´ rēd´) To mark editing changes on paper using proofreading marks (p. 400)

Proper adjective (prop´ ər aj´ ik tiv) A proper noun used as an adjective, or an adjective made from a proper noun (p. 91)

Proper noun (prop´ ər noun) The name of one particular person, place, thing, event, or idea (p. 27)

Publish (pub´ lish) To share your writing with others (p. 411)

Q

Quotation marks (" ") (kwō tā´ shən märks) The marks placed at the beginning and end of a direct quotation (p. 369)

R

Reflexive pronoun (ri flek´ siv prō´ noun) A pronoun that ends in -*self* or -*selves* (p. 61)

Regular verb (reg´ yə lər vèrb) A verb whose past tense and past participle end with -*ed* or -*d* (p. 122)

Relative pronoun (rel´ ə tiv prō´ noun) One of these pronouns: *who, whom, whose, that,* or *which* (p. 63)

a	hat	e	let	ī	ice	ô	order	ù	put	sh	she	ə	a in about
ā	age	ē	equal	o	hot	oi	oil	ü	rule	th	thin		e in taken
ä	far	ėr	term	ō	open	ou	out	ch	child	ᴛʜ	then		i in pencil
â	care	i	it	ò	saw	u	cup	ng	long	zh	measure		o in lemon
													u in circus

Report (ri pôrt′) An organized summary of information about a topic; usually involving research (p. 411)

Research (ri sėrch′) To find information about a topic (p. 411)

Revise (ri vīz′) To change a piece of writing to make it better (p. 381)

Run-on sentence (run ôn sen′ təns) Two or more ideas written as one without proper punctuation or conjunctions (p. 295)

S

Second-person pronoun (sek′ ənd pėr′ sən prō′ noun) A pronoun that refers to the person who is being spoken to (p. 58)

Sentence (sen′ təns) A group of words that expresses a complete thought (p. 3)

Sentence fragment (sen′ təns frag′ mənt) A group of words that does not express a complete thought (p. 3)

Series (sir′ ēz) A list of three or more words, phrases, or clauses (p. 220)

Simple sentence (sim′ pəl sen′ təns) One independent clause (p. 277)

Simple tense (sim′ pəl tens) The present, past, or future form of a verb (p. 118)

Singular noun (sing′ gyə lər noun) The name of one person, place, thing, event, or idea (p. 34)

State-of-being verb (stāt ov bē′ ing vėrb) A verb that links the subject of a sentence to a word or phrase that tells something about it (p. 149)

Subject (sub′ jikt) The word or words in a sentence that tell who or what the sentence is about (p. 7)

Subordinating conjunction (sə bôrd′ n āt ing kən jungk′ shən) A word that begins a dependent clause and connects it to an independent clause (p. 228)

Subtopic (sub′ top′ ik) A division or part of a larger topic (p. 414)

Superlative form (sə pėr′ lə tiv fôrm) The form of an adjective used to compare more than two people or things (p. 103)

T

Tense (tens) The time when an action takes place (p. 118)

Third-person pronoun (thėrd pėr′ sən prō′ noun) A pronoun that refers to the person or thing that is being talked about (p. 58)

Topic sentence (top′ ik sen′ təns) A sentence that states the main idea of a paragraph; usually the first sentence in a paragraph (p. 329)

Transition (tran zish′ ən) A change from one thing to another; often a change in time, place, situation, or thought (p. 391)

V

Variety (və rī′ ə tē) A collection of things that are different or vary in some way (p. 388)

Verb (vėrb) The word or words in a sentence that express action or state of being or that link ideas (p. 8)

Verb phrase (vėrb frāz) A main verb plus a helping verb (p. 120)

Verbal (vėr′ bəl) A verb used as a noun, adjective, or adverb (p. 307)

Verbal phrase (vėr′ bəl frāz) A verbal and its complements (p. 309)

W

Writing prompt (rīt ing prompt) The directions for a writing assignment (p. 441)

Index

not in, 176
possessive nouns *vs.*, 90
Conventions as writing trait,
14, 76, 266, 457, 465. *See also*
Writing traits
Coordinating conjunctions, 218,
219–24, 279
Correlative conjunctions, 218,
225–27

D

Dates
capitalization rules for, 468
plural forms of, 41
punctuation rules for, 471
Declarative sentences, 2, 11, 17
Definite articles, 84, 86, 88
Demonstrative adjectives, 84,
101–2
Demonstrative pronouns, 54,
69–71
Dependent clauses, 218, 228
Dialogue, 352, 369–72
Dictionaries, 16, 57, 322
Direct objects, 242, 248–51
Direct quotations, 352, 369, 474
Do, 135–37
Double negatives, 168, 175–76
Doubling consonants, 71, 104
Drafts, drafting, 380, 411,
457, 460–62. *See also*
Writing process
body, 461
conclusions, 462
final drafts, 463
introductions, 461
speeches, 476–77

E

Editing, 380, 399–402,
411, 458, 463–64. *See also*
Writing process
checklist for, 399
E-mail, 438, 444
End punctuation, 2, 4, 11, 17
English in Your Life
giving directions, 403
giving instructions, 185

job applications, 321, 451
letters of complaint, 15
résumés, 141
telling what happened, 235
thank-you letters, 77
to-do lists, 345
Essays, 438, 440
Exclamation marks, 2, 4, 11, 17
Exclamatory sentences, 2, 11, 17
Experts, 212

F

Facts, 352, 358. *See also*
Information sources
Fiction, 352, 365
Final drafts, 463
First-person pronouns, 54, 58
Footnotes, 432
Formal *vs.* informal language,
450

G

Gender, 56
Gerund phrases, 306, 312–15
Gerunds, 306, 312–15
Grammar reference books, 452
Grammar Tip, 276, 331, 356, 366,
389, 396, 445
Graphic organizers, 48, 481
Group Activity, 17, 49, 79, 109,
143, 163, 187, 213, 237, 269,
301, 323, 347, 375, 405, 433,
453

H

Helping verbs, 114, 119
Homographs, 423
Homophones, 262
Hyphens, 22, 25, 475

I

Ideas
as writing trait, 46, 160, 344,
430, 456, 459, 463. *See also*
Writing traits
choosing, 459
developing, 460

Idioms, 393
Imperative sentences, 2, 11
Indefinite articles, 84, 88
Indefinite pronouns, 54, 72–74
subject-verb agreement with,
131–32
Indent, 328, 329
Independent clauses, 218, 228
Indexes, 78
Indirect objects, 242, 252–55,
260–62
Indirect quotations, 352, 371
Inferencing as reading strategy,
148, 149, 153, 320, 328, 332,
338, 339, 342, 482
Infinitive phrases, 306, 307–11
Infinitives, 114, 122, 307–11
Inform, 352, 353
Informal *vs.* formal language,
450
Information sources, 108, 162,
417–20
Interjections, 218, 232–34
Internet, 300, 311, 418
Interrogative pronouns, 54,
66–68
Interrogative sentences, 2, 11, 17
Intransitive verbs, 242, 243–47
Invitations, 79, 449
Irregular plural nouns, 22, 39
Irregular verbs, 114, 122–26

J

Job applications, 321, 451

K

Keywords, 410, 418

L

Letters. *See* Business letters,
Letters of complaint, Personal
letters, Thank-you letters
Letters of complaint, 15
Letters, plural forms of, 41
Library catalogs, 268, 410,
415, 417

Acknowledgments

Photo Credits

Cover, © Fotolia; page 5, © Bananastock/Punchstock; page 13, © Corbis/Jupiter Images; page 15, © Image 100/Punchstock; page 27, © Corbis/Jupiter Images; page 41, © BananaStock/Alamy; page 47, © Tiburon Studios/Shutterstock; page 59, © Comstock/Jupiter Images; page 70, © Adam Tinney/Shutterstock; page 77, © Lorelyn Medina/Shutterstock; page 88, © Superstock/Jupiter Images; page 96, © DAJ/Getty Images; page 107, © Thinkstock/Punchstock; page 125, © Comstock Images/Alamy; page 132, © Image 100/Punchstock; page 141, © Ron Chapple/Jupiter Images; page 154, © Kayte M. Deioma/Photoedit; page 159, © First Class Photos PTY LTD/Shutterstock; page 161, © Jose Luis Pelaez, Inc/Jupiter Images; page 173, © Elena Elisseeva/Shutterstock; page 183, © Thinkstock/Jupiter Images; page 185, © Rubberball Productions/Jupiter Images; page 194, © Brand X Pictures/Jupiter Images; page 209, © Thinkstock/Punchstock; page 211, © David R. Frazier Photolibrary, Inc./Alamy; page 220, © Douglas Pulsipher/Alamy; page 232, © Image Source/Punchstock; page 235, © Blend Images/Jupiter Images; page 258, © Brand X Pictures/Jupiter Images; page 265, © Redchopsticks.com LLC/Alamy; page 267, © Kayte M. Deioma/Photoedit; page 280, © Blend Images/Jupiter Images; page 291, © Jeff Greenberg/Photoedit; page 299, © Chuck Franklin/Alamy; page 314, © Creatas Images/Jupiter Images; page 319, © Ableimages/Getty Images; page 312, © Image 100/Jupiter Images; page 336, © Veer; page 340, © Mike Watson Images/Punchstock; page 342, © Blend Images/Alamy; page 345, © Image Source/Jupiter Images; page 355, © Doug Menuez/Getty Images; page 367, © Comstock Images; page 373, © Marmaduke St. John/Alamy; page 381, © Corbis/Jupiter Images; page 401, © Ablestock/Jupiter Images; page 403, © SW Productions/Jupiter Images; page 412, © Blend Images/Superstock; page 426, © Creatas Images/Punchstock; page 431, © Stephen Coburn/Shutterstock; page 449, © Photodisc/Punchstock; page 451, © Corbis/Jupiter Images

Staff Credits

Melania Benzinger, Karen Blonigen, Nancy Condon, Barbara Drewlo, Daren Hastings, Brian Holl, Jan Jessup, Mariann Johanneck, Bev Johnson, Mary Kaye Kuzma, Julie Maas, Daniel Milowski, Carrie O'Connor, Deb Rogstad, Morgan Russell-Dempsey, Julie Theisen, Peggy Vlahos, Charmaine Whitman, Sue Will, Jen Willman